Excel 5 for Windows Spreadsheet Databases

JOHN DRANCHAK

John Wiley & Sons, Inc.
New York • Chichester • Brisbane • Toronto • Singapore

This book is dedicated to my father, John Dranchak,
who never got to see my work in print.

Publisher: Katherine Schowalter
Editor: Tim Ryan
Managing Editor: Frank Grazioli
Editorial Production & Design: Inpressions, a division of Edwards Brothers, Inc.

Designations used by companies to distinguish their products are often claimed as trademarks. In all instances where John Wiley & Sons, Inc. is aware of a claim, the product names appear in Initial Capital or all CAPITAL letters. Readers, however, should contact the appropriate companies for more complete information regarding trademarks and registration.

This text is printed on acid-free paper.

Copyright © 1994 by John Wiley & Sons, Inc.

All rights reserved. Published simultaneously in Canada.

This publication is designed to provide accurate and authoritative information in regard to the subject matter covered. It is sold with the understanding that the publisher is not engaged in rendering legal, accounting, or other professional service. If legal advice or other expert assistance is required, the services of a competent professional person should be sought.

Reproduction or translation of any part of this work beyond that permitted by section 107 or 108 of the 1976 United States Copyright Act without the permission of the copyright owner is unlowful. Requests for permission or further information should be addressed to the Permissions Department, John Wiley & Sons, Inc.

Library of Congress Cataloging-in-Publication Data:

Dranchak, John, 1964–
    Excel 5 for Windows spreadsheet databases / by John Dranchak
      p.   cm.
    Includes index.
    ISBN 0-471-30360-7 (paper)
    1. Microsoft Excel for Windows. 2. Business—Computer programs. 3. Electronic spreadsheets. I. Title.
  II. Title: Excel 5 for Windows spreadsheet databases.
HF5548.4.M523D73 1994
650'.0285'5369—dc20   94-7802
                                                                               CIP

Printed in the United States of America
10 9 8 7 6 5 4 3 2 1

Acknowledgments

Brian Baczyk, for contributing the core material for Chapters 7, 14, and 15, keeping Logic Control clients happy, and for being a great friend! Tim Ryan for believing in me enough to publish this book; Ed Finley, Barbara Murphy, and John Halvey at Milbank, Tweed, Hadley & McCloy for their guidance; Dan Williams, for convincing me not to write this book about Excel 4.0, but to wait for 5.0. It was a long wait, but well worth it! Eric Wells, Excel Product Manager, who was always able to cut through the red tape; Ian Warhaftig of Microsoft for encouraging me to become an Excel Consulting Partner way back in the stone age; Pete Thompson, of Microsoft, who's been my champion since day one.

In closing I'd like to thank my mother, Lorraine Dranchak, for encouraging me to always pursue my dreams, and my closest friends: Mary C. Doyle, Joe and Teri LaCroce, and Ed Ross, for dealing with me while I went through the trials and tribulations of composing this work, and for always being there. Last but not least, thanks to Natasha and Ginger.

Vendor Acknowledgments

I'd like to thank Microsoft. In addition to the fact that this book would not exist if Excel wasn't on the market, Microsoft has provided a set of tools that allow me to make my living at something I truly enjoy doing, while providing my clients with great solutions!

I'd also like to thank Halcyon Software for providing me with DoDot. All of the screen shots were taken with DoSnap, and all of the images were cataloged with DoThumbnail, both part of the DoDot graphics package. Although the final book has less, there were originally over 350 screen captures taken! It would have been a nightmare to create and manage this collection without DoDot. You can contact Halcyon Software directly at 408-378-9898 for more information on their great products.

Contents

CHAPTER 1

What Is a Database? 1

Introduction 1
Data versus Information 1
Lists 3
Databases 8
Internal Data versus External Data 11

CHAPTER 2

Sorting 13

Sort Keys 13
Advanced Sort Options 31
Custom Sort Orders 33
Sorting Data in an Outline 41

CHAPTER 3

Filtering 43

Introduction 43
Filtering 43
AutoFilter 46
Advanced Filter 54
Summary 68

CHAPTER 4
Data Forms — 69

Introduction	69
What a Data Form Is	69
Using a Data Form	72
Restricting Data Entry/Editing	77
Summary	81

CHAPTER 5
Database Functions — 83

Introduction	83
Summary	91

CHAPTER 6
Data Tables — 93

Introduction	93
What a Data Table Is	93
One-Input Data Tables	94
Two-Input Data Tables	100
Lookup Tables	103
Summary	115

CHAPTER 7
Reading and Writing Other Data Formats — 117

Introduction	117
Importing Data	117
Exporting Data	127
Symbolic Link Files	133
Combining Data from Multiple Files into a Single File	134
Things to Watch For	135
Summary	136

CHAPTER 8
Custom Data Forms — 138
Using VBA to Create a Custom Data Form — 138
Excel 4.0 Style Dialogs — 149

CHAPTER 9
Pivot Tables — 151
What a Pivot Table Is — 151
Creating a Pivot Table — 155
Refreshing a Pivot Table — 176
Creating Charts from Pivot Tables — 179

CHAPTER 10
Advanced Pivot Tables — 186
Adding and Removing Existing Fields — 186
Changing the Layout of a Pivot Table — 188
Using Page Fields to Change Your View of Data — 194
Working with Totals in a Pivot Table — 199
Formatting a Pivot Table — 212
Grouping Items in a Pivot Table Field — 216
Hiding and Showing Detail in a Pivot Table — 228

CHAPTER 11
Macros/VBA — 233
Working with Text — 233
Using Pivot Table Methods in VBA Code — 235

CHAPTER 12
MS Query Overview — 238
External Data — 238
What MS Query Is and How It Works with Excel — 238

Windows Open Services Architecture (WOSA)   240
Data Access from an Excel Worksheet   246

CHAPTER 13

Microsoft Query as a Stand-Alone Application   249

Starting MS Query   249
Parts of the MS Query Workspace   250
Building a Simple Query   261
Building Advanced Queries   272

CHAPTER 14

Structured Query Language Basics   298

Introduction   298
Relational Database Fundamentals   299
Basic Data Retrieval   299
Joining Multiple Tables   306
Sorting Information with SQL   310
Summarizing Information with SQL   310
Scalar Functions   312
Data Updating   314

CHAPTER 15

Using SQL Server   318

Introduction   318
Introduction to Client/Server Computing   318
Attaching to SQL Server   320
Views   321
Stored Procedures   323
Transact/SQL Query Extensions   326
Transacts/SQL Programming Language Extensions   329

INDEX   335

CHAPTER 1
What Is a Database?

Introduction

Microsoft Excel 5.0 is a Windows-based worksheet which offers features and functions for manipulating rows and columns of information. One common use of worksheets is list storage and manipulation. This is sometimes referred to as database management. Excel 5.0 offers a wide range of features to help you work with lists and databases. In this chapter you will learn:

- The difference between data and information.
- What a list is.
- What a database is.
- What Excel's database/list management features are.
- How Excel takes advantage of the Windows environment.
- Why you should use Excel to meet your list and database needs.
- When you should use Excel to meet your list and database needs.

Data versus Information

Data

Examine the data illustrated in Table 1.1. Although it is fairly safe to assume that these are abbreviations for January, February, and March, you do not know that just by looking at the table. **Jan**, **Feb**, and **Mar** could be the names that a hippie gave his first three children. Even though the children

TABLE 1.1

Jan
Feb
Mar

may have been named after the first three months of the year, you would still not understand this table's true meaning. That is because **data** consists of raw, isolated facts. Unless you see data in context, you really do not know what those facts mean.

Information

By putting a simple column heading on this table, as illustrated in Table 1.2, the data is suddenly placed in context. Somewhat. By labeling this column as **Month**, you know that you have the correct items in the list. But what do you know about these months? Are they just the first quarter of the year? Or do they represent the three months that a college student is going to spend in Paris?

Table 1.3 sheds a little more light on the matter, by adding a second column and a caption. The more data that is combined, the closer those facts come to becoming information. **Information** is data which has meaning. Data, in context, makes a whole greater than the sum of the parts.

Lists and Databases

Lists and databases are organized collections of data. The more organized your list or database is, the better equipped you will be to assemble your data in meaningful ways. A well organized list or database can help convert

TABLE 1.2

Month
Jan
Feb
Mar

TABLE 1.3
First Quarter 1994
Widget Sales

Month	Sales
Jan	$25M
Feb	$33M
Mar	$34M

meaningless data into rich information by allowing you to sort your list, view only parts of your list, and perform summary calculations on the data in your list.

How Does Excel 5.0 Fit into This?

Excel is designed to help you quickly and easily create, edit, maintain, and view your data. It is especially useful for transforming boring old data into useful information. With tools such as **AutoFilter, Advanced Filter, Sorting, Pivot Tables,** the ability to import and export data to other formats, and the ability to link to external data sources via MS Query, Excel provides a robust interface for transforming data into information.

Why Use Excel?

Why should you use Excel 5.0 to handle your data and list management? First of all, if you're reading this book, you probably already own it. At the time this book was written, there were over five million registered copies of Excel in use! Although database applications like Microsoft Access offer great power and ease of use—and definitely have their place—they are often overkill for most list and database activities. Since Excel 5.0 includes MS Query, you can gain access to data that exists in true database applications like MS Access and SQL Server. You can actually use Query to create and populate Access databases and tables.

Secondly, by starting with Excel 5.0 and Query, if your data management needs ever require the power of MS Access, it will be an easy migration, since MS Query was derived from Access. Everything you learn about building queries in MS Query can be easily transferred to Access, when the time is appropriate.

Last but not least, Excel provides tools for performing mathematical, statistical, and charting operations that no database package can come near! If performing analytics on data sets is important to you, Excel is unquestionably the tool of choice, especially with the new list and database functions, which make working with large and complex data sets easier than ever before.

Lists

A **list** is a series of worksheet rows that contain related data. Lists consist of one or more columns. Although not required, the top row of most lists contains column headings which identify the contents of the columns.

These are known as **column labels**. Each row contains information about an entity. An **entity** is a person, place, or thing. Essentially, all lists are databases.

Creating a List

Creating a list in Excel is a cinch. Just choose a cell where you want your list to begin, type a column heading to help you identify what you are listing, and then start typing entries in the cells below.

Identifying Lists

Excel 5.0 has built-in intelligence to figure out what you think a list is. Sometimes it makes the right guess; sometimes it makes the wrong guess, and you get unexpected results. To insure that Excel correctly interprets the range you want to use, there are two ways to help it out:

- Use column labels to let Excel identify the beginning of a list.
- Use the reserved name *Database* to manually mark the list.

How Excel Identifies Your List When Selecting a Single Cell

Excel identifies the 'top' boundary of your list because it has a column label and blank cells in the row directly above the column label. Excel also identifies the other three boundaries of your list by finding blank cells. If your list contains one or more blank ranges (especially a blank row or column), Excel may incorrectly interpret those blank cells as the end of the list.

Column Labels

The concept of column labels is very important to the way Excel handles sorting and filtering. If you have created a range named *Database*, the top row contains field names or column names. If you are using a list and have not gone through the process of formally defining it as a database, Excel takes a guess as to whether or not the range you have selected includes column labels.

Consider the data illustrated in Table 1.4. At a quick glance, the information in this table should be fairly meaningful to you. You understand that **Jan**, **Feb**, and **Mar** are all abbreviations for months, and the column label **Month** confirms this for you. The top row of a table usually contains labels that describe the contents of the columns in that table. Yet, there are many times when a column label is not used.

Consider the data illustrated in Table 1.5. You still know that this is a table that lists the abbreviations for three months, even though there is no column label. How do you know this? Once again, you know that **Jan**, **Feb**, and **Mar** are abbreviations for months. In this case, because the table is small, it is easy to identify the entities in the column.

It is also standard convention to separate column labels from the contents of a column. How is this done? One of the oldest and simplest ways is to underline the label. In the past, you often could not underline a character as part of the printed character set, so a line of dashes was inserted between the label and the first row of data. If you are used to using a character-based spreadsheet package, such as the first several versions of Lotus 1-2-3, this concept should be quite familiar to you. Table 1.6 illustrates an example of this, using a mono-spaced font, Courier 12.

With the advent of WYSIWYG software and the wide-scale adaptation of Graphical User Interfaces (GUI), this old standard has been replaced with more contemporary character formatting such as underlining, bold, font size, and font type, as well as background formatting. A more contemporary representation of the table which has been used for these examples is illustrated in Table 1.7.

How Excel Identifies Column Labels

It is a standard convention to format a column label different than the actual data in a table or to use a different datatype. Based on this convention, the Excel development team decided that instead of forcing you to select man-

TABLE 1.4

TABLE 1.5

TABLE 1.6

```
Month
—
Jan
Feb
Mar
```

TABLE 1.7

ually the whole range you want to sort (as was the case in previous releases of Excel), you could select only one cell in the range (or even no cells in the range, if you wanted to sort a whole list). The following rule is used by Excel to identify the column label:

RULE

Label Identification Rule (LIR)

If the first row of a list is formatted differently from the rest of a list or is a different datatype, Excel assumes that the first row is a column label.

WARNING

Excel actually recognizes up to two rows as column labels since many users split long labels into two vertical cells. Although this works with 'simple lists,' if you want to use any of Excel's advanced database features, such as data forms or database functions, the name of the field (column label) must be contained in the top row. Names that span two rows are not permitted.

How Column Labels Affect Sorting

Why is it important to identify the column labels when performing a sort? If, in the previous examples, the first row **Month** was not identified as the column label, it would be included in the sort range. After all, how is Excel to know that **Month** is a label that describes **Jan**, **Feb**, and **Mar** rather than just another string of random characters? If you were using the Sort Ascending tool, and Excel did not correctly identify **Month** as the label, the list illustrated in Table 1.8 would be the result. Definitely not the expected result!

Helping Excel Identify Your Column Labels

By knowing that this is how Excel tries to identify sort ranges, you can easily prepare your lists to help Excel out. If you work frequently with lists, a little effort up front will save a lot of time. Based on the LIR, the following rule will help you to work more efficiently with Excel:

What Is a Database? 7

RULE **Dranchak's First Table Rule**

Always apply a different formatting style to the column labels of a list.

The simplest way to do this is to use Excel's **AutoFormat** command every time you create a list. To apply an **AutoFormat** to a list, follow the steps below.

STEPS **Using AutoFormat to Format a List**

1. Select any cell in the list (**AutoFormat** actually looks at the list as a table).
2. Select **Format→AutoFormat...** . The dialog box illustrated in Figure 1.1 will be displayed.
3. Select a style from the **Table Forma**t list box. Notice how the display changes.
4. Select **OK** when you have found a style that you like.

For some users, the styles which **AutoFormat** offers will meet all of their formatting needs. If they do not meet your needs, you can modify the default styles by selecting the **Options**⟩⟩ button in the **AutoFormat** dialog box. If this still does not meet your needs, you can create custom styles (such as 'List Header') which you can apply to any range. You can even create your own 'AutoFormat' by writing a macro that looks at the selection

TABLE 1.8

| Feb |
| Jan |
| Mar |
| Month |

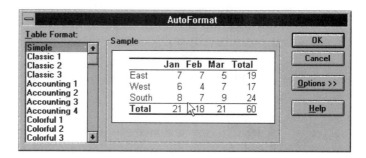

FIGURE 1.1 AutoFormat dialog box.

and then applies different styles based on rules that you create. For more information on **AutoFormat**, **Styles**, and **Macros**, see Excel's on-line help.

Selecting a List to Sort or Filter

Before you can perform a sort or filter, you must first select the range on which you wish to perform the sort. There are two ways that you can do this:

- List **AutoSelect**
- Define a **Database**.

If you have already created a list and followed the guidelines recommended earlier in this chapter for helping Excel identify the list's column headings, all you have to do is select any cell in the list, and then select **Data→Sort…** . Excel automatically selects the complete list for you (most of the time) and decides whether or not there is a labels row. If Excel 'thinks' there is a labels row, it selects all of the rows except the first one, and when the **Sort** dialog box is displayed, the **Header Row** option is selected from the **My List Has** option group. If Excel 'thinks' there is no labels row, it selects all of the rows in the list, including the first one, and when the **Sort** dialog box is displayed, the **No Header Row** option is selected from the **My List Has** option group. If you select a cell which is not part of a list, the message box illustrated in Figure 1.2 will be displayed.

Databases

Lists are very informal databases. By formalizing your list, you can become more efficient in how you process your data. In Excel, you need only take a few seconds to make sure your database is set up correctly, and then tell Excel that it is a database.

Parts of a Database

Databases have two major components:

- Fields
- Rows.

In each row in a database you store information about a single entity. For each piece of different information, you use a separate column. Each

What Is a Database?

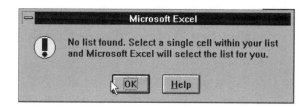

FIGURE 1.2
No List Found message box.

column holds a particular piece of information about the entity that identifies it. These columns are called the entity's **attributes**. A more common name for the attributes are **fields**. Each entity, or row, has one or more fields, or columns. You identify what the attribute is by placing a **field name**, or column label, at the top of each row. Table 1.9 illustrates a simple list, or database.

Here, the fields are **First Name**, **Last Name**, **Company**, and **Phone**. It should be evident that the entities contained in the rows are **John Smith**, **Melinda Hayes**, and **Tom Jones**. In Excel, this is already a list. To make it a database, all you would have to do is identify it as such, by naming the range *Database*. There is one other slight change you need to make. Since the names of fields in Excel database can't have blanks, you must change the text of the column labels so that there are no blanks. The most common way to do this is to substitute underscores for blanks.

Manually Defining a Database Range

If you are familiar with using range names, you can perform this operation manually. To manually define the Database range, follow the steps below.

STEPS

Manually Defining a Database Range, Using the Name Box

1. Select the range which contains the list.
2. Select the **Name Box**. The cell address will be highlighted.
3. Type *Database* over the cell address.
4. Press **Enter**.

TABLE 1.9

First Name	Last Name	Company	Phone
John	Smith	Acme Widgets	555-1234
Melinda	Hayes	Acme Widgets	555-4321
Tom	Jones	Qapmoc Inc.	123-7777

STEPS — **Manually Defining a Database Range, Using the Define Name Command**

1. Select the range that you want to define, including the column labels. (This must be a contiguous range.)
2. Select the **Insert→Name→Define...** . The dialog box illustrated in Figure 1.3 will be displayed. Notice that the worksheet name and cell reference for your selection are listed in the **Refers To** text box, in the format = *'Worksheet Name'!CellAddress*.
3. Type *Database* in the **Names in Workbook** edit box.
4. Select **OK**

Selecting a Range While the Define Name Dialog Box is Open

Although the method above uses the technique of first selecting the range that you wish to define as the database, you can select the range after you have opened the **Define Name** dialog box. This is because the **Define Name** dialog box is a **Modeless** window. Unlike some other dialog boxes which do not allow you to interact with the current worksheet (such as the **Save As** dialog box), the **Define Name** dialog box allows you to have the dialog open on the screen while you make selections in your workbook. To use a mouse to define a database after the **Define Name** dialog box has been opened, follow the steps below.

STEPS — **Defining a Database, Using the Mouse, Selecting the Range After Opening the Define Name Dialog.**

1. Select **Insert→Name→Define**. The **Define Name** dialog box will be displayed.
2. Type *Database* in the **Names in Workbook** text box.
3. Select the worksheet name and cell reference for the current selection in the **Refers To** text box by highlighting all of the text in the **Refers To** text box.
4. Select the contiguous range which you want to define, including the column labels. Notice that the **Define Name** dialog box stays on the screen and that the contents of the **Refers To** text box dynamically changes as your selection changes.

What Is a Database?

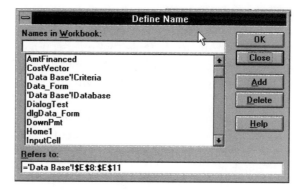

FIGURE 1.3
Define Name dialog box with Database range.

*You could also manually type in the range to use for your database in the format ='WorksheetName'!StartCell:EndCell. Your selection does not have to be in the current spreadsheet (or workbook!). Simply navigate to the workbook/worksheet of your choice by pointing and clicking on the workbook you wish to use (or selecting it from the **Window** menu). Select the worksheet of your choice by clicking on the proper tab, and then selecting the range that you want to use.*

5. When you are satisfied with the results, select **OK**.

Internal Data versus External Data

There are two kinds of data that you can work with in Excel:

- Internal Data
- External Data.

Internal data is any list or database that is stored as an Excel Workbook. Whether the list starts life as an Excel worksheet or whether you imported it from a Lotus 123 spreadsheet, once the data is saved as part of an Excel Workbook, it is internal.

External data is any database, stored outside of an Excel Workbook, that you create a link to via Microsoft Query. Essentially, external data is a snapshot, or copy, of the original data. Some examples of external data are:

- A SQL Server for Windows NT view that exists on an enterprise server
- An Oracle table that exists on a departmental DEC mini-computer
- A dBASE file which exists on your own machine
- An Access database which resides on a Netware file server.

Remember that when you look at a worksheet that contains external data, it looks just like a worksheet that contains internal data. This means you can perform any operation on it that you would perform on an internal database.

There are several advantages to using external data. The first advantage is data integrity. Since you are working with a copy of the data, you cannot 'edit' or destroy the underlying source data. You can manipulate the data without worrying about its integrity. Similarly, if you are the 'owner' of a particular source of data (say a forecasting database that resides on a SQL Server NT server), you can feel comfortable giving access to users, without the fear that they might modify data they shouldn't be modifying.

Most database servers do provide security. The database administrator (DBA) can restrict a user to viewing data, and users can modify only the data they are authorized to modify. Although this is the case, the fact that Excel external databases cannot be edited provides an additional layer of security.

On the other side of the coin, by 'attaching' to data sources, you can guarantee that your data is always up to date simply by refreshing the query. If you design a quarterly forecast spreadsheet around a query which accesses a sales database, you can do a presentation with the most up-to-date numbers, provided you connect to the data source and refresh your query right before your presentation. Compare this to the more traditional method of getting an extract from the mainframe several weeks before your presentation, and seeing the numbers change the day before, and being unable to get a new extract in time for your presentation.

It is possible, assuming the DBA has assigned the correct authorization, to create an application using Excel dialog boxes and Dynamic Data Exchange (DDE) that allows users to edit the underlying data. This will not be covered in this book.

CHAPTER 2
Sorting

Sort Keys

Sorting is the process of ordering the contents of a list or database, based on some hierarchy that you define. The item that you choose to sort by is known as the **Sort Key**. If, for example you wish to sort a list of contacts by the contact's state, **State** would be the sort key. Many sorts that you perform will only have a single sort key. Other sorts will require several sort keys. Excel 5.0 supports up to three sort keys in a single sort. With three possible sort keys, you can easily perform most sorts that are required for list management. If you need to use more than three keys, Excel allows you to create **nested sorts.** Nested sorts allow you to sort by more than three keys by sequentially performing several sorts, using different sort keys.

Excel 5.0 allows you to:

- Sort a list using a single key.
- Sort a list using multiple keys.
- Sort a list using nested sorts.
- Sort a subset of a list.
- Sort one or more complete columns in a worksheet.
- Sort a list which contains graphic objects.
- Sort a list which contains OLE objects.

Before getting into the meat and potatoes of sorting, a quick look at **Sort Orders** will be helpful.

Sort Orders

Although the concept of an ascending or descending sort is seemingly straightforward, all is not what it appears to be! If your sort key contains only numbers, or only alphabetic text (A through Z), as many sorts do, things appear straightforward. Numbers are actually straightforward, but text is a little more complex. If you have been sticking to the 26 characters of the alphabet, you have only been working with a subset of the available characters. But what if your key contained a question mark? When you perform an ascending sort, would you expect the row with the question mark to be placed at the beginning of the sorted list, or at the end? No matter what your expectations are, in an ascending sort, a question mark will always be placed before all 26 characters of the English alphabet. What is the exact order by which text is sorted? What about lists which contain other types of data such as logicals, error values, and blanks? What about keys which contain multiple datatypes?

Ascending Sorts

In an ascending sort, with a single datatype:

- Text is sorted in the following order:
  0 1 2 3 4 5 6 7 8 9 (space) ! " # $ % & ' ( ) * + , - . / : ; < = > ? @ [\ ] ^ _ ` { | } ~ A B C D E F G H I J K L M N O P Q R S T U V W X Y Z

  The numbers listed above do not refer to numeric datatype, but to cells in which a number is 'forced' to be treated as 'text.' This is accomplished by placing an apostrophe (') as the first character in a cell.

- Numbers are sorted from the smallest negative number to the largest positive number.
- Dates and times are sorted from the earliest value to the latest value.
- Logical Values are sorted with False placed before True.
- Error values are sorted in the order in which they are found.
- Blanks are sorted last.

> **NOTE**
>
> *Excel 5.0 selects a sort order based on the sorting rules for the country defined in the International section of the **Windows Control Panel**. All examples and text in this work assume that the United States is the selected country. Versions of Excel prior to 3.0a used a different sort order. If your application requires compatibility with a sort order prior to Excel 3.0a, add the line **SORT = 2** to your **EXCEL5.INI** file, using a text editor such as **Notepad**. Be sure to make a backup copy of this file before you modify it!*

In a list which contains a mix of datatypes, if you apply an ascending sort, the contents will be grouped in the following order, and then sorted according to the rules defined above:

- Times
- Numbers
- Dates
- Text
- Logical Values
- Errors
- Blank cells.

Figure 2.1 illustrates a list with all the datatypes listed above. Figure 2.2 illustrates the same list after applying an ascending sort.

Descending Sorts

In a descending sort, with a single datatype:

- Text is sorted in the following order:
  Z Y X W V U T S R Q P O N M L K J I H G F E D C B A ~ } | { ` _ ^] \ [@ ? > = < ; : / . - , + *) (' & % $ # " ! (space) 9 8 7 6 5 4 3 2 1 0
- Numbers are sorted from the largest positive number to the smallest negative number.
- Dates and times are sorted from the latest value to the earliest value.
- Logical Values are sorted with True placed before False.
- Error values are sorted in the order in which they are found.
- Blanks are sorted last.

In a list which contains a mix of datatypes, if you apply a descending sort to the list, the contents will be grouped in the following order, and then sorted according to the rules defined above:

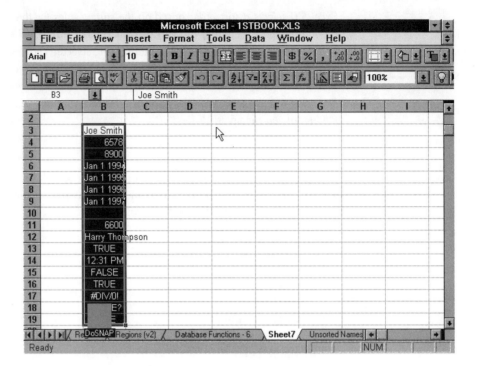

FIGURE 2.1
Unsorted List.

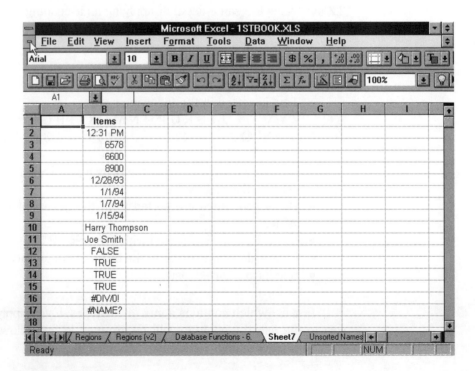

FIGURE 2.2
Sorted List.

- Errors
- Logical Values
- Text
- Dates
- Numbers
- Times
- Blank cells.

Note that in all cases, blank cells are sorted last. It should also be noted that a cell with a 'space' (i.e., to clear the contents of a cell, you pressed the spacebar) is not the same as a 'blank' cell. To make sure that a cell is blank, you should always use the **Clear** command select (**Edit**→**Clear** or press **del**).

Sorting by a Single Key

To sort a list using a single key, you have two basic options:

- Use the **Sort Ascending/Descending** buttons on the toolbar.
- Use the **Data**→**Sort** command.

Sort Ascending/Descending Buttons

The quickest way to perform a single key sort is to use the sort buttons on the toolbar. The sort buttons are identified by the callouts in Figure 2.3. The advantage of using these buttons is that with a single mouse click, you can perform the actions of several mouse clicks (or keyboard strokes), and thus save time. The disadvantage of using these buttons is that they do not give you as much flexibility. They do not give you the ability to sort on more than one column, or to interactively set advanced sort options. To sort by a single key, using the **Sort Ascending/Descending** buttons, follow the steps below.

STEPS Performing an Ascending Quick Sort

1. Within the list you wish to sort, select any cell in the column you wish to sort by.
2. Select the **Sort Ascending** button.

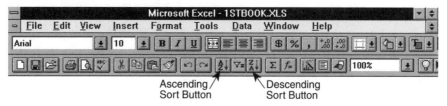

FIGURE 2.3
Sort buttons on the standard toolbar.

STEPS

Performing a Descending Quick Sort

1. Within the list you wish to sort, select any cell in the column you wish to sort by.
2. Select the **Sort Descending** button.

HINT

*Holding down the shift key while you select either the **Sort Ascending** or **Sort Descending** buttons causes the list to be sorted in the opposite order. In other words, if you simultaneously hold down the **Shift** key and select the **Sort Ascending** button, a descending sort will be applied to the list.*

The Sort Command

Although the **Sort Ascending/Descending** buttons can save time, they can also be somewhat limiting. They do not allow you to interactively modify your sort options, and they can only be used to sort by a single key. To solve these 'problems,' you must use the **Sort** command.

Another advantage of the **Sort** command is that the sort key and sort order options that you set will be used by subsequent sort operations within the same Excel session. In other words, if you select a field named *State* to perform a descending sort on, the next time you use **Data→Sort** (no matter which column contains the active cell within the list), the **Sort By** drop-down list box will default to *State,* and the sort order will default to **Descending.** Excel also 'remembers' these settings for multiple sort keys and the advanced sort options, both of which will discussed later in this chapter. Excel does not store the setting from the **My List Has** option group, which is used to identify whether or not the list contains labels.

Remember, these settings are only stored for the current session. If you exit from Excel at the end of the day and start up again the following day, you are back to ground zero—the settings are no longer remembered. Also, if you use the **Sort Ascending** or **Sort Descending** button subsequent to using the **Sort** command, the settings will be overwritten by the selection that you make. To perform a single-key sort using the **Sort** command, follow these steps:

Sorting

STEPS

Performing a Single-Key Sort, Using the Sort Command

1. Within the list you wish to sort, select any cell in the column you wish to sort by.
2. Select any cell within the list.
3. Select **Data→Sort**. The dialog box illustrated in Figure 2.4 will be displayed.
4. Select the field you wish to sort from the **Sort By** drop-down list box. Notice that the name defaults to the column which contains the active cell. If your list has no column headings, the Excel column name will appear.
5. Select the option button from the **Sort By** option group that corresponds to the sort order you wish to apply.
6. If Excel did not correctly identify whether or not your list has column labels, select the appropriate option button from the **My List Has** option group.
7. Select **OK**.

Sorting on a list using multiple keys and **Advanced Sort Options**, accessible from the **Options...** button, are both discussed later in this chapter.

Sorting on Up to Three Multiple-Keys

Often you will find it necessary to perform a sort on more than one key. Examine the data illustrated in Table 2.1. First, notice that there are two Mary Smiths: one who works for Borlus, and one who works for Holmes, Inc. Also notice that there are three different Smiths who work for Borlus.

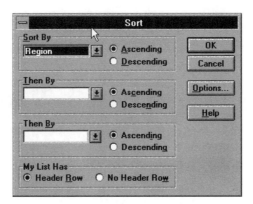

FIGURE 2.4
Sort dialog box.

TABLE 2.1
Unsorted Sample Data

Company	Last Name	First Name
Borlus	Smith	John
Borlus	Smith	Mary
Borlus	Smith	Stephen
Holmes, Inc.	Smith	Mary
Borlus	Jones	Jerry

What if you wanted to sort these contacts, first by **Company**, then by **Last Name**, and then by **First Name**? Table 2.2 illustrates the data this sort would result in (if all sorts were all ascending). To perform a sort which uses more than one key, follow the steps below.

STEPS

Performing a Sort, Using Three Keys

1. Select a cell in the list that you wish to sort.
2. Select **Data→Sort**. The dialog box illustrated in Figure 2.5 will be displayed.
3. Select the first key that you wish to sort by from the **Sort By** list box.

TABLE 2.2
Sample Data Sorted in Ascending Order

Company	Last Name	First Name
Borlus	Jones	Jerry
Borlus	Smith	John
Borlus	Smith	Mary
Borlus	Smith	Stephen
Holmes, Inc.	Smith	Mary

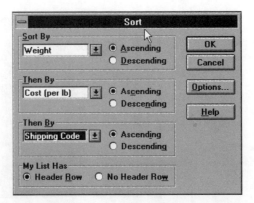

FIGURE 2.5
The **Sort** dialog box.

Notice that if your list has no column labels, the name of the column that contains the active cell is the selected choice in the **Sort By** list box.
4. Select the option button for the sort order of your choice.
5. Select the second key that you wish to sort by from the **Then By** list box.
6. Select the option button for the sort order of your choice.
7. Select the third key that you wish to sort by from the **Then By** list box.
8. Select the option button for the sort order of your choice.
9. Select **OK**.

Performing Nested Sorts—Sorting by Four or More Keys

If you want to perform a sort by more than three keys, you must use a **Nested Sort**. Because Excel 5.0 can only sort by three keys at a time, you must perform two or more sorts to achieve the correct sort order. For example, take the data illustrated in Table 2.3. What if you wanted to sort by **State**, **Last Name**, **First Name** and then **SAT Math** score?

The solution is a two-step process. First, sort the list by the key of least importance (**SAT Math**), and then sort the newly ordered list by **State**, **Last Name**, and **First Name**. Just remember that you cannot simply undo your 'two-stage' sort. It, therefore, makes sense to make a copy of the original list, and then perform your sorting on the duplicate. When you are satisfied with the results, you can then choose to replace the original list with the new one. To perform a four-key sort, follow the steps below.

STEPS Sorting by Four Keys

1. Select the entire list that you wish to sort.
2. Copy the list to another location (within the same sheet or on another sheet).
3. Select any cell within the new list.

TABLE 2.3
Sample Data

State	Last Name	First Name	SAT Math	SAT English
CT	Smith	Tom	670	650
MA	Smith	Mary	510	640
CT	Smith	Tom	510	470
CT	Smith	Martin	730	800
CT	Smith	Tina	740	760
MA	Jones	Tom	540	760

4. Select **Data→Sort...** .
5. Select **SAT Math** from the **Sort By** list box.
6. Select **(none)** from the **Then By** list box.
7. Select **(none)** from the **Then By** list box.
8. Select **OK**. Notice that the list will be resorted.
9. Select **Data→Sort...** .
10. Select **State** from the **Sort By** list box.
11. Select **Last Name** from the **Then By** list box.
12. Select **First Name** from the **Then By** list box.
13. Select **OK**. Notice that the list will be resorted.
14. Replace the original list with the new list.

If you find yourself frequently performing sorts on four or more keys, you should probably consider using another tool for your sorting operations. One option is to use MS Query (which ships with Excel 5.0. Using an Excel ODBC driver, you can attach to Excel files and easily perform multiple key sorts. It should be noted that as of the writing of this book, an Excel ODBC driver does not ship with Excel 5.0. You must purchase one either from Microsoft, or another ODBC driver vendor, such as Q+E Software. For more information on using MS Query, see Chapter 11, An Overview of External Data.

Microsoft Access is a relational database tool which offers a more comprehensive solution. MS Access allows you to import and export Excel files, as well as to attach to them via ODBC, provided you have an Excel ODBC driver. You can also read and write Access tables via the ODBC driver which ships with MS Query. As such, you can access all of the data you store in Access tables from Excel 5.0, via MS Query. For more information on Access, see **Building Access Applications Using Point and Click Programming**, also by this author.

Sorting a Subset of a List

Sometimes you do not want to sort a complete list. When you want to sort part of a list, you need to select the subset of the list which you wish to sort, and then apply the sort. To sort a subset of a list, follow these steps:

FIGURE 2.6
Sort Warning
dialog box.

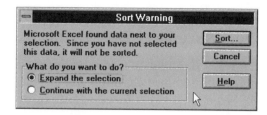

STEPS Sorting a Subset of a List by Using the Sort Ascending/Descending Buttons

1. Select the range you want to sort.
2. Select either the **Sort Ascending** or **Sort Descending** button, as appropriate.

STEPS Sorting a Subset of a List by Using the Sort Command

1. Select the range you want to sort.
2. Select **Data→Sort**.
3. Select the options that are appropriate for the outcome you desire.
4. Select **OK**.

If the range you have selected is a subset of a larger list (as it usually will be) and contains only a single row or single column, the dialog box illustrated in Figure 2.6 will be displayed. Since users most commonly sort a complete list, Excel recognizes that you have selected only a subset of a list. Since this is not the most common behavior, Excel prompts you to ask if this is really what you want to do.

Selecting **Expand the selection** in the **What do you want to do?** option group will change the selected range to include the complete list. Selecting **Continue with the current selection** allows you to sort just the range which you have selected. After either of these selections are made, select **Sort...** to continue with the sorting operation.

Sorting One or More Complete Columns

There will be times when you want to sort one or more complete columns, not just a list, or a subset of a list. When you do this, if there are any blank rows at the top of the column, they will be moved to the bottom of the range, and the data will move up to start at Row 1. To sort a complete column, follow these steps:

STEPS

Sorting One or More Complete Columns, Using the Sort Ascending/Descending Buttons

1. Select the column heading(s) for the column(s) you wish to sort. Notice that the whole column(s) will be selected, as illustrated in Figure 2.7.
2. Select either the **Sort Ascending** or **Sort Descending** button, as appropriate.

STEPS

Sorting One or More Complete Columns, Using the Sort Command

1. Select the column heading(s) for the column(s) you wish to sort.
2. Select **Data→Sort**.
3. Select the options that are appropriate for the outcome you desire.
4. Select **OK**.

If you select a single row, the dialog box discussed in the previous section (Sorting a Subset of a List) will be displayed. In addition to sorting complete columns, you can also sort one or more complete rows. Follow the meth-

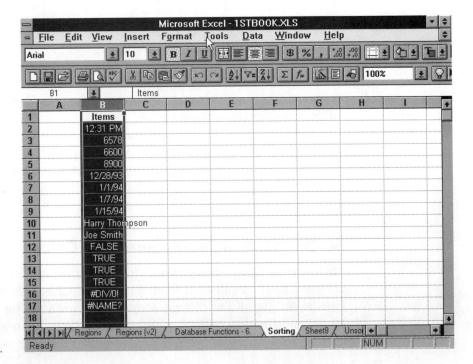

FIGURE 2.7
Worksheet with a column **B** selected.

odology detailed in the Sort Orientation section of this chapter when setting your options in Step Three of the above procedure.

Sorting with Graphic Objects

If you have graphic objects (i.e., buttons, text boxes, pictures, etc.), you can include them in sorts. If there is an object in a cell adjacent to or within your list when you perform a sort on the list, the object will be moved with the row (or column, if you are performing a horizontal sort) if you have correctly set the objects' properties. As a result, you can actually use Excel as a 'multi-media' or graphical database.

To include a graphic object as part of a sort, there are two requirements which must be met:

- The graphic object must be positioned in (actually on or over) a cell which is in the list, or directly adjacent to the list.
- The graphic object's **Object Postitioning** property must be set to either **Move and Size with Cells** or **Move but Don't Size with Cells**.

The object's **Object Positioning** property is what determines whether or not an object is 'attached' to a particular cell, and if it is, whether or not the object will be re-sized when the cell is re-sized. When a sort is performed, the cells are actually moved into a new order. Thus, for an object to be sorted, it must be 'attached' to a cell so that it can be moved with the cell when sorting occurs.

Figure 2.8 illustrates how you can use Excel 5.0 as a catalog for graphic objects. This particular example uses Excel as a 'storehouse' for Windows Metafile graphic objects. To create a catalog for pictures, using an Excel list, follow the steps below.

STEPS

Creating a Graphics Catalog with Metafiles

1. Select **Insert→Picture...** . The dialog box illustrated in Figure 2.9 will be displayed.
3. Create or select a new worksheet.
4. Select cell **B3**, and then type **Picture**.
5. Select cell **C3**, and then type **Description**.
6. Select **B3:C3**.
7. Select **Format→Cells...** and then apply the formatting changes that you wish to use to identify this row as the column labels.

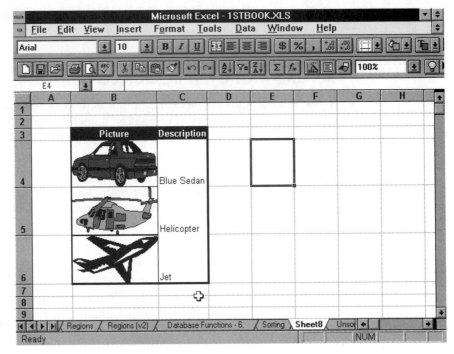

FIGURE 2.8
Using a worksheet as a database to store graphical objects. **Catalog.xls/Catalog** worksheet.

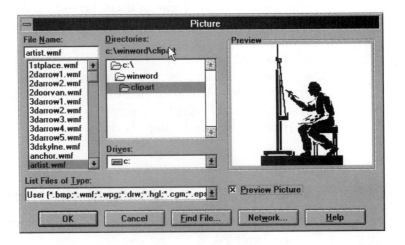

FIGURE 2.9
Picture dialog box.

8. Select the next available cell in the Picture column.
9. Select a directory which has graphics which you wish to import. If you have Microsoft Word and have done a complete installation, the **C:\Word\Clipart** *directory* should have a variety of metafiles. This is where all examples in this book came from.
10. Select a file from the **File Name** list box, and then select **Preview Picture** to preview the file you have selected. If you are satisfied with that picture, select **OK**. The picture will be inserted into your worksheet.
11. Double-click on the picture. The dialog box illustrated in Figure 2.10 will be displayed.
12. Select the **Properties** tab, if it is not already selected.
13. Select **Move but Don't Size with Cells** (or **Move & Size**) from the **Object Positioning** option group, and then select OK.
14. If you want, add a description for the picture in the adjacent cell.
15. Select **Format→Cells**, and then apply the formatting that you wish to use to the cell.
16. Repeat steps 8 through 15 until your list contains all of the pictures that you want to include. When you're done, don't forget to save your worksheet immediately.

You can now select any cell in the description column and apply a sort to it. The description and the objects in the adjacent cells will then be sorted according to the sort you apply. You could create a macro that would automate steps 9 through 20, prompt you to add a new picture to the list, and then assign it to a command button which you place next to the list.

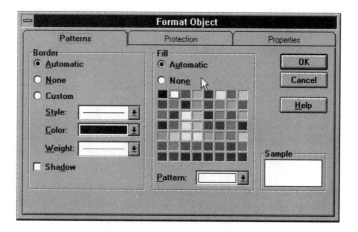

FIGURE 2.10
Format Object dialog box.

Sorting with OLE Objects

Excel 5.0 does not limit this behavior only to graphic objects. It also works with OLE objects. Figure 2.11 illustrates a worksheet which contains three Word 6.0 document objects, in an unsorted order. Two of them display the actual contents of the Word object, while the third simply displays a Word icon. To create a list which can be used for storing and/or cataloguing OLE objects, follow the steps below.

STEPS

Creating a List to Catalog MS Word 6.0 Document OLE Objects

1. Select as many rows as you initially expect your "database" to have.
2. Select **Format→Row→Height**.
4. Type in height that will be large enough to display your objects (25 is a good starting point for this example), and then select **OK**.
5. In cell **A1**, type **Document**; in cell **A2**, type **Description**.
6. Select cells **A1** and **A2** and change the typeface to bold. Then adjust the widths of columns 1 and 2 to allow your document and description to fit.

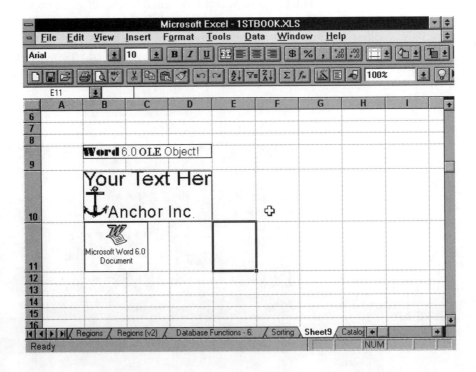

FIGURE 2.11
Catalog of Word 6.0 OLE objects.

7. Select **Insert→Object...**. The dialog box illustrated in Figure 2.12 will be displayed.
8. Select the **Create New** tab, if it is not already selected, and then select **Word 6.0 Document** from the **Object Type** list box.
9. Select the **Display as Icon** check box if you wish to display an icon instead of the actual object contents. Select **OK**. Notice that Excel's menu bar and toolbars change to Word 6.0's menu bar and toolbars, as illustrated in Figure 2.13. This is called **In-Place** editing, and is a feature of OLE 2.0.
10. Resize the Word object by dragging its **Sizing** handles.
11. Add whatever text you would like to have displayed, and then click anywhere in the Excel 5.0 workspace outside of the Word object. This will close the Word object's editing window.
12. Select the Word object you just added, and then select **Format→Object**.
13. Select the **Properties** tab, and then select **Move but Don't Size with Cell** from the **Object Positioning** option group. Select **OK**.
14. Select a cell to the right of the object, and then type a description of the object.
15. Select the next cell where you want to insert an object, and repeat steps 7 through 14 until your list is populated.
16. Apply any formatting to the list which you wish to use, and then save the worksheet.

You can now select any cell in the description column and apply a sort to

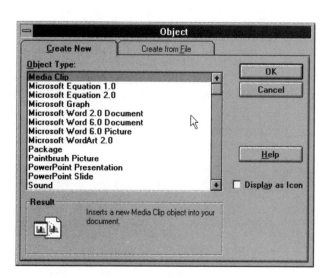

FIGURE 2.12
The **Create Object** dialog box.

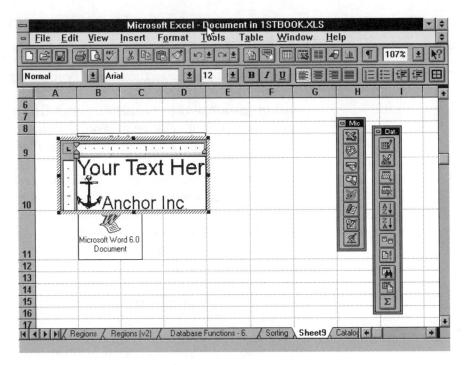

FIGURE 2.13
In-Place editing of a Word object inside Excel 5.0.

it. The description and the objects in the adjacent cells will then be sorted according to the sort you apply.

By using a technique like this, you can create a 'database' which contains all documents related to a single client or project. Remember, you can have different OLE servers in the same client application (in this case, your Excel worksheet). This means that in addition to Word documents, you can store other OLE objects together in the same list. Thus, if you are an architect, you might store all of the CAD objects, Word objects, and Excel objects related to a particular project, all in the same list. In other words, you would be using Excel as a repository and object manager for everything related to the project. If you made each of the cells 'page size' (so that a complete page of the document would be displayed), you could use this technique to print out reports with multiple Word 6.0 objects, in which you could very quickly change the page order via drag-and-drop or by applying a new sort order.

Advanced Sort Options

In addition to the basic sort options (choosing each of the three keys, whether each is ascending or descending, and whether or not there is a **Header Row**), there are several user configurable sort options available. These are:

- First Key Sort Order
- Case Sensitivity
- Sort Orientation.

Once set, each of these options will be used for all sorts (even if you use the **QuickSort** buttons) until they are reset, or until you end your Excel session.

First Key Sort Order

The **First Key Sort Order** allows you to use custom sort orders for situations when standard ascending/descending sorts do not meet your needs. To use a custom sort order, simply select it from the **First Key Sort Order** list box. For more information on creating and using custom sort orders (custom lists), see the section **Custom Sort Orders**, later in this chapter.

Sort Orientation

When most users think of sorting a list, they think of sorting it vertically. In other words, the sort is either performed top-to-bottom, or bottom-to-top. Although this is the default behavior for Excel 5.0, **Sort Orientation** is a user configurable option. Thus, you can have a list sorted horizontally as well as vertically.

Take, for example, the data illustrated in Table 2.4. This table was manually entered with the column labels in the order that would typically be expected (ascending, based on numeric equivalent—1 through 4).

What if you, instead, wanted to sort the columns, on a horizontal alphabetic sort? If you choose the top row (column labels) as the **Sort By**

TABLE 2.4 Sample Data Sorted in Ascending Order

Column One	Column Two	Column Three	Column Four
66	70	68	69
45	50	53	55
51	40	20	10

key, and set the **Orientation** option to **Sort Left to Right**, the list illustrated in Table 2.5 will be the result. To define Orientation of your sort, follow the steps below.

STEPS

Defining a Horizontal Sort Orientation

1. Select a cell in the list you wish to sort.
2. Select **Data→Sort...** and then select **Options...**.
3. Select **Sort Left to Right** from the **Orientation** option group, and then select **OK**.
4. Select the column you wish to apply the sort to, from the **Sort By** list box, and then select **OK**. The sort will be applied.

STEPS

Defining a Vertical Sort Orientation

1. Select a cell in the list you wish to sort.
2. Select **Data→Sort...** and then Select **Options...**.
3. Select **Sort Right to Left** from the **Orientation** option group, and then select **OK**.
4. Select the column you wish to apply the sort to, from the **Sort By** list box, and then select **OK**. The sort will be applied.

Case Sensitivity

When sorting duplicate items, Excel 5.0 ignores capitalization, by default. In other words, **John**, **JOHN** and **jOHN** are considered of equal value when sorting. If case sensitivity is critical to your sorting, it is an option which you can turn on. To turn case sensitivity on, follow these steps.

TABLE 2.5
Sample Data Sorted Left to Right, by the Column Label Row

Column Four	Column One	Column Three	Column Two
69	66	68	70
55	45	53	50
10	51	20	40

SORTING   33

STEPS   **Turning Case-Sensitivity On**

1. Select a cell in the list.
2. Select **Data→Sort...** and then select **Options....** The dialog box in Figure 2.14 will be displayed.
3. Select **Case Sensitive**, and then select **OK**.

Custom Sort Orders

Excel 5.0 allows you to create custom sort orders, so that you can create sorts that are specific to your application, by defining **Custom Lists**. Take, for example, a business which looks at sales by region: North East, South East, North West, and South West. If you were to apply a standard ascending sort to a list which contained these four entries, you would get the result illustrated in Table 2.6. This is clearly not the way you want the sort to come out!

To solve problems like this, Excel 5.0 allows you to create custom sort lists, in which you define the items to be sorted, and how they are sorted. Thus, to solve the problem of the sort order by region, you can build a list that orders the four regions in the order you want them to appear. You can then recall this sort order, and apply it to any list in your workspace. The result of applying this custom sort list to Table 2.6 would result in the list illustrated in Table 2.7.

Custom sort orders are stored globally, in EXCEL5.XLB. As such, they

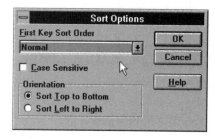

FIGURE 2.14
Sort Options dialog box.

TABLE 2.6
Standard Ascending Alpha Sort for Regions

Region
Northeast
Northwest
Southeast
Southwest

TABLE 2.7
Custom Sort
for Regions

Region
Northeast
Southeast
Northwest
Southwest

are not stored with a workbook. This can be either an advantage or a disadvantage, depending on your point of view. If you want to use the same custom sort order across more than one workbook in your own Excel environment, it is an advantage, because the custom list only has to entered once. After it has been entered, it is accessible by all workbooks you use. On the other hand, if you want to create a distributable workbook with a database, and one or more custom sort orders, it is a disadvantage because the custom sort orders are not stored in the workbook. Thus, if you distribute the workbook file to others, their **Sort** functions will not have the same custom sort order available unless everyone shares the same EXCEL5.XLB on a network. To get around this problem, you can create a custom macro which automatically adds the custom sort order to the user environment, the first time the workbook is opened.

Working with custom lists is a two step process:

- Define a custom list.
- Apply a custom list to the range you wish to sort.

The following sections teach you how to define the custom list and then how use it.

Defining a Custom List

There are three different ways that you can define a custom sort list:

- Manually enter a list.
- Import a list from a range of cells in an Excel workbook.
- Import a list from an external file.

Manually Entering a List

If the list you would like to create is short (and does not exist as part of a range of cells), the most efficient way to define the custom list is to enter it manually, in the **Custom Lists** tab of the **Options** dialog box. To enter a list manually, follow these steps.

STEPS

Entering a Custom List Manually

1. Select **Tools...→Options.Custom Lists**. The dialog box illustrated in Figure 2.15 will be displayed.
2. Select **NEW LIST** from the **Custom Lists** list box. Notice that as soon as you make this selection, a blinking I-Beam cursor appears in the **List Entries** list box.
3. Type the text for the first entry of your list, and then press **Enter**. This puts a break between list items.
4. Repeat step 3 until your list is complete.
5. Select **Add**. Notice that the list you just created appears at the bottom of the **Custom Lists** list box.
6. Repeat steps 2 through 5, if you wish to add additional lists. Select **OK**.

NOTE

If you wish to create a custom list which includes numbers, the only way to do it is by manually entering the list, using the method described above. As you will see in the next section, if you try to 'import' a range of cells which contain numbers (in other words, cells without text) they are ignored. Thus you have to 'force' Excel into using numbers by manually entering them.

Importing a List from a Range of Cells

If you wish to define a custom list, the contents of which exist in a range of cells within the same (or another) Excel workbook, the quickest way to define the list is to 'import' the range. To import a range of cells as a custom list, follow the steps below.

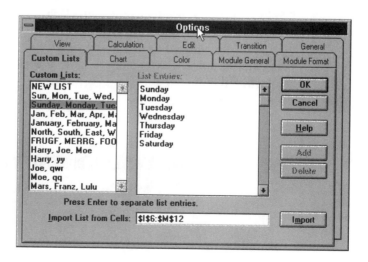

FIGURE 2.15
Options.Custom Lists dialog box.

STEPS — **Importing a List from a Range of Cells**

1. Select the range of cells that you wish to import.
2. Select **Tools...→Options.Custom Lists**. Notice that the range you have selected is listed in the **Import List from Cells** text box.
3. Select **Import**. Notice that the contents of the range you have selected appears in the **List Entries** list box and at the bottom of the **Custom Lists** list box.
4. Select **Add**. If you wish to define any more lists at this point, do so now.
5. Select **OK**.

X-REF

The **Options.Custom Lists** dialog box is modeless, just like the **Define Name** dialog box described in Chapter 1. If you wish to add another list, but do not wish to close the dialog box, you may interact with the Excel workspace as described in **Selecting a Range While the Define Name Dialog Box is Open** section of Chapter 1, and applying the same technique.

If you try to import a range of cells which contains only numbers, or a combination of text and numbers, the dialog box illustrated in Figure 2.16 will appear when you select **Import**.

This is to warn you that only cells which contain text will be imported into the custom list. At this point, this is only a warning dialog, and you cannot cancel the operation. You must select **OK**. This feature is actually quite handy, because it allows you to select ranges of cells that have both text and numbers, and only to import the text, which is probably what you want 99% of the time. As such, you do not have to 'reorganize' your data just to group all of the text values together.

In the method listed above, it is assumed that you selected a range of cells that were either in a single row or a single column. When most users first think of a list, they usually think of a vertical one-dimensional array, as illustrated in Figure 2.17, or a horizontal one-dimensional array, as illustrated in Figure 2.18.

There will be times, however, when you either intentionally or acci-

FIGURE 2.16
Cells without simple text were ignored. dialog box.

SORTING

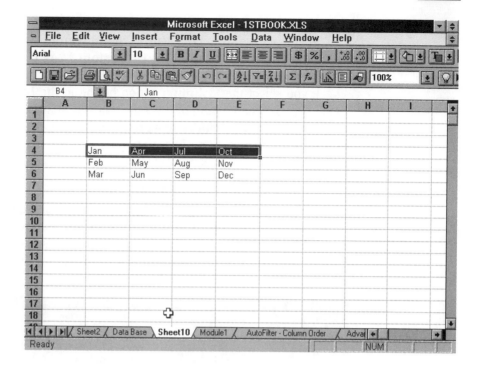

FIGURE 2.17
A vertical one-dimensional array, selected in a worksheet.

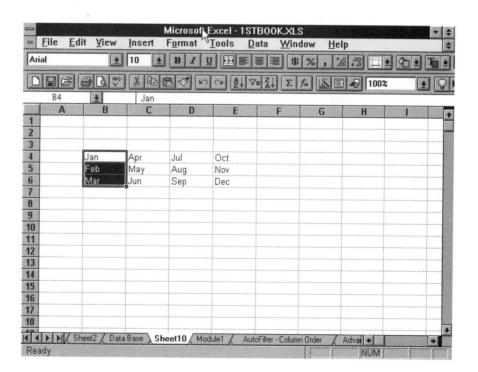

FIGURE 2.18
A horizontal one-dimensional array, selected in a worksheet.

dentally select a two-dimensional array, such as the one illustrated in Figure 2.19, as the source to import your custom list from. When this happens, after you select **Import**, the **Import Custom Lists** dialog box, which is illustrated in Figure 2.20, will be displayed.

If you select the **Columns** option button in the **Import Lists From** option group, each column of the selection will be imported as a separate list, starting with the leftmost column first. If you select the **Rows** option button in the **Import Lists From** option group, each row of the selection will be imported as a separate list, starting with the topmost column first.

Importing a List from an External File

If the list is long and exists outside of the Excel environment in another file format (such as a dBase or text file), the suggested method is to import the file into an Excel workbook, and then 'import' this result set as a custom list. For example, someone in your department might have created a dBase

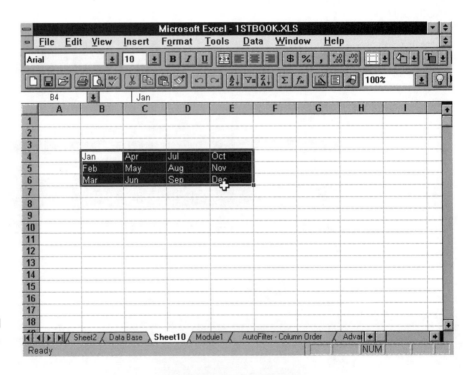

FIGURE 2.19
A two-dimensional array, selected in a worksheet.

FIGURE 2.20
Import Custom Lists dialog box.

file, which you have access to on a file server. This file contains a list of products which you wish to use for a custom sort order. Instead of printing out a copy of this list, and then re-keying it, you can simply import it into Excel.

STEPS — Importing a Custom List from a dBase File

1. Identify the target source file. Make sure that you know the file format, in this case dBase.
2. Select **File→Open**. The dialog box illustrated in Figure 2.21 will be displayed. Then select **dBase Files (*.DBF)** from the **List Files of Type** drop-down list. Notice that the text in the **File Name** combo box changes to ***.dbf**.
3. Use the **Drives** and **Directories** controls to select the drive and directory where your source file is located.
4. Select the file you wish to import from the **File Name** combo box, and then select **OK**. The file will be read into a new workbook, with the field names appearing in the top row of the worksheet.
5. Select the range of cells that you wish to 'import' as your custom list, and then select **Tools…→Options.Custom Lists**.
6. Select **Import**. Notice that the contents of the range you selected appear in the **List Entries** list box and at the bottom of the **Custom Lists** list box, and then select **OK**.
7. Select **File→Close**. Note that you did not, and should not, save the file in an XLS format.

You can now use the custom sort list with any workbooks in your Excel workspace.

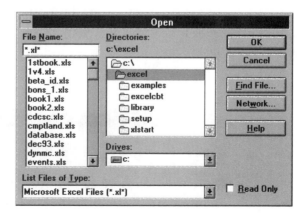

FIGURE 2.21
Open dialog box.

Although this example uses a dBase file format (which was used as an example at this point because Excel can read a dBase file without having to parse it manually), you can choose any file format which Excel supports. For more information on importing foreign file formats, see Chapter Seven, **Reading and Writing Other Data Formats.** You could also use MS Query to bring the contents of any database supported by ODBC into a workbook, instead of just importing the data directly via Excel's **File→Open** command. For more information on using MS Query to bring data into Excel, see Chapter 11, **An Overview of Using External Data.**

Removing a Custom List

There will, of course, be times when you decide that you no longer want to use a custom list. Excel allows you to remove any custom list that you may have added. To remove a custom list, follow the steps below.

STEPS   Removing a Custom List

1. Select **Tools→Options.Custom Lists**.
2. Select the list you want to remove from the **Custom Lists** list box.
3. Select **Delete**, and then select **OK**. The dialog box illustrated in Figure 2.22 will be displayed.
4. Repeat steps 2 through 3 until all of the lists that you want removed have been deleted.
5. Select **OK**.

Using a Custom List

Once you have defined a custom list using one of the above methods, you can apply it to any sort that you wish to perform. To use a custom list, follow these steps.

FIGURE 2.22
Lists will be permanently deleted! dialog box.

STEPS   Using a Custom List

1. Select the range you wish to sort, and then select **Data...→Sort**.
2. Select the column you wish to sort from the **Sort By** combo box if the default is not what you want.
3. Select **Options...** and then select the custom list you wish to use for the sort from the **First Key Sort Order** drop-down list box. Figure 2.23 illustrates the **Sort Options** dialog box.
4. If appropriate, modify the **Case Sensitivity** and **Orientation** options, and then select **OK**.

NOTE

*Once you have used a custom list, the options that you have just selected will be re-used every time you use the **QuickSort** tool for the remainder of the current Excel session unless you reset them again via the **Sort** dialog box.*

Sorting Data in an Outline

Worksheet outlining, introduced in Excel 4.0, allows users to organize data in a fashion which allows them to provide summary reports. Figure 2.24 illustrates an example of a worksheet which contains an outline, which is expanded, and shows both detail and summary information. Figure 2.25 illustrates the same worksheet with the outline collapsed, so that only summary information is displayed.

When Excel performs a sort on a list that contains an outline, it keeps rows and/or columns that are grouped together, together, and sorts based on the value of the group total. Thus, in the example illustrated above, if an ascending sort was performed on the list, using Jan as the sort key, **Cars** (and all of the corresponding detail rows) would be moved to the top of the list. For more information on creating and using Excel outlines, see **Excel 5 Insider**, also published by Wiley.

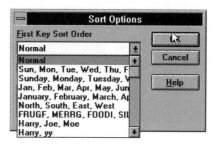

FIGURE 2.23
Sort Options dialog box.

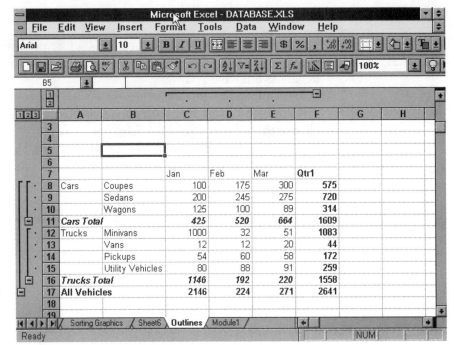

FIGURE 2.24
A worksheet with its outline expanded to display detail and summary information.

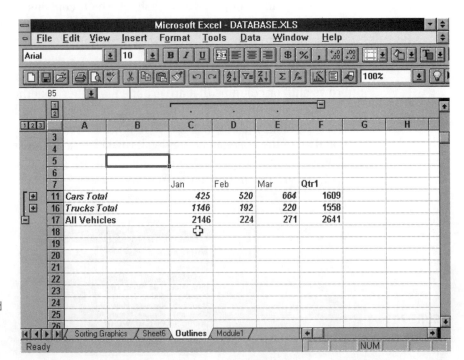

FIGURE 2.25
A worksheet with its outline collapsed to display only summary information.

CHAPTER 3
Filtering

Introduction

In Chapter Two, you learned how to sort your lists. Now that you understand how Excel's sorting can help you increase your productivity, it is time to introduce a feature of Excel which will let you work with subsets of your list: **Filtering**. In this chapter you will learn:

- What a filter is.
- What **Filter Mode** is, and how it affects your work.
- How to use an **AutoFilter**.
- How to define and use a **Custom AutoFilter**.
- How to define and use an **Advanced Filter**.

Filtering

As your list grows in size, you will find yourself frequently wanting to work on a subset of the list, not the complete list. Excel allows you to apply a **Filter** to your list which will screen out or filter out all rows which don't meet a comparison criteria which you specify.

Filter Mode

When you apply a filter, Excel switches into **Filter Mode. Filter Mode** allows you to edit, format, chart, and print your data, without rearranging it or moving it. For example, if you have a chart linked to your list and you apply a filter to it, only the data which meets your criteria will be displayed in the chart. Figure 3.1 illustrates a chart linked to a list, with all records shown. Figure 3.2 shows a subset of the list, after a criteria has been applied. To show that you are in filter mode, Excel gives you several reminders:

- The status bar displays either the text **Filter Mode** or indicates the number of rows in the list, and the number of rows that match your criteria.
- The drop-down arrow in the column heading(s) appears blue.
- The headings of the rows which meet the criteria appear blue.

When you are in **Filter Mode**, some commands work differently than when you are in one of Excel's other modes. If you use **AutoFill** (or **Edit→Fill →**), Excel will enter values only in the visible cells. In addition, the **Edit →Fill→Series...** command is not available. If you use the **AutoSum button**, when you are in **Filter Mode**, it only sums the visible cells. Thus, if you change the filter to **Show All**, the **AutoSum** will respond accordingly. The **Format→Cells...** (or **Format Cells...** from the **Shortcut** menu) will only format visible cells in the selection. The **Chart Wizard** button will create a chart only from the visible cells in the selection. The **Edit→Clear**

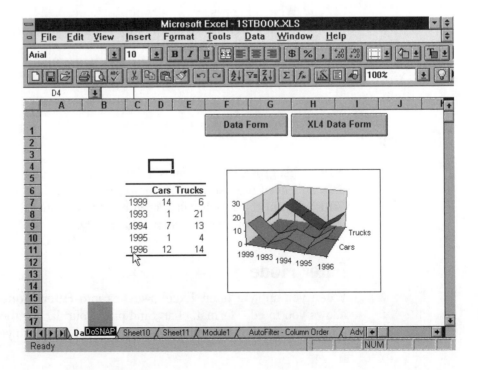

FIGURE 3.1
Chart and list, before filtering.

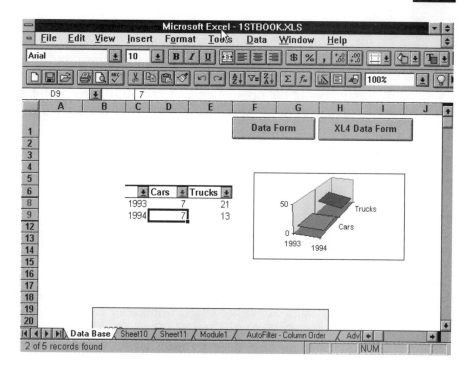

FIGURE 3.2
Chart and list, after applying a filter.

command will clear only the visible cells in the selection. The **Edit→Copy** command will copy only the visible cells in the selection. The **Edit→Delete** command becomes **Edit→Delete Row**, which deletes only visible rows in the selection. You cannot delete individual cells in a filtered worksheet, only complete rows. The **Insert** command (**Shortcut** menu) becomes **Insert Row**. The **Insert→Cells** command is not available. The **Insert Copied Cells** (**Shortcut** menu) becomes **Insert Pasted Rows** (assuming there is data in the clipboard). The **File→Print** command prints only visible cells. The **Data→Sort** command sorts only visible cells. The **Data→Subtotals** command calculates subtotals only for visible cells.

Excel 5.0 offers two features which allow you to use filters with lists:

- **AutoFilter**
- **Advanced Filter.**

Filters screen out all of the rows which you don't want, by comparing the values in the list, against a **Comparison Criteria** which you specify. Comparison criteria contain one or more values in one or more columns that you wish to search for in your list. If a row in the list matches your criteria, it is displayed in the filtered list. If it does not match the criteria, the row is hidden. **AutoFilter** provides an easy-to-use interface for specifying your search criteria, by allowing you to select your criteria from a drop-down list, with limited matching options. **Advanced Filter**, on the other hand, provides you with more options, but uses a more complex interface. Traditionally, ease of use comes at the price of power, and power comes at the price of ease of use. **AutoFilter** and **Advanced Filter** are both relatively easy to use, once you understand their interfaces, and AutoFilter will probably satisfy all but the most demanding of your filtering requirements. The following sections detail both features.

AutoFilter

AutoFilter is the simplest way to apply a filter to your list and screen out all unwanted rows by placing drop-down lists directly on your worksheet, in place of your column headings, which allow you to select your criteria from the drop-down. Examine the data illustrated in Figure 3.3. What if you only wanted to view contacts who were located in New York? If you applied an **AutoFilter** to the list, and then selected the arrow next to the **State** column heading, the drop-down list illustrated in Figure 3.4 would be displayed.

If you selected NY from the drop-down list, all of the rows which did

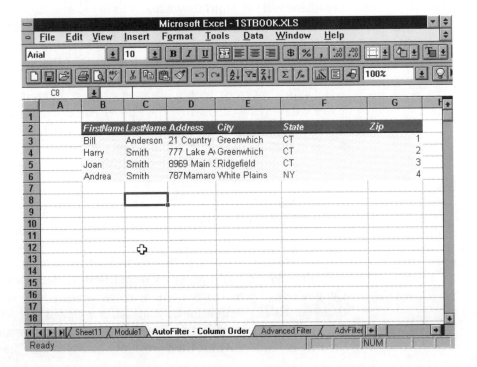

FIGURE 3.3
Contacts list.

FILTERING 47

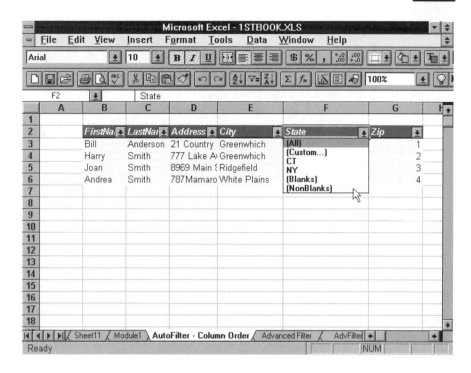

FIGURE 3.4
Contacts list,
AutoFilter, drop-down list for State.

not contain NY would be hidden, and the list illustrated in Figure 3.5 would be displayed. Using an AutoFilter is a two-step process. First you must apply an **AutoFilter** to the list. Once this is done, you can define comparison criteria for the **AutoFilter**. To apply an **AutoFilter** to a list, follow the steps below.

STEPS   Applying an AutoFilter to a List

1. Select any cell within the list.
2. Select **Data→Filter→AutoFilter**. Notice that drop-down arrows appear on your worksheet, next to the column headings.

That's it! Now you are ready to define your comparison criteria for the **AutoFilter**.

Comparison Criteria

Comparison criteria are the values that you wish to compare to the values in the rows. If you wanted to find all rows in a list where the **State** column contained the value 'NY', (in English), **State = NY** would be your com-

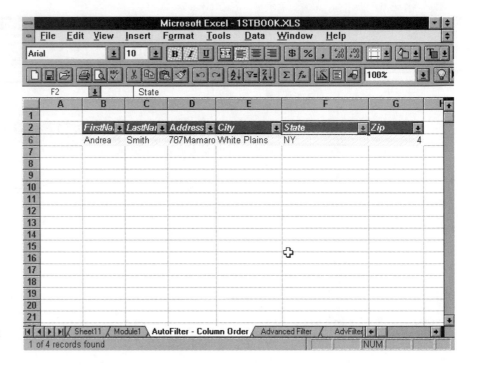

FIGURE 3.5
Collapsed Contact List—NY only.

parison criteria. Although it helps to be able to verbalize your comparison criteria in this manner, **AutoFilter** allows you to define your comparison criteria simply clicking on the arrow next to the column heading, and selecting from a list of values. When you click on the arrow next to the column heading you wish to set the criteria for, Excel displays the criteria drop-down list for this column. When you display the criteria drop-down list, Excel reads through your list, identifies all of the unique values in the list, and then displays them in the drop-down. If a value occurs in more than one row in your list, the criteria list will only list it once. No matter what order the items are really sorted in, when you display the criteria drop-down box, they will be sorted in ascending order, following the rules described in Chapter Two, **Sorting**. Besides the contents of your list, the criteria drop-down always contains four standard entries:

- (All)
- (Custom)
- (Blanks)
- (NonBlanks).

Selecting **(All)** will remove the criteria from the column you are working with, and will display all of the rows. **(Custom)** allows you to define custom criteria, and is covered below. Selecting **(Blanks)** will display all rows that contain no values (nulls). This is useful for identifying incomplete rows within your list. Selecting **(NonBlanks)** will display all rows which contain data, including blank text **("")**. Selecting any other entry will hide all of the rows which do not meet the criteria. To apply a criteria to a column, follow the steps below.

STEPS

Applying Criteria to a Column

1. If you have not already defined an **AutoFilter**, do so now, following the steps detailed in the previous section.
2. Click on the drop-down arrow that appears to the right of the column heading for the column you wish to apply the criteria to. The criteria drop-down list will be displayed.
3. Select the criteria that you wish to apply. All of the rows which match your criteria will be displayed.

For navigating through long list, there are several shortcuts which can be used, once the criteria drop-down is open. Pressing **Home** moves the cursor to the top of the list. Pressing **End** moves the cursor to the bottom of the list. Pressing **Page Up** scrolls up the list one 'page' at a time. Pressing **Page Down** scrolls down the list one 'page' at a time. Pressing the key that corresponds with any of the 26 letters of the alphabet moves the cursor to the first entry that matches, presuming the list contains entries which start with an alphabetic character (entries like addresses, which start with a number, do not follow this behavior). Repeatedly pressing the key will scroll through all entries which match the key.

Custom AutoFilter

If you like the simplicity of AutoFilter and the ease of making selections from drop-down list boxes, but need to apply slightly more complex criteria, then you should try using a **Custom AutoFilter**. Whereas a normal **AutoFilter** will allow you to select rows based on a single equi-match, **Custom AutoFilter** allows you to easily create criteria which:

- Use comparison operators other than equality (=).
- Contain either of two comparison values.
- Contain two different comparison values.

Comparison Operators

A **comparison operator** is the sign which is used to compare two values. In all of the examples in the previous sections of this chapter, the only comparison operator has been =, or **Equal To**. When you build your criteria, Excel compares the criteria which you specify against the value in the cell(s) that you are examining, based on the comparison operator. It is common to want to find all values in a range which exceed a certain value (greater than the comparison operator), or are not equal to a certain value (not equal to the comparison operator). For example, you might want to apply a filter to a list which contains sales information, and only look at rows where a person's sales for a period are below quota (the less than comparison operator). Table 3.1 lists the six standard comparison operators which are available in Excel.

In addition to the six standard comparison operators listed in Table 3.1, **AutoFilter** allows for two additional comparison operators which allow you to combine two criteria in a single Custom **AutoFilter**. These operators are:

- And
- Or.

These two operators are used to join the two individual criteria together to create one 'Meta Criteria', which is used for the comparison. The **And** operator is used to select rows which meet **both** criteria. The **Or** operator is used to select rows which meet **either** criteria.

Query by Example

The interface which Excel provides to define your criteria for a **Custom AutoFilter** is called **Query By Example (QBE)**, because you to define your criteria by specifying an example. When you select a value from the drop-down list in 'standard' **AutoFilter**, you are actually using a simple version of QBE, because you simply give Excel an 'example' of what to match, and Excel takes care of all the behind-the-scenes mechanics of the

TABLE 3.1 Standard Comparison Operators

Operator	Meaning
=	Equal to
>	Greater than
<	Less than
>=	Greater than or equal to
<=	Less than or equal to
<>	Not equal to

FILTERING

query. When using **Custom AutoFilter**, you create your examples by interfacing with the dialog box. To create your **QBE**, all you have to do is select your comparison operators, and enter (or select) your criteria values.

The **Custom AutoFilter** dialog box has three major components:

- **Comparison Operator** list boxes
- **Comparison Value** combo boxes
- **And/Or** comparison operator option buttons.

The **Comparison Operator list boxes** are used to select the comparison operators. The **Comparison Value combo boxes** are used to enter/select the criteria value which you want to compare. The **And/Or option buttons** are used only when you use two criteria, to determine which of these two comparison operators will be used to join the criteria together. To create a **Custom AutoFilter**, follow the steps below.

STEPS Creating a Custom AutoFilter

1. If you have not already defined an **AutoFilter**, do so now.
2. Select **(Custom)** from the criteria drop-down for the column you wish to apply the criteria to.
3. Select the comparison operator(s), comparison value(s) you wish to use.
4. Select **OK**. All of the rows which match your criteria will be displayed.

Wildcards

Wildcard characters can also be used to create criteria which will find values which share some (but not necessarily all) characters. For example, if you wanted to find all rows in a list of first names which start with the letter 'J,' you could use a wildcard character in the search. All you have to do is substitute the characters you don't know with the wildcard(s) described in Table 3.2.

Table 3.3 illustrates a list of names, sorted alphabetically. Table 3.4

TABLE 3.2
Wildcards

Character	Character Name	Description
*	Asterisk	Represents any number of characters
?	Question mark	Represents any single character

TABLE 3.3
List of Names

Name
Gerry
James
Jane
Janet
Jerry
Jill
Joe
John
Terry

illustrates the results of using various wildcards in criteria, when applied against this list.

If you wish to match an actual question mark, asterisk, or tilde(~), you must precede the special character with a tilde(~).

Applying an AutoFilter to Select Columns in a List

Excel's default behavior is to apply filters to every column in the list when you use an AutoSort. Although this will often be what you want, there will be times when you want to apply a filter only to one or more selected columns, not to all of them. Follow the steps below to apply an **AutoFilter** to a subset of the columns in a list.

STEPS — **Applying an AutoFilter to Only One Column in a List**

1. Select the column heading, and at least one cell directly below it.
2. Select **Data→Filter→AutoFilter**.
3. Set your criteria.

STEPS — **Applying an AutoFilter to Two or More Columns in a List**

1. Select the column headings of the columns you wish to filter.
2. Select **Data→Filter→AutoFilter**.
3. Set your criteria.

TABLE 3.4
Use of Wildcards in Criteria

Criteria	Returned Value(s)
J*	John, James, Jerry, Jane, Jill, Joe, Janet
J???	John, Jane, Jill
J?n	Jane, Janet
?erry	Gerry, Jerry, Terry

Removing an AutoFilter

When you are finished working with an AutoFilter, you can either:

- Turn the filter off, to show all of the data.
- Completely remove the filter from the list.

If you plan on using the filter again, you should just turn the filter off. The easiest way to do this is to Select **Data→Filter→Show All**. This will result in all hidden rows being displayed again. You can also select **(All)** from the drop-down list box of a column you have applied a filter to. If you have criteria for more than one column set, this will remove only the criteria for that column. In order to remove all of the criteria, you must set each column's criteria to **(All)**. Thus, if you have two or more columns with criteria, and you want to turn the filter off on all of them, the **Data→Filter→Show All** method is usually quicker.

If you are finished using an AutoFilter with a list, you can completely remove it by selecting **Data→Filter→AutoFilter**. Notice that the drop-down arrows are removed from the list's column headings.

Copying Filtered Data

While AutoFilter provides a quick way to view and manipulate data via in-place filtering, there will be many situations in which you will want to copy the filtered data to another worksheet, and then manipulate it. This guarantees that the underlying data remains intact. To copy a list which has an AutoFilter applied to it, follow the steps below.

STEPS

Copying a List Which Has AutoFilter Applied to It to Another Worksheet

1. Apply the **AutoFilter** and **Criteria** as defined above.
2. Select the range you wish copy.
3. Select **Edit→Copy**.

4. Select the new worksheet that you wish to copy the range to.
5. Select **Edit→Paste**.

> **HINT** You can use the **Copy** button and **Paste** button tools on the toolbar, or Excel's drag-and-drop capabilities to copy the range. See Excel's online help, or printed documentation for more information on these subjects.

You can also copy the range within the same worksheet, or to another workbook. Copying within the same worksheet is not recommended because it is easy to confuse the original data and the copy. Also, as **AutoFilter** hides and unhides rows, if you place the duplicate next to the original, you may get views which are not what you really desire, without realizing it. Since Excel 5.0 supports a true three-dimensional workbook model, it is easier than ever to put the duplicate range in another worksheet. Using the sheet-naming capability of Excel, it is easy to create several worksheets within the same workbook, with names such as *List* and *Duplicate List*. When you copy your data, you can also use **Edit→Paste Link** or **Edit→Paste Special** to paste dynamic links, so that if you change a value in the original list, the copy will be updated automatically.

Advanced Filter

If your filtering needs are beyond the capabilities that **Custom AutoFilter** provides, you should try using **Advanced Filter**. There are four main reasons why you would want to use **Advanced Filter**:

- You want to define multiple criteria across multiple columns, in a single step.
- You want to use more than two criteria on a single column.
- You want to use an expression in your criteria. This includes referencing a cell outside of the list, or within the list.
- You want to automatically extract the filtered data to another range.

The major components of the **Advanced Filter** dialog box are:

- **Action** option group
- **Criteria Range:** text box
- **List Range:** text box
- **Copy to:** range text box
- **Unique Records Only** check box.

When you apply an **Advanced Filter** to a list, there are two possible outcomes which you can choose from, which are determined by the option you select in the **Action** option group. You can:

- Filter the list in place.
- Automatically extract the rows which match the criteria to another range.

Filtering In Place hides all rows which do not meet the comparison criteria. **Extracting** automatically copies the rows of the filtered list to another range within the same worksheet, to a different worksheet within the same workbook, or to another workbook all together. Selecting **Copy to Another Location** will extract the filtered list. Selecting **Filter the List, in-place** will filter the list in place.

There are three main components which are necessary for **Advanced Filter** to work if you want to automatically copy the filtered records to another range:

- The **Criteria Range**
- The **List Range**
- The **Extract Range**.

If you do not want to copy the filtered records to another range, only two of these components are required:

- The **Criteria Range**
- The **List Range**.

The **Criteria Range** is the range of cells which you use to enter your criteria. It is where you specify the comparison operators as well as the comparison values. The **List Range** is the range of cells which contains the list against which you wish to perform the **Advanced Filter**. The **Extract Range** is the range of cells to which you wish to copy the filtered rows, if you are using **Advanced Filter** to perform an extract.

If you use the **Data→Filter→Advanced Filter** command, Excel handles the creation, naming and management of these ranges for you, based on the values you enter in the **Advanced Filter** dialog box. Alternatively, you can manually create and modify these three ranges, and exercise more control over the entire filtering operation.

The **Unique Records Only** check box determines whether Excel will display duplicate rows in the result set. If the **Unique Records Only** check box is checked, duplicate rows will not be displayed. If the **Unique Re-**

cords Only check box is not checked, duplicate rows will be displayed. The latter is the default behavior.

List Range

The **List Range** is used to identify the list which the **Advanced Filter** will be applied against. It makes sense that before you can filter a list, you must have already created your list. For Advanced Filter to work correctly, Excel must define the list name using the reserved range name *Database*. There are two ways you can define a criteria range:

- Automatically, using the **Advanced Filter** dialog box's **List Range:** edit box
- Manually, using **Range Names**.

Automatically Defining List Ranges

The quickest and easiest way to define a list range is to allow Excel to do it for you by selecting or entering a range in the **Advanced Filter** dialog box's **List Range:** edit box. To define the list range using the **Advanced Filter** dialog box, follow the steps below.

STEPS

Using the Advanced Filter Dialog Box to Define the List Range

1. Select any cell in your list.
2. Select **Data→Filter→Advanced Filter....** Notice that Excel automatically selects the entire list, and a reference to the range which contains the list appears in the **List Range:** edit box.
3. If Excel does not correctly identify your list, select the range on your worksheet which contains your list.
4. Define the **Criteria Range:** and **Copy to:** range.
5. Select **OK.**

X-REF

The **Advanced Filter** dialog box is modeless, just like the **Define Name** dialog box, described in Chapter 1. You may interact with the Excel workspace as described in **Selecting a Range While the Define Name Dialog Box is Open** section of Chapter 1, and applying the same technique.

As soon as you have completed this operation, Excel automatically defines a range named *Database* for the **List Range:** you just defined. You can verify this via the **Define Name** dialog box, or the **Name Box**.

X-REF *Manually defining a Database Range was covered in Chapter One.*

Now, when you use the **Advanced Filter** command, you can simply type the text *Criteria* in the **List Range:** edit box. Note that when you do this, Excel automatically converts the text to the cell address, although you will not see this until the next time that you view the **Advanced Filter** dialog box.

Criteria Range

Instead of the drop-down lists which are used by **AutoFilter**, **Advanced Filter** uses a range of the worksheet called the **Criteria Range**, in which you manually define your comparison criteria. The criteria range is an array of at least two rows and one column. The interface which Excel uses for the criteria range is known as a **Query By Example** grid. This is because you define the comparison criteria by placing examples of what you want to search for in the **QBE** grid. The **QBE** grid consists of two parts:

- One row that defines criteria labels
- One or more rows that define comparison criteria.

Criteria labels are simply cells that contain the column headings from the list you wish to filter, and are used to identify the columns you wish to match. **Comparison criteria** are contained in cells below the criteria labels. Each cell in the grid which contains comparison criteria contains two components:

- The Comparison Operator
- The Comparison Value (or formula).

To enter a comparison criteria, all you do is type the comparison operator, followed by the comparison value, in a cell below the **Criteria Label** you wish to match. Unlike **AutoFilter**, you can also use expressions. A simple criteria range could be *Select all rows where **LastName** is Smith and **Sales** are greater than 2100.*

Comparison Operators

Aside from **And** and **Or**, the six comparison operators detailed earlier in this chapter behave exactly alike. The only difference is that instead of selecting them from a drop-down list as you did in the **Custom AutoFilter** dialog box, you must type them into the **QBE** grid. If no comparison operator is specified, equality is assumed. Thus, if you want to perform a match using the equality (=) comparison operator, you do not have to explicitly declare it (except for exact text matches, as detailed below).

If you would like to use the **And** comparison operator, you place all of the criteria which should be joined together by the **And** in the same row. If for example, you want to select all rows where **FirstName** *equals Harry,* **and LastName** *equals Smith,* **and State** *equals CT,* use the criteria illustrated in Table 3.5.

If you would like to use the **Or** comparison operator, you place the criteria in another row. If for example, you want to build upon the previous example, and also say **FirstName** *equals Harry,* **and LastName** *equals Smith,* **and State** *equals CT,* **or FirstName** *equals Joan,* use the criteria illustrated in Table 3.6.

If you really want to find all rows in which **FirstName** *equals Harry* or *Joan,* **and LastName** *equals Smith,* **and State** *equals CT,* use the criteria illustrated in Table 3.7.

If you would like to use the **And** comparison operator on the same column more than once, you must repeat the column label. If, for example, you want to find rows with zip codes which fall between 06000 and 07000, you would use the criteria illustrated in Table 3.8.

TABLE 3.5 Criteria Built Using **And** and **Or** Comparison Operators

FirstName	LastName	Address	City	State	Zip
Harry	Smith			CT	

TABLE 3.6

FirstName	LastName	Address	City	State	Zip
Harry	Smith			CT	
Joan					

TABLE 3.7

FirstName	LastName	Address	City	State	Zip
Harry	Smith			CT	
Joan	Smith			CT	

TABLE 3.8

Zip	Zip
>06000	<07000

Although the criteria in the first two examples include labels for all of the columns in the list, it is only necessary to include the columns you wish to match, as example in Table 3.8 illustrates.

Building a Criteria Range

There are two requirements for building your criteria range:

- Build the QBE grid.
- Identify the range as the criteria.

Assuming that you already have a list in place, the first step is to identify the range you wish to use as the criteria range, and to build your **QBE** grid. To build a **QBE** grid, follow the steps below.

STEPS

Building the QBE Grid

1. Insert as many rows as necessary at the top of the worksheet, to hold the criteria range.
2. Copy the necessary column labels from the list that you wish to filter, to the top row of the criteria range.
3. Enter the comparison operators and values to the **QBE** grid.

Once you have built the **QBE** grid, you must define it as the criteria range, so that Excel can use it correctly. There are two ways you can define a criteria range:

- Automatically, using **Advanced Filter**'s **criteriaRange** argument.
- Manually, using **Range Names**.

Automatically Defining Criteria Ranges

The quickest and easiest way to define a criteria range is to allow Excel to do it for you, based on the **criteriaRange** argument of **AdvancedFilter** method. Although you can access the **AdvancedFilter** method's **criteriaRange** programmatically, you can also set it simply by selecting or entering a range in the **Advanced Filter** dialog box's **Criteria Range:** edit box. To define the criteria range using the **Advanced Filter** dialog box, follow these steps:

STEPS

Using the Advanced Filter Dialog Box to Define the Criteria Range

1. Select **Data→Filter→Advanced Filter...**.
2. Select the **Criteria Range:** edit box.
3. Select the range on your worksheet which contains your **QBE** grid. Notice that a reference to the range you select appears in the **Criteria Range:** edit box, which includes the workbook name.
4. Define the **List Range** and **Copy to:** range, as described elsewhere in this chapter.
5. Select **OK**.

X-REF

*The **Advanced Filter** dialog box is modeless, just like the **Define Name** dialog box, described in Chapter 1. You may interact with the Excel workspace as described in **Selecting a Range While the Define Name Dialog Box is Open** section of Chapter 1, and applying the same technique.*

As soon as you have completed this operation, Excel automatically defines a range named *Criteria* for the **Criteria Range:** range you just defined. You can verify this via the **Define Name** dialog box, or the **Name Box**.

Manually Defining Criteria Ranges

If you are comfortable with using range names, you can perform this operation manually. To manually define the criteria range, follow the steps below.

STEPS

Manually Defining a Criteria Range, Using the Name Box

1. Select the range which contains the **QBE** grid.
2. Select the **Name Box**. The cell address will be highlighted.
3. Type *Criteria* over the cell address.
4. Press **Enter**.

STEPS   Manually Defining a Criteria Range, Using the Define Name Command

1. Select the range which contains the **QBE** grid.
2. Select the **Insert→Name→Define…**. Notice that the text box contains a reference to the range you have selected in the format = *'Worksheet Name'!CellAddress*.
3. Type *Criteria* in the **Names in Workbook** edit box.
4. Select **OK**.

Now, when you use the **Advanced Filter** command, you can simply type the text *Criteria* in the **Criteria Range:** edit box. Note that when you do this, Excel automatically converts the text to the cell address, although you will not see this until the next time that you view the **Advanced Filter** dialog box.

RULE   Dranchak's Criteria Identification Rules (DCIR)

Here are some general rules/recommendations which you should follow when defining your criteria range (Figure 3.6):

- Always place the criteria range above or below the list, if the list and criteria are in the same worksheet. If you place them side by side and use **Filtering In Place**, you may hide rows of your criteria range, which will yield unexpected results.
- Always copy your column names to the criteria range to reduce the likelihood of typing errors.
- Clearly identify the criteria range using different formatting, such as a double outline border.
- Identify the column headings by applying a different format to them.
- Identify the criteria range by placing a label above it and applying a different format.
- If you are using one or more **Or** comparison operators, type a text label that specifies **Or** in the column to the left of the criteria range, to make the criteria range more 'readable.'

You can also place your **QBE** in a separate workbook, and create a **QBE** window, which contains buttons which will invoke **Advanced Filter**. By making calls to the Windows API, via an Excel Module, you can make the workbook **Modeless**, so that it would be a **Floating QBE Window**. Figure 3.7 illustrates an example of a workbook being used as a **QBE** window.

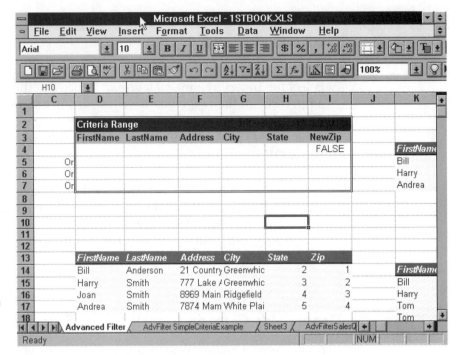

FIGURE 3.6
Criteria range which follows **Dranchak's** Criteria Identification Rules.

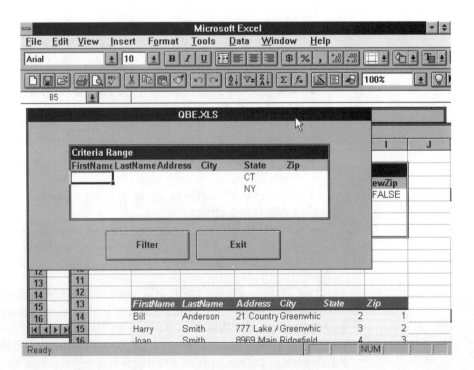

FIGURE 3.7
Floating QBE Window—**QBE.XLS**.

Comparison Values Criteria
Exact Text Matches
When using a **Custom AutoFilter**, if you did not know the exact text which you wanted to match, you had to use wildcard characters in your criteria definition. When using **Advanced Filter**, Excel finds all items which begin with the text which you specify in the criteria. Thus, if your list contains **Greens Farms** and **Greenwich** in the **City** column, and your criteria specifies **Green**, Excel will select both of these rows. If you want to perform an exact match, you must specify the text using the expression

$$="=text"$$

where **text** is the complete text you wish to match. If, for example, you only want the rows with **Greenwich** returned, you would have to use the expression $="=Greenwich"$.

Wildcards are still required if you do not know the starting character(s) of the text, or if you want to search for a single character. For more information on wildcards, see the **Wildcards** discussion in the **AutoFilter** section, earlier in this chapter.

Calculated Criteria
In addition, to allow the use of constants and constants intermixed with wildcards as criteria values, **Advanced Filter** also supports **Calculated Criteria**. **Calculated Criteria** are expressions which evaluate to **True** or **False**. Within a calculated criteria, you can use any mix of constants, functions, and cell references, as long as the expression can evaluate to **True** or **False**. If the expression evaluates to **True**, the row which contains it will be returned to the filtered data set. If the expression evaluates to **False**, the row will not be included. In addition to evaluating to **True** or **False**, the expression must contain a reference to at least one column on the list. To refer to a column in a list, use a relative address which refers to the first column in the list (column heading). In addition, if you are using a calculated criteria, you should not use a criteria heading which matches a column heading in your list. If you do, Excel may evaluate the wrong range, and return incorrect and/or unexpected results.

If you want to compare the contents of a cell in your list with a cell that contains a constant value, you should use an absolute cell reference. An example of this is illustrated in Figure 3.8. The expression in the **BelowQuota** criteria compares the **Sales** column to the value in the **Sales Quota** cell. Note that to reference a column with a relative address, you use the address of the first row of the list, which falls below the column headings. Also note the formula in the **Formula** bar, as well as the fact

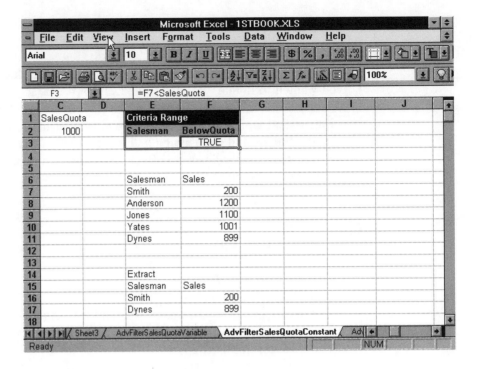

FIGURE 3.8
AdvFilterSales-
QuotaConstant.

that the cell displays the value **TRUE**. You can also use a range name as the absolute reference. If the cell which contained the **Sales Quota** constant was named **SalesQuota**, you could use the expression =*F7<SalesQuota* in the **BelowQuota** criteria.

If you want to compare the contents of a cell in your list with another cell in the list, you should use a relative cell reference. An example of this is illustrated in Figure 3.9. The expression in the **BelowQuota** criteria compares the **Sales** column to the value in the adjacent **Quota** column. Once again, note that to reference a column with a relative address, you use the address of the first row of the list, which falls below the column headings. Thus, as Excel evaluates each row in the list, the reference keeps changing. Also note the formula in the **Formula** bar, as well as the fact that the cell displays the value TRUE.

Extract Range

As defined earlier in this chapter, the **Extract Range** is the range of cells to which the data will be copied, if you select **Copy to Another Location** option button in the **Action** option group.

An extract can have one of several possible outcomes, based upon the size, shape content, and location of the range you select:

- If you select a single cell, Excel will copy the column labels, and

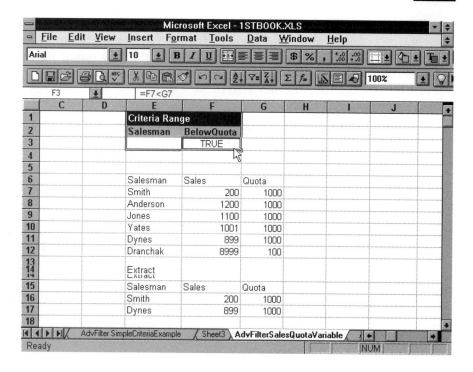

FIGURE 3.9
AdvFilterSales-
QuotaVariable.

all of the filtered data for every column in the list, regardless of which columns are in the criteria. If there are cells below or to the right of this cell which contain data, they will be overwritten without warning. It is important to make sure that you leave enough room for the extract.
- If you select a range of more than one cell, Excel copies as many rows as will fit in the range. If there is not enough room in the range to copy all of the rows, Excel displays the dialog box. If the range does not have enough columns to hold all of the columns in the list, only the number of columns in the range will be copied.
- If you select a range of more than one cell, and the first row contains one or more column labels which correspond to the list, only those columns will be pasted to the new range.

There are two ways you can define an extract range:

- Automatically, using **Advanced Filter**'s **copyToRange** argument.
- Manually, using **Range Names.**

Automatically Defining Extract Ranges

The quickest and easiest way to define an Extract range is to allow Excel to do it for you, based on the **copyToRange** argument of **AdvancedFilter** method. Although you can access the **AdvancedFilter** method's **copy-**

ToRange programmatically, you can also set it simply by selecting or entering a range in the **Advanced Filter** dialog box's **Copy to:** edit box. To define the **Extract Range** using the **Advanced Filter** dialog box, follow the steps below.

STEPS: Using the Advanced Filter Dialog Box to Define the Extract Range

1. Select **Data→Filter→Advanced Filter…**.
2. Select the **Copy to Another Location** option button in the **Action** option group.
3. Select the **Copy to:** edit box.
4. Select the range on your worksheet that you wish to copy to. Notice that a reference to the range you select appears in the **Copy to:** edit box, which includes the workbook name.
5. Define the **List Range** and **Criteria Range**, as described elsewhere in this chapter.
6. Select **OK**.

> **X-REF**
> The **Advanced Filter** dialog box is modeless, just like the **Define Name** dialog box described in Chapter 1. You may interact with the Excel workspace as described in **Selecting a Range While the Define Name Dialog Box is Open** section of Chapter 1, and applying the same technique.

As soon as you have completed this operation, Excel automatically defines a range named *Extract* for the **Copy to:** range you just defined. You can verify this via the **Define Name** dialog box, or the **Name Box**.

Manually Defining Extract Ranges

If you are comfortable with using range names, you can perform this operation manually. To manually define the extract range, follow the steps below.

STEPS: Manually Defining an Extract Range, Using the Name Box

1. Select the range you would like to copy the filtered list to.
2. Select the **Name Box**. The cell address will be highlighted.
3. Type *Extract* over the cell address.
4. Press **Enter**.

STEPS Manually Defining an Extract Range, Using the Define Name Command

1. Select the range you would like to copy the filtered list to.
2. Select the **Insert→Name→Define…**. The **Define Name** dialog box will be displayed. Notice that the **Refers To** text box contains a reference to the range you have selected in the format = *'Worksheet Name'!Cell Address*.
3. Type *Extract* in the **Names in Workbook** edit box.
4. Select **OK**.

Now, when you use the **Advanced Filter** command, you can simply type the text *Extract* in the **Copy to:** edit box. Note that when you do this, Excel automatically converts the text to the cell address, although you will not see this until the next time you view the **Advanced Filter** dialog box.

Extracting to Another Worksheet

Excel 5.0 Advanced Filter does not allow you to directly copy the filtered range to another worksheet in a single step. The most obvious way to try this would be to use a reference to another worksheet in **Advanced Filter**'s **Copy to:** text box. If you try to use a reference to another worksheet in the text box, Excel will display a message box informing you that this is an illegal operation.

There is, however, a way around this 'limitation.' Although Excel 5.0 does not allow the use of a reference to another worksheet in **Advanced Filter**'s **Copy to:** text box, it does allow the use of external references in the **Criteria Range:** and **List Range:** text boxes. To extract filtered records to another worksheet, follow the steps below.

STEPS Extracting to Another Worksheet

1. Set up your criteria and list in one worksheet (They can actually be in separate worksheets).
2. Switch to the destination worksheet and select **Data→Filter→Advanced Filter…**.
3. Select the **Criteria Range:** text box and specify an external reference to the criteria range.
4. Select the **List Range:** text box and specify an external reference to the list range.

5. Select the **Copy to Another Location** option button in the **Action** option group and select the **Copy to:** edit box.
6. Select the range on the destination worksheet that you wish to copy to and select **OK**.

This method works not only for worksheets in the same workbook, but also for worksheets in other workbooks.

Summary

In this chapter you have learned:

- When you apply a filter to a list, Excel switches to **Filter Mode**.
- Excel has two features to help you with filtering: **AutoFilter** and **Advanced Filter**.
- **AutoFilter** provides an easy-to-use interface for specifying your search criteria, by allowing you to select your criteria from a drop-down list.
- **Comparison Criteria** are the values that you wish to compare the values in the row with.
- A **Comparison Operator** is the sign which is used to compare two values.
- After you apply an **AutoFilter**, you can copy the filtered list to another range.
- **Advanced Filter** provides you with advanced filtering options which are not available using **AutoFilter**, but uses a more complex interface.
- The **Criteria Range** is the range of cells which you use to enter your criteria to be used with **Advanced Filter**.
- The **List Range** is the range of cells which contains the list on which you wish to perform the **Advanced Filter**.
- The **Extract Range**, is the range of cells to which you wish to copy the filtered rows, if you are using **Advanced Filter** to perform an extract.
- **Calculated Criteria** are expressions which evaluate to **True** or **False**.
- **Advanced Filter** uses a **Query By Example** grid, which is located on a worksheet to define comparison criteria. This is also known as the **QBE** grid.

CHAPTER 4

Data Forms

Introduction

Although the grid interface of an Excel worksheet is useful for moving through large amounts of data, it is not always the most ideal interface. Excel provides another interface which is forms-based. These **Data forms** allow you to work with your lists and databases. In this chapter you will learn:

- What a Data form is.
- Why you would want to use a Data form.
- What the parts of a Data form are.
- How to add, edit and delete data using a Data form.
- How to find one or more records using the **QBE** capabilities of a Data form.
- How to limit data entry/editing by protecting cells.

What a Data Form Is

Users are often concerned with a single record, or a single row of data. Also, there are many times when all of the columns (or fields) in a list do not fit on a single screen, even if you are running at a very high video resolution such as Super VGA, XGA, or 1024 x 768. For both of these 'problems,' there is a simple solution: **Data Forms**. Data forms allow the user to view the contents of a list one row at a time, with the fields being laid out vertically instead of horizontally. In other words, the fields and their

CHAPTER 4

labels are transposed. Figure 4.1 illustrates a sample list, and a data form to view the first record of the list.

You can use a data form to:

- Browse your list.
- Add new records to your list.
- Delete records from your list.

Parts of the Data Form

Figure 4.2 illustrates the seven major components which a data form is comprised of. These components are:

- **Data Form** system menu
- **Data Form** title bar
- **Data Form** field names
- **Data Form** fields
- **Data Form** scroll bar
- **Data Form** record number indicator
- **Data Form** command buttons.

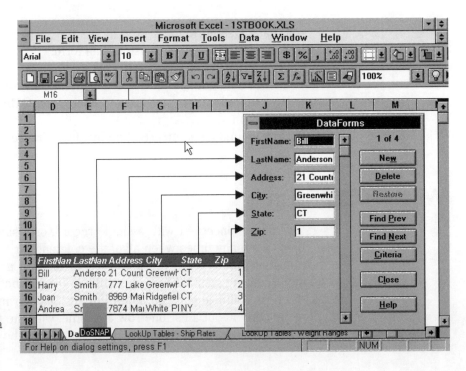

FIGURE 4.1
Sample list and data form with arrows connecting fields.

DATA FORMS

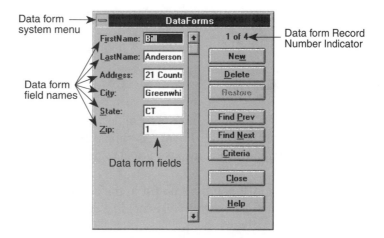

FIGURE 4.2 Data Form components.

The **Data Form system menu** is used to **Move** and **Close** the data form. The **Data Form title bar** displays the name of the worksheet that contains the list. The **Data Form field names** are the text labels that correspond to the field names or column labels for your list. The **Data Form fields** represent the actual data in your list. If a field is editable, it appears on the data form as an **edit box**. If a field is calculated, or protected, it simply appears as a text label, which cannot be edited. The **Data Form scroll bar** is used to indicate the relative position of the current record in the list, and to navigate through the list. The **Data Form record number indicator** tells you which record you are currently on, and how many records there are in the list.

Also, when you toggle into **Criteria Mode** (more on this later!) by selecting Criteria, the Record Number Indicator changes to say *Criteria*.

The **Data Form command buttons** are used to add new records, delete the current record, undo changes you just made to the current record, navigate among adjacent records, toggle into **Criteria Mode**, exit from the **Data Form**, or display **Help.** Table 4.1 identifies and describes all of the Data Form's command buttons.

Data forms do not have maximize or minimize buttons. This is because data forms are **modal**, and as such behave like dialog boxes. In other words, you must complete your work in the data form, and close it, before focus can be transferred to another window or object in the Excel workspace. Since the data form must be closed before you can continue, it does not make any sense to be able to minimize or maximize it.

Note: Data forms can only display 32 fields. If you are using a list with more than 32 fields, you should consider using a relational database product, such as Microsoft Access to break your list into smaller tables, and/or provide a more robust forms-based user interface. If you try to use a data form on a list which has more than 32 fields, the dialog box illustrated in Figure 4.3 will be displayed.

Using a Data Form

Using a data form is as simple as selecting a cell in your list, and then selecting **Data→Form**. As simple as this is, there are three common scenarios which can cause Excel to display an error message:

- If you have no list in the active worksheet.
- The active cell is not in a list, and there is no database in the active worksheet.
- There is a range named *Database* elsewhere in the workbook, but not on the active worksheet.

If you try to invoke a data form, any of these three scenarios will cause Excel to produce an error. This will result in the displaying of the dialog box illustrated in Figure 4.4. If the active cell is not in a list, all you need to do is move it to a list. If you have a range named *Database* in the current worksheet, your active cell does not have to be in a list. If one of the other

TABLE 4.1
Data Form
Command Buttons

Button Name	Action	Notes
New	Toggles into data entry mode	
Delete	Deletes the current record	
Clear	Removes the current criteria	**Criteria Mode** Only
Restore	Undoes edits to the current record	Not available until after an edit has been made
Find Prev	Moves to the previous record	
Find Next	Moves to the next record	
Criteria	Toggles into **Criteria Mode**	
Form	Returns to the default **DataForm**	**Criteria Mode** only
Close	Closes the **DataForm**	
Help	Displays **Help** on the **DataForm**	

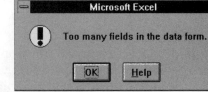

FIGURE 4.3
Too many fields dialog box.

FIGURE 4.4
Database or list range is not valid dialog box.

two circumstances is at the root of your problem, then you must make sure that your list/database is properly defined. For more information on properly defining a list or a database see Chapter One.

Browsing Data

Browsing is the act of viewing and/or editing data. When you browse data using a data form, you scroll through your list one record, or one row, at a time. If you see a piece of data which should be edited, you simply select the appropriate field's edit box, and type your changes. When you move to another record, the edit will be made to the underlying list. If you make changes to several fields in the same record, and then realize you didn't want to make any changes, you can undo your changes by selecting **Restore**. This will 'restore' the current record to its previous state.

There are three ways to navigate from record to record using a data form:

- The **Find Prev/Find Next** command buttons.
- The **Up** and **Down** arrow keys.
- The Data Form scroll bar.

Once the data form is displayed, selecting the **Find Next** command button will move you to the next record, whereas selecting the **Find Prev** command button will move you to the previous record. If you are on the last record of your list, selecting **Find Next** will create a new record, and toggle you into Data Entry mode. Pressing the **Down Arrow** key will move you to the next record, while pressing the **Up Arrow** key will move you to the previous record. Alternatively, you can use the **Data Form scroll bar** to navigate through the list. Table 4.2 summarizes the various actions you can use with the scroll bar, and which record you will be moved to when the corresponding action is taken. To browse through your list using a data form, follow these steps:

STEPS

Browsing through a List, Using a Data Form

1. Select a cell in the list, or make sure that you have a range named *Database* defined in the active worksheet.
2. Select **Data→ Form...**.
3. Navigate through the list, making whatever edits are required.
4. Select **Close**.

Finding One or More Records Using Criteria Mode

To find a particular record or set of records in the database, Excel will search through the database and find matches, based on a **Comparison Criteria**. Instead of choosing from a drop-down list of values as with **AutoFilter**, criteria in data forms use a **QBE** grid like **Advanced Filter**. The main difference is that the skeleton of the **QBE** grid is built for you when you display the data form, and the field names are arranged vertically, not horizontally. In addition, the data form is not quite as flexible. Although you can use the same comparison operators listed in Table 4.3, you cannot use the **Or** operator or have multiple criteria on a single field. If you still wish to use the data form, you can avoid these limitations by applying a filter (**AutoFilter** or **Advanced Filter**) to your list, before you invoke the data form.

All you need to do is to type the comparison operator and a comparison value into the edit box for the field(s) you wish to match. If no operator is typed, equality is assumed, and the **Equal to** (=) operator is used. To

TABLE 4.2 Data Form Scroll Bar Action/Result Table

Action	Moves To
Clicking the down scroll arrow in scroll bar	The same field in next record
Clicking the up scroll arrow in scroll bar	The same field in previous record
Clicking below the scroll box in scroll bar	The same field, 10 records forward
Clicking above the scroll box in scroll bar	The same field, 10 records back
Dragging the scroll box to bottom of scroll bar	The last record
Dragging the scroll box to top of scroll bar	The first record

TABLE 4.3 Standard Comparison Operators

Operator	Meaning
=	Equal to
>	Greater than
<	Less than
>=	Greater than or equal to
<=	Less than or equal to
<>	Not equal to

find a record, specifying a criteria through a data form, follow the steps below.

X-REF *For more information on comparison operators, comparison values, and comparison criteria in general, see Chapter 3, **Filtering**.*

STEPS ## Finding a Record Using a Data Form

1. If the data form is not already displayed, select **Data→Form...**.
2. Select **Criteria**. Notice that the text of the record indicator changes to *Criteria*, the scroll bar is inactive, and that a 'blank record' appears, as illustrated in Figure 4.5, all of which indicate that you are in **Criteria Mode**.
3. Type in the criteria value(s) and operator(s) for the field(s) you wish to match. This criteria will be in effect until you close the data form, or manually reset it.
4. Select **Find Next** to move to the next record which matches the criteria (if there is more than one record).
5. You can now perform the desired operation on the current record.
6. Select **Close**.

To reset the criteria, select **Clear** before closing the data form. To return to the default data form, select **Form**.

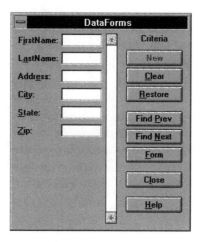

FIGURE 4.5
Criteria DataForm dialog box.

Adding a New Record

When you select the **New** command button, press **Enter**, or press **Page Down**, you toggle the data form into **Data Entry Mode**. When you use a data form to add new records, Excel automatically inserts a blank row at the bottom of your list. If you have a range named *Database*, Excel automatically changes the cell references for the range named to include the new row. You are essentially inserting a new record. To add a new record using a data form, follow the steps below.

STEPS   Adding a New Record Using a Data Form

1. If the Data Form is not already displayed, select **Data→Form...**.
2. Select **New**. Notice that the text of the record indicator changes to *New Record*, and that a 'blank record' appears, as illustrated in Figure 4.6.
3. Add data to the first field (It will be selected by default).
4. Move to the next field.
5. Add data for this field.
6. Repeat steps 3 through 5 until your record is complete.
7. Repeat steps 2 through 6 until you are finished adding new records.
8. Select **Close**.

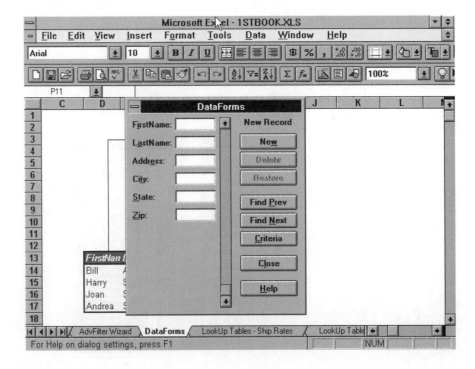

FIGURE 4.6
New Record dataform dialog box.

Deleting a Record

Deleting a record using the data form is simply a matter of selecting the record you want to delete, and then deleting it. You can only delete one record at a time using a data form. To delete a record using a data form, follow the steps below.

Deleting a Record Using the Data Form

1. If the data form is not already displayed, select **Data**→**Form....**
2. Navigate to the record you wish to delete, using **Criteria** and the **Find Next/Prev** command buttons.
3. Select **Delete**. The dialog box illustrated in Figure 4.7 will be displayed.
4. Select **OK**. The record will be permanently deleted.

Restricting Data Entry/Editing

There will be times when you wish to restrict access to the data in your list. There are three levels of security which you can use:

- Workbook protection
- Worksheet protection
- Cell/Object protection.

Although these protections exist 'separately,' it is when they are combined together that a flexible security environment is created. **Workbook protection** prohibits changing the way a workbook is displayed and/or arranged. **Worksheet protection** prohibits the modification of a worksheet's contents. **Cell/Object protection** prohibits the modification of cells and/ objects. For Cell/object protection to work, worksheet protection must be turned **on**.

Workbook protection will not be discussed further in this chapter, because there is no direct relationship between it and cell protection. As

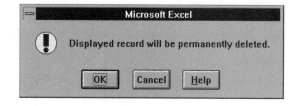

Figure 4.7
Displayed record will be permanently deleted dialog box.

such, it has no impact on limiting data entry. In addition to these three levels of security, there is an additional level of security which can be used to allow only an authorized user to open/modify a worksheet. Although this feature is not to be overlooked, it is assumed that you want the user to open the worksheet, and then have restricted access to part of the worksheet. As such, password-protecting the file is not part of this discussion.

Cell Protection

If you lock a cell, and try to view it using a data form, the field will appear as a text label, not an edit box. If you try to edit a locked cell on the worksheet (in place), the dialog box illustrated in Figure 4.8 will be displayed. By default, all cells in an Excel worksheet are locked, but worksheet protection is turned **off**. It is not until protection is turned **on**, that the cells are really **locked**. As such, protecting cells is a two-step process. First, you must properly set the protection for every cell in your workbook. Then you must turn the worksheet's protection **on**. To lock a range of cells, follow the steps below.

Locking a Range of Cells

1. Select the cell(s) that you wish to lock.
2. Select **Format→Cells…**.
3. Select the **Protection** tab.
4. Select the **Locked** check box if it is not already selected (remember that by default, all cells are locked).
5. Select **OK**.

Worksheet Protection

Worksheet protection allows you to password-protect worksheet:

- Contents

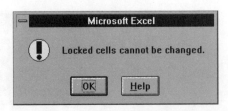

FIGURE 4.8
Locked cells cannot be changed dialog box.

- Objects
- Scenarios.

Protecting a worksheet's **Contents** protects worksheet cells and chart items. This is not applicable to Dialog Sheets (XL5 or XL4 macro sheets) or Visual Basic modules. Protecting **Objects** prohibits graphical objects on worksheets and charts from being moved, edited, resized, or deleted. Protecting **Scenarios** prohibits changes to the definitions of scenarios on a worksheet. Although it is recommended that you use a password, it is not required.

Now that you have locked the cells that you wish to protect, you must actually turn the worksheet's **Protection on**, to make your cell level locking effective. To turn a worksheet's protection **on**, follow the steps below.

STEPS

Protecting a Worksheet

1. Select **Tools→Protection→Protect Sheet...**. The dialog box illustrated in Figure 4.9 will be displayed.
2. Select the **Contents** check box, if it is not already selected.

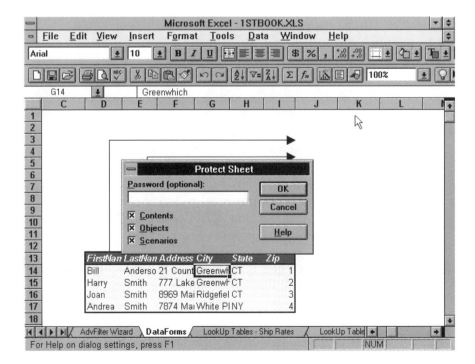

FIGURE 4.9
Protect Sheet dialog box.

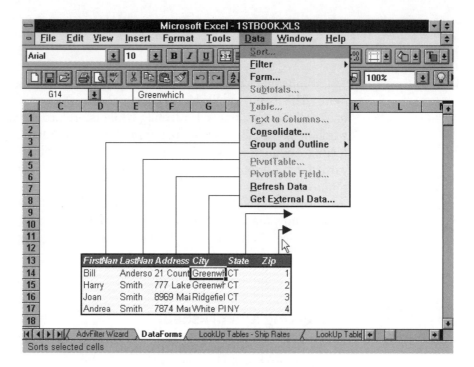

FIGURE 4.10
Data menu on a protected worksheet.

3. Type a password in the **Password** text box (optional, but highly recommended).
4. Select **OK**.

Your worksheet is now 'protected.' Examine your menus. All menu choices related to editing are greyed out and unavailable. Figure 4.10 illustrates the **Data** menu, with worksheet protection turned **on**. You might ask why the Filter menu is not greyed out. If you opened up the **Filter** sub-menu, you would see that all of its choices are greyed out. With worksheet protection, you must open the sub-menu to see whether or not its menu selections are available or not. If you use a data form, the values of any cells which are protected will be displayed as labels, not as editable text boxes (which is how cells that are not locked are displayed). Figure 4.11 illustrates a data form in which all cells are locked.

Although you will probably use protection to restrict another user's movement in a worksheet, the day will come (probably sooner than you think) when you will want to turn the worksheet's protection **off**. To turn a worksheet's protection **off**, follow these steps:

Data Forms

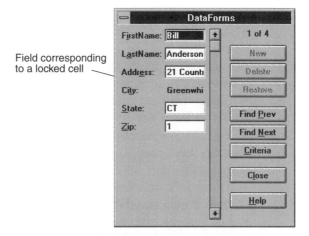

FIGURE 4.11
Data form displaying locked cells.

FIGURE 4.12
Unprotect Sheet dialog box.

 Unprotecting a Worksheet

1. Select **Tools→Protection→Unprotect Sheet...**. The dialog box illustrated in Figure 4.12 will be displayed.
2. Type the password in the **Password** edit box.
3. Select **OK**.

Summary

In this chapter you have learned:

- You should use a data form when there are more fields than fit on a screen in your list, and/or it is important to view data one record at a time.
- You can use a data form to **Browse**, **Add** and **Delete** records from your list.
- The major components of a data form are the **Data form system menu**, the **Data form title bar**, the **Data form field names**, the **Data form fields**, the **Data form scroll bar**, the **Data form record number indicator**, and the **Data form command buttons**.

- If a field is editable, it appears on the data form as an **edit box**.
- If a field is calculated, or protected, it simply appears on the data form as a text label, which cannot be edited.
- Data forms are **modal**. That is, focus must remain on the form (within the application's workspace) until it is closed.
- A data form can contain a maximum of 32 fields.
- **Browsing** is the act of viewing and/or editing data.
- You can use the **Find Prev/Find Next** buttons, the **Up** and **Down** arrow keys, and the **Data Form scroll bar** to navigate through your list.
- The data form's **Criteria Mode** allows you to find records using criteria using a **QBE** paradigm.
- You can enter **data entry mode** by selecting **New**, pressing **Enter**, or pressing **Page Down**.
- When you insert records using a data form, Excel automatically inserts a new row at the bottom of your list.
- You can delete a record using a data form by navigating to the record, and selecting **Delete**.
- You can use Excel's **Cell protection** and **Worksheet protection** in tandem, to restrict data entry/editing to certain cells.

CHAPTER 5
Database Functions

Introduction

Although **Sorting** and **Filtering** help you analyze your data, the real power of using Excel is as a data analysis tool, by taking advantage of Excel's built-in functions. Although a discussion of how all of Excel's several hundred functions can be applied to lists and databases is beyond the scope of this book, Excel provides a category of functions specifically for working with databases. In this chapter you will learn:

- What a function is.
- The general syntax of all functions.
- The syntax of database functions.
- How to use the **Function Wizard**.
- What the twelve database functions are.

What Is a Function?

A **function** is a pre-written routine which accepts one or more values as arguments, performs an operation, **and** returns a value or values. You can think of a function as a black box to which you feed arguments (input). It performs one or more operations using these arguments, and then returns one or more values (output).

One of the simplest functions Excel has, which you are probably familiar with, is the **SUM** function. Examine the data in Table 5.1. If you wanted to add all of the values between cell A1 and A8 together, and display them in cell A9, you could type the formula:

TABLE 5.1
Table to be used for SUM() Example.

	A
1	8
2	12
3	6767
4	84
5	348
6	2342
7	2342
8	24234
9	

$$A9 = A1 + A2 + A3 + A4 + A5 + A6 + A7 + A8$$

Alternatively, Excel provides a function which will summarize all of the values in a range of cells which you specify, **SUM()**. Instead of the formula listed above, in cell A9 you would type:

$$= SUM(A1:A8)$$

Using either method, the result would be exactly the same: 36,137. The difference would be in the amount of typing which you need to do. Although this does not seem like much typing, the less typing the better. Less typing means less time to enter your formula, and the likelihood of error is lower. If this list were 5,000 rows long, the benefits would be a little more obvious.

Syntax of the Database Functions

In Excel, all functions have the following syntax:

$$= FunctionName(Argument, Argument2, Argument3,...)$$

where:

- The **equal sign** (=) is a required keyword.
- **FunctionName** is the name of the function.
- The **parentheses** tell Excel where the arguments begin and end.
- The **commas** are delimiters which separate arguments.
- The **Arguments** are constants or formulas that are passed to the

function, to be used in performing whatever operation the function performs.

In the above example, using the SUM function:

- **SUM** is the **FunctionName**.
- The **equal sign**, and **parentheses** are required delimiters.
- The **range A1:A8** is the first and only argument which the SUM function takes.

Excel has twelve built-in functions for working with databases to help you with your work. These are collectively known as **Dfunction**, and have the syntax:

$$=\text{Dfunction(Database, Field, Criteria)}$$

where:

- **Dfunction** is the name of the database function.
- **Database** refers to any valid database, as defined in Chapter One. Acceptable values include the reserved name *Database*, a reference to the cells which contain the database, or the name of a range which contains the database.
- **Field** is the name of the field which the function will perform the operation on. Remember that field name and column heading are the same, provided you have followed the rules outlined in Chapter One. Acceptable values are the name of a field (same as a column heading), or a reference to a cell which contains a column heading. If you use the name of a field, it must be enclosed within quotes.
- **Criteria** is the range of cells which contains the **comparison criteria**. Valid values for criteria include a reference to the cells which contain the criteria, the reserved range name *Criteria*, or the name of a range which refers to the criteria. Criteria always refers to a range of cells, and must be defined as described in the **Advanced Filter** section of Chapter Three.

Function Wizard

Although you can manually type functions into the formula bar, it is usually quicker to use the **Function Wizard** to walk you through entering a function. The **Function Wizard** is a tool which allows you to select functions based on their functional usage, and then prompts you for values for their arguments, giving you hints along the way. Rather than spending your time learning the syntax and arguments for each one of Excel's several hundred functions, you can spend your time focusing on solving your business problems. To use the **Function Wizard** for the **Dfunction**, follow the steps below.

STEPS Using the Function Wizard

1. Select the cell where you wish to place the function.
2. Type an Equal sign (=). Notice that as soon as you do this, the formula bar changes to display the **Cancel** button, **Enter** button, and **Function Wizard** button, as illustrated in Figure 5.1.
3. Click on the **Function Wizard** button. The dialog box illustrated in Figure 5.2 will be displayed.
4. Select **Database** from the **Function Category** list box. Notice that the **Function Name** list box dynamically changes to list only database functions.
5. Select the function that you wish to use from the **Function Name** list box. Notice that as you select different functions, the syntax and a short description appears below the **Function Category** list box.

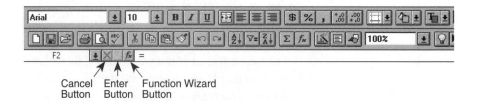

FIGURE 5.1
Formula bar, in edit mode.

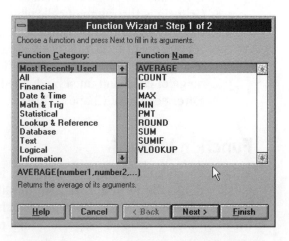

FIGURE 5.2
Function Wizard Step 1 of 2 dialog box.

Database Functions

6. Select **Next>**. The dialog box changes as illustrated in Figure 5.3. Notice the description of the function, and the first argument.

   - Select the **database** edit box, if it is not already selected, and enter the name of the range which contains your database, or select the appropriate range on your worksheet.
   - Select the **field** edit box (Notice that the dialog changes to include a description of the argument), and enter the name of field that you wish to use the function on, or select the column heading on your worksheet.
   - Select the **criteria** edit box and enter the name of the range which contains your criteria, or select the appropriate range on your worksheet. Notice that the value that the function will return appears in the **Value** control, in the upper right hand corner of the dialog box.

7. Select **Finish** and Press **Enter**.

X-REF

The **Function Wizard—Step 2 of 2** dialog box is modeless, just like the **Define Name** dialog box, described in Chapter 1. You may interact with the Excel workspace as described in **Selecting a Range While the Define Name Dialog Box is Open** section of Chapter 1, and applying the same technique.

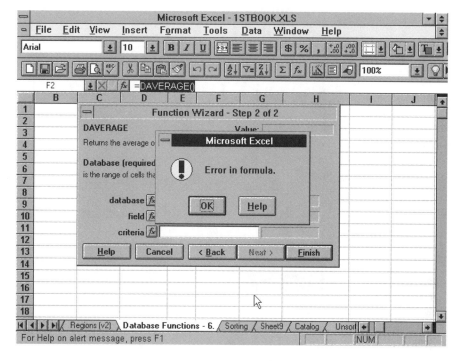

FIGURE 5.3
Function Wizard—
Step 2 of 2
dialog box.

The Database Functions

Table 5.2 illustrates a set of sample data which will be used for all of the examples in this chapter. The database argument will always refer to the range which encompasses these cells. The criteria argument will always refer to the range illustrated in Table 5.3. The **Field** argument, will refer to the **Sales** column, where it is required.

In other words, in the examples for each of the 12 **Dfunctions** discussed below, the syntax will be:

=Dfunction(Database,"Salesman",Criteria)

The twelve **Dfunctions** are:

- **DAVERAGE**
- **DCOUNT**
- **DCOUNTA**
- **DGET**
- **DMAX**
- **DMIN**
- **DPRODUCT**
- **DSTDEV**
- **DSTDEVP**
- **DSUM**
- **DVAR**
- **DVARP**.

TABLE 5.2 Sample Data for the Rest of the Chapter

Salesman	Sales
Jones	1000
Smith	1100
Smith	800
Roarty	1400
Jones	1200
Kinko	1500
Thomas	1200

Table 5.3 Sample Criteria Range

Salesman
Jones

DAVERAGE

The **DAVERAGE** function calculates the average value of all of the rows, for the specified field, which match the specified criteria. If you used the DAVERAGE function on the data illustrated in Table 5.2, and the criteria-specified **Salesman = Jones**, the result would be 1,100.

DCOUNT

The **DCOUNT** function counts the number of rows, for the specified field, which contain numbers that match the specified criteria. The field argument is optional. If you used the **DCOUNT** function on the data illustrated in Table 5.2, and the Criteria specified **Salesman = Jones**, the result would be 2.

DCOUNTA

The **DCOUNTA** function counts the number of non-blank cells, for the specified field, that match the specified criteria. The field argument is optional. If you used the **DCOUNTA** function on the data illustrated in Table 5.2, and the Criteria specified **Salesman = Jones**, the result would be 2.

DGET

The **DGET** function retrieves the value of a single row, for the specified field, that meets the specified criteria. If you specify a criteria which returns more than one row, Excel will return a **#NUM!** error. If there are no rows which meet the criteria, Excel will return a **#Value!** error. If you used the DGET function on the data illustrated in Table 5.2, and the criteria specified **Salesman = Jones**, the result would be **#NUM!**, because more than two rows are returned. If you changed the criteria to **Salesman = Kinko**, the result would be 1500.

DMAX

The **DMAX** function returns the largest value, for the specified field, which meets the specified criteria. If you used the **DMAX** function on the data illustrated in Table 5.2, and the criteria specified **Salesman = Jones**, the result would be 1,200.

DMIN

The **DMIN** function returns the smallest value, for the specified field, which meets the specified criteria. If you used the DMIN function on the data illustrated in Table 5.2, and the criteria specified **Salesman = Jones**, the result would be 1000.

DPRODUCT

The **DPRODUCT** function multiplies all of the values, in the specified field, that meet the specified criteria, and returns the product. If you used the **DPRODUCT** function on the data illustrated in Table 5.2, and the criteria specified **Salesman = Jones**, the result would be 1,200,000 (1,200 × 1,000).

DSTDEV

The **DSTDEV** function calculates the standard deviation of a population, based on a sample, using the values in the specified field, of rows in the database which meet the specified criteria. If you used the **DSTDEV** function on the data illustrated in Table 5.2, and the criteria specified **Salesman = Jones**, the result would be 141.

DSTDEVP

The **DSTDEV** function calculates the standard deviation of a population based on the entire population, using the values in the specified field, of rows in the database which meet the specified criteria. If you used the **DSTDEVP** function on the data illustrated in Table 5.2, and the criteria specified **Salesman = Jones**, the result would be 100.

DSUM

The **DSUM** function summarizes the values, in the specified field, of all of the rows which meet the specified criteria. If you used the **DSUM** function on the data illustrated in Table 5.2, and the criteria specified **Salesman = Jones**, the result would be 2,200 (1000 + 1200).

DVAR

The **DVAR** function calculates the variance of a population, based on a sample, using the values in the specified field, of rows in the database which meet the specified criteria. If you used the **DSUM** function on the data illustrated in Table 5.2, and the criteria specified **Salesman = Jones,** the result would be 10,000.

DVARP

The **DVARP** function calculates the variance of a population based on the entire population, using the values in the specified field, of rows in the database which meet the specified criteria. If you used the **DVARP** function on the data illustrated in Table 5.2, and the criteria specified **Salesman = Jones**, the result would be 10,000.

Summary

In this chapter you have learned that:

- A **function** is a pre-written routine or formula which accepts one or more values as arguments, performs an operation, **and** returns a value or values.
- The SUM() function takes one argument, the range to sum, and summarizes all values in that range.
- All Excel functions have the syntax:

    =FunctionName(Arg,Arg2,Arg3,...).

- The twelve database functions are collectively known as **Dfunction**.
- All of the **Dfunctions** have the syntax:

    =Dfunction(Database,Field,Criteria).

- The **Function Wizard** walks you through the process of entering a function into a formula.
- The **DAVERAGE** function calculates the average value of all of the rows, for the specified field, which match the specified criteria.
- The **DCOUNT** function counts the number of rows, for the specified field, that contain numbers which match the specified criteria.
- The **DCOUNTA** function counts the number of non-blank cells, for the specified field, that match the specified criteria.
- The **DGET** function retrieves the value of a single row, for the specified field, that meets the specified criteria.
- The **DMAX** function returns the largest value, for the specified field, which meets the specified criteria.
- The **DMIN** function returns the smallest value, for the specified field, which meets the specified criteria.
- The **DPRODUCT** function multiplies all of the values, in the specified field, that meet the specified criteria, and returns the product.
- The **DSTDEV** function calculates the standard deviation of a population, based on a sample, using the values in the specified field, of rows in the database which meet the specified criteria.
- The **DSUM** function summarizes the values, in the specified field, of all of the rows which meet the specified criteria.
- The **DVAR** function calculates the variance of a population, based

on a sample, using the values in the specified field, of rows in the database which meet the specified criteria.
- The **DVARP** function calculates the variance of a population based on the entire population, using the values in the specified field, of rows in the database which meet the specified criteria.

CHAPTER 6
Data Tables

Introduction

In previous chapters, you learned that using **Advanced Filter**, you could automatically extract a subset of a list to another range, or that you could use the **DGET()** database function to extract a single value of a field, provided that the set returned by the specified criteria was only a single row. But what if you want to do the opposite? What if you want to change a variable and see the result propagated through a table? What if you want to change two variables?

In this chapter you will learn:

- What a data table is.
- What the differences between a **One-Input Data Table** and a **Two-Input Data Table** are.
- How to create and fill in a **One-Input Data Table**.
- How to create and fill in a **Two-Input Data Table**.
- What a **Lookup Table** is.
- How to create a **Lookup Table**.

What a Data Table Is

A **data table** is a special kind of list, the contents of which Excel fills in, by varying the value of one or two input cells, referenced in one or more formulas. There are two kinds of data tables:

- One-input
- Two-input.

A **one-input data table** is used to input values for one variable, and to see the effect on one or more formulas. A **two-input data table** is used to input values for two variables, and to see the effect on one formula.

One-Input Data Tables

Assume that you've decided to buy a new car, and you would like to have Excel help you calculate what your monthly payments will be. As such, you have created the range illustrated in Figure 6.1, which uses the PMT() function to calculate the monthly payment.

You've already decided on a car which is going to cost $25,000, you are going to put $5,000 down, and you are going to finance it over sixty months (five years) to keep the monthly payments as low as possible. The only variable is the interest rate which you will finance at. Although you want to minimize this number, all you want to do is get a quick fix on how the interest rate will affect the monthly payment. You could manually input all of the iterations within a certain range (say all interest rates between

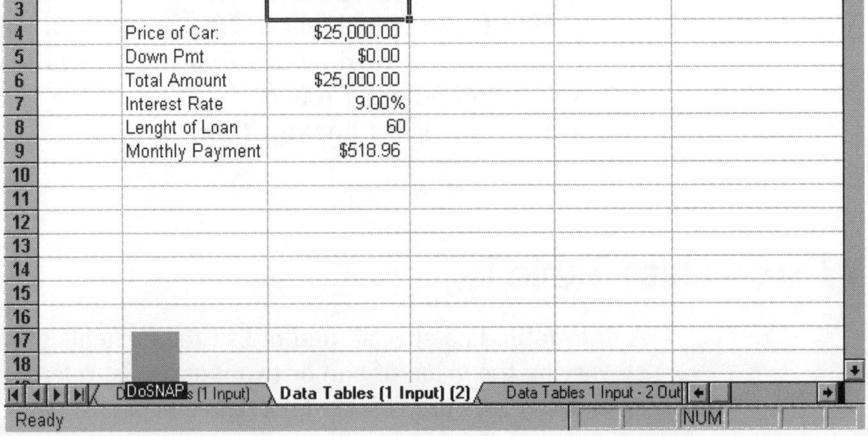

FIGURE 6.1

nine and eleven percent, in quarter point intervals). This would be time consuming, and would not give you a list which could be used for comparison. Instead, you could let Excel create a list for you, using a one-input data table. A one-input data table allows you to specify a formula, an input cell, and a list of values to plug into the input cell.

A one-input data table consists of four components:

- **Input Cell**
- **List Range**
- **Data Table Formula Cell**
- **Output Range**.

The **Input Cell** is the cell which contains the variable which you want to change. The **List Range** contains the list of values which you want to substitute into the input cell. The **Data Table Formula Cell** contains a formula which includes a reference to the input cell, and will be used to fill the output range. The data table formula cell can also contain a reference to a cell which contains a reference to the input cell. The data table formula cell is always located one row above, and one column to the right of the top cell of the list range. The **Output Range** is the range of cells where the values in the list range will be substituted for the input cell reference, in the data table formula. Figure 6.2 illustrates these four components, using the previous example as the starting point.

Creating a one-input data table is a two step process:

- Set Up the data table.
- Fill the data table in.

Setting Up a One-Input Data Table

The first step in creating a one-input data table is to create the data table itself, as well as the input range and any formulas which the data table formula cell will reference. Follow the steps below to set up the data table.

STEPS

Setting Up the Data Table

1. Name the cell you wish to use as the input cell *InputCell*.
2. Create the formula which you wish to plug the variable into, and use the name *InputCell* in the proper argument.
3. Fill the list range with all of the values you wish to use. If it is a serial list, use **AutoFill** to speed this process.

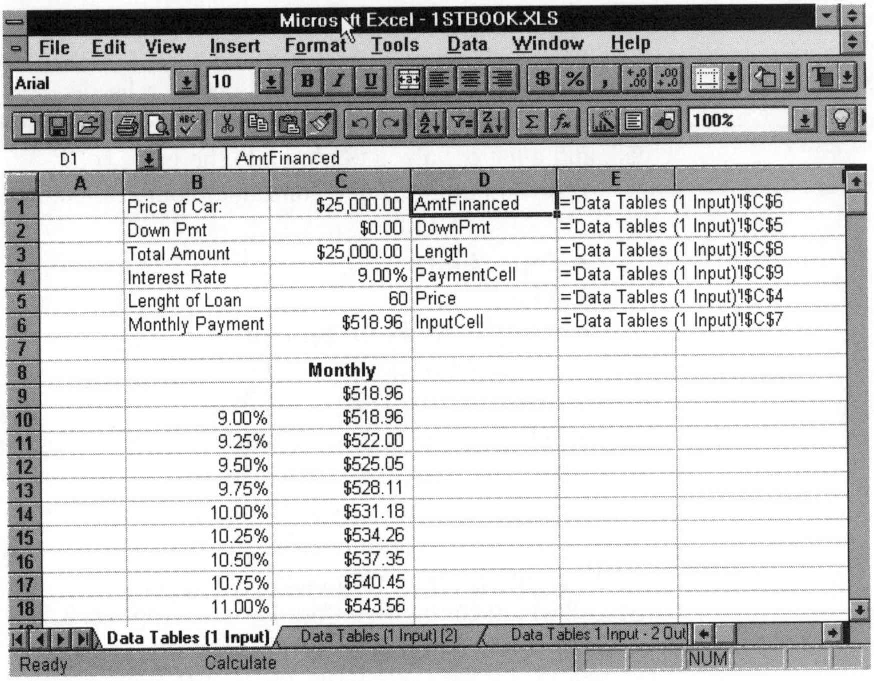

FIGURE 6.2
The components of a one-input data table.

4. In the data table formula cell, enter a reference to the cell which contains the formula you created in Step two.

Figure 6.3 illustrates how the **Car Payment** data table would look after the data table components are set up, but before the values are filled in. Table 6.1 lists the contents of the data table formula cell, and the cell it references. Note that the range names and their addresses are directly on the worksheet.

Filling a One-Input Data Table

Once the data table has been properly set up, you have to fill it in. To fill in the data table, follow the steps below.

STEPS   Filling In the Data Table

1. Select the range which contains the list range and data table formula.
2. Select **Data→Table**. The dialog box illustrated in Figure 6.4 will be displayed.
3. If list range in the data table is vertically oriented (fills a column), type

Data Tables

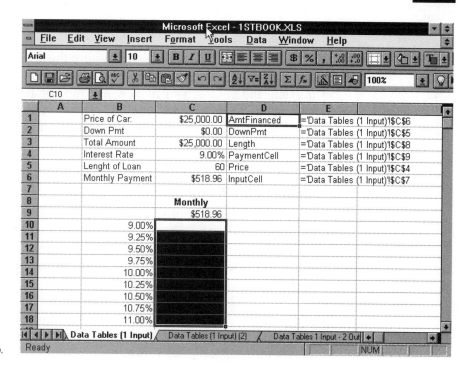

FIGURE 6.3
Data Tables [one input]—Basic setup.

TABLE 6.1 Contents of Data Table Formula Cell, and the Cell It References

Cell	Formula
C6 (PaymentCell)	=PMT(InputCell/12,Length,–AmtFinanced)
C9	=PaymentCell

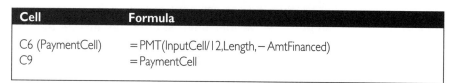

FIGURE 6.4
Table dialog box.

InputCell (or whatever you named the range) in the **Column Input Cell** edit box. If list range in the data table is horizontally oriented (fills a row), type *InputCell* (or whatever you named the range) in the **Row Input Cell** edit box.

4. Select **OK**.

The output range will be filled with the new values. Note that each cell in the output range contains the following array reference:

$$\{=TABLE(,C4)\}$$

In this case, C4 is the **InputCell**. Because the complete output range is an array, you cannot edit or delete any cells in this range. If you would like to delete the results, you must select the complete array (**Output Range**). Only then can you clear the cells' contents, or delete them. Even though it is an array, you can still clear or modify an individual cell's formatting.

Adding Additional Formulas and Input Values

One-input tables allow you to use more than one data table formula cell. There are only two restrictions:

- Each data table formula cell must directly or indirectly reference the input cell.
- Each additional data table formula cell must be located to the right of existing data table formula cells if they are arranged horizontally (in a row), or below existingd Data table formula cells if they are arranged vertically (in a column).

Using the car payment model again, what if you also wanted to see the impact of various interest rates, not just on the monthly payment, but on the total payments and the total interest? You could place formulas in the two cells to the right of the existing data table formula cell, with the formulas for these calculations. Figure 6.5 illustrates this, with the output range filled in. Table 6.2 details the formulas for the new cells. Follow the steps below to add additional data table formula cells to a data table.

STEPS — Adding Additional Data Table Formula Cells

1. Add the new data table formula cell(s).
2. Select the range which contains the list range and all of the data table formula cells.
3. Select **Data→Table**.
4. Input either the **Column Input Cell** or **Row Input Cell**, as is appropriate for the orientation of your data table.
5. Select **OK**.

You can also expand the list range after the data table has been created.

DATA TABLES

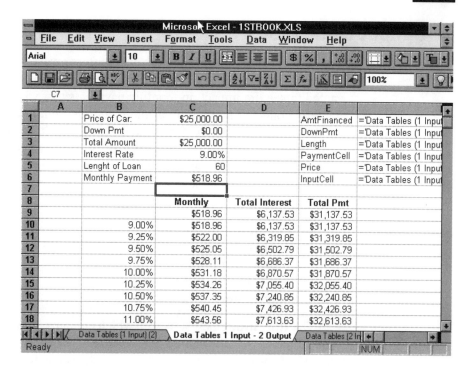

FIGURE 6.5
One-input data table with several data table formula cells.

All you have to do is add the new values, and then re-fill the data table. To add additional input values to the list range, follow the steps below.

STEPS   Adding Additional Input Values to the List Range

1. Add the new values to the list range.
2. Select the range which contains the list range and all of the data table formula cells.
3. Select **Data→Table**.
4. Input either the **Column Input Cell** or **Row Input Cell**, as is appropriate for the orientation of your data table.
5. Select **OK**.

TABLE 6.2
Contents of New Data Table Formula Cells

Cell	Formula
D9	= PaymentCell*Length
E9	= PaymentCell*Length − AmtFinanced

Two-Input Data Tables

What if you would like to see how changing two values would impact the values returned by a formula? Using the car payment model, what if you wanted to see the impact on monthly payments that various combinations of interest rate and number of payment periods would have? If you want to see these combinations in a list, Excel can create it for you, using a two-input data table. A two-input data table allows you to specify a formula, two input cells, and a list of values to plug into each input cell.

A two-input data table consists of six components:

- **Row Input Cell**
- **Column Input Cell**
- **Row List Range**
- **Column List Range**
- **Data Table Formula Cell**
- **Output Range**.

The **Row Input Cell** is the cell which contains the variable which you want to change, which will be placed on the horizontal (x) axis of your data table. The **Column Input Cell** is the cell which contains the variable which you want to change, which will be placed on the vertical (y) axis of your data table. The **Row List Range** contains the list of values which you want to substitute into the row input cell. The **Column List Range** contains the list of values which you want to substitute into the column input cell. The **Data Table Formula Cell** contains a formula which includes either a direct or indirect reference to the both the row and column input cells, and will be used to fill the output range. The data table formula cell is always located at the intersection of the row list range and column list range. The **Output Range** is the range of cells where the values in both the row and column list ranges will be substituted for the row and column input cell references, in the data table formula cell. Figure 6.6 illustrates these six components, again using the car payment model.

Creating a two-input data table is a two step process:

- Set up the data table.
- Fill the data table in.

Setting Up a Two-Input Data Table

The first step in creating a two-input data table is to create the data table itself, as well as the input range and any formulas which the data table formula cell will reference. Follow the steps below to set up a two-input data table.

Data Tables

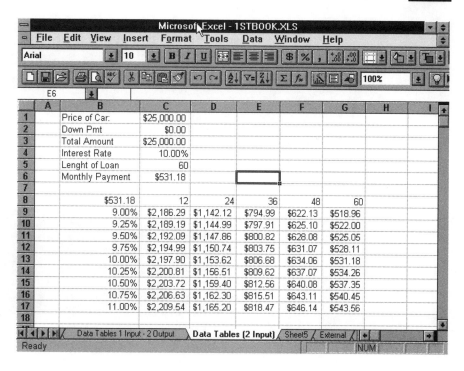

Figure 6.6
The components of a two-input data table.

Setting Up a Two-Input Data Table

1. Name the cell you wish to use as the row input cell *RowInputCell*.
2. Name the cell you wish to use as the column input cell *ColumnInputCell*.
3. Create the formula which you wish to plug the two variables into, and use the names *RowInputCell* and *ColumnInputCell* in the proper arguments.
4. Fill the row list range and column list range with all of the values you wish to use. If these are serial lists, use **AutoFill** to speed this process.
5. In the data table formula cell, enter a reference to the cell which contains the formula you created in Step 3.

Figure 6.7 illustrates how the two-input car payment data table would look after the data table components are set up, but before the values are filled in. Table 6.3 lists the contents of the data table formula cell, and the cell it references.

Filling In a Two-Input Data Table

Once the two-input data table has been properly set up, you have to fill it in. To fill in a two-input data table, follow these steps:

FIGURE 6.7
Data Tables [two input]—Basic setup.

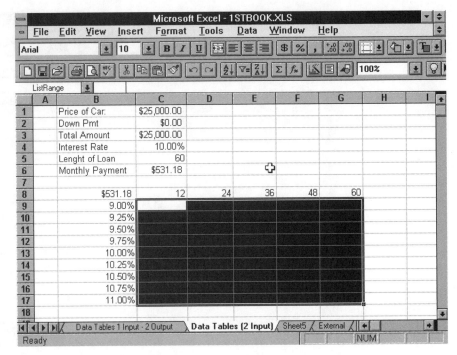

TABLE 6.3
Contents of Data Table Formula Cell, and the Cell It References

Cell	Formula
C6 (PaymentCell)	=PMT(ColumnInputCell/12,RowInputCell,−AmtFinanced)
C8	=PaymentCell

STEPS Filling In a Two-Input Data Table

1. Select the range which contains the list ranges and data table formula.
2. Select **Data→Table**. The **Table** dialog box will be displayed.
3. Type *RowInputCell* (or whatever you named the range, or the corresponding cell address) in the **Row Input Cell** edit box.
4. Type *ColumnInputCell* in the **Column Input Cell** edit box.
5. Select **OK**.

The output range will be filled with the new values. Note that each cell in the output range contains the following array reference:

$$\{=TABLE(C5,C4)\}$$

In this case, **C5** is the **ColumnInputCell**, and **C4** is the **RowInputCell**. Because the complete output range is an array, you cannot edit or delete any cells in this range. If you would like to delete the results, you must select the complete array (output range). Only then can you clear the cells' contents, or delete them. Even though it is an array, you can still clear or modify an individual cell's formatting.

Data Table Performance Considerations

Every time you make an entry on a worksheet, Excel automatically recalculates every formula. Although this is not any issue for many 'small' worksheets, when your worksheets start to grow in size, recalculation time can become problematic. Similarly, on small data tables, recalculation times will probably not be an issue. But, there will reach a point, as your data table grows, when the size will affect the amount of time it takes to recalculate. Most lookup tables are static. In other words, the formula has to be calculated only the first time you fill the output range. After this, every time a data table recalculates, it is usually just wasting CPU cycles. Because of this, Excel allows you to control calculation so that you can automatically recalculate everything in a worksheet, except for tables. You can then force a manual calculation of the active worksheet (including all tables) by pressing **Shift+F9**. Pressing **F9** forces calculation of all worksheets in all open workbooks. To turn auto calculation of data tables **off**, follow the steps below.

STEPS **Setting Table Calculation to Manual**

1. Select **Tools→Options...**.
2. Select the **Calculation** tab.
3. Select the **Automatic Except Tables** option button, in the **Calculation** option group.
4. Select **OK**.

Lookup Tables

A **lookup table** is a special list in which you use one value, which you know, to find another value, which you don't know. In other words, you use the value of one column to find the value of another column, for the same row or record. The value that you are trying to match is known as the **search value**. Take, for example, the data illustrated in Table 6.4. Assume that the value that you know is the **Weight**, and that the value which

TABLE 6.4
Shipping Costs, Based on Weights

Weight	Cost (per lb.)	Shipping Code
1	$5.00	Blue
5	$3.00	Red
25	$1.50	White
100	$0.75	Green

you are seeking is the **Cost (per lb.)** that corresponds to a weight. To have Excel do this for you, you need to use the **VLOOKUP()** function, which has the syntax:

VLOOKUP(*lookup_value,table_array,col_index_num,range_lookup*)

where:

- *lookup_value* is the search value, or the value that you want to match. Although you can code in a constant, it usually refers to a range which contains the value.
- *table_array* is the range which contains the list you wish to search.
- *col_index_num* is the index number, of the column whose value you seek. The **col_index_num** for the first column (the match column) is zero, and increases incrementally by one, for each column to the right.
- range_lookup is a logical value, which specifies whether an exact match must be made, or whether an approximate match can be made.

If the **col_index_num** is less than one, a **#VALUE! Error** is returned. If the **col_index_num** is greater than the number of columns in the list, a **#REF! Error** is returned.

Figure 6.8 illustrates a simple business application for lookup tables. If you have a business which ships out packages and pre-charges customers for shipping, you must be able to calculate shipping charges, based on the weight of the package, and include it in the amount due. From your shipper of choice, you get a rate schedule, which has the per pound rates for packages, based on weight classes, as well as a shipping code. What you want to be able to do is input this schedule once, and then be able to input the weight of an order. From this input, Excel should then 'look up' the proper shipping charge per pound (based on the order's weight), return the shipping cost per pound, the shipping code, and then calculate the total shipping cost.

In the worksheet illustrated in Figure 6.8, the range named *Database* refers to cells C6:E10, which contain the rate schedule provided by the carrier. This is the **Lookup Table**. In addition to the actual lookup table, there is another range which is used for the input of the search value, and returns shipping cost per pound, shipping code, and the total shipping cost. This range is formatted differently from the rest of the worksheet. The cell which is used to input the search value, H6, is a range named *InputCell*. Note that this range was also formatted differently, by applying a 3D effect. Cell H7, which returns the cost per pound, contains the formula:

= VLOOKUP(*InputCell,Database,2,FALSE*)

This formula looks through the lookup table, until it matches the contents of *InputCell*. When it does, it returns the value of the second column for the same row, **Cost (per lb.)**. Because the **range_lookup** argument is set to **FALSE**, an exact match is required. Table 6.5 lists the other cells in

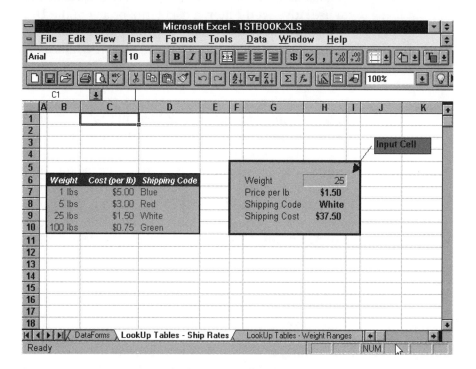

FIGURE 6.8
LookUp Tables—
Ship Rates
worksheet.

TABLE 6.5
VLOOKUP()
Function Used to
Calculate Shipping

Cell	Formula
H8	=VLOOKUP(InputCell,Database,3,TRUE)
H9	=VLOOKUP(InputCell,Database,2,TRUE)*InputCell

this range, and their formulas, which are used to return the corresponding **Shipping Code** and total **Shipping Cost**.

Creating Lookup Tables

Creating a lookup table is a two step process:

- Create the list which will be used as the lookup table.
- Build the **Lookup I/O Range**, which will be used to input the search value and output matching values.

Creating the list which will be used is as simple as typing in the values for list, and your column headings. After this is done, you should use **Auto-Format** to make your list stand out from the rest of your worksheet. Once this has been completed, you should name the range *Database*. Although you do not have to use this name, it comes in handy in case you would like to use **Advanced Filter**, a data form, or any of the **Dfunctions**.

Once the actual lookup table has been created, you need to identify a range which will be used to input search values and monitor output values, by applying a unique format to it. This is called the **Lookup I/O Range**. You should not name this range *Lookup I/O Range*. If you try to, you will get an error because you are not allowed to use spaces or the / character in range names. Within this range, you should name a cell *InputCell*, and refer to this cell whenever you need to use the **lookup_value** argument. This cell should be formatted differently from all the other cells in this range. The final step is to create the lookup functions that are going to return values from the lookup table. As the previous example illustrates, you can use the **VLOOKUP()** function by itself, or can combine it with others within a larger formula, as was done with formula that calculates **Total Shipping Cost**. To create a lookup table and lookup I/O range, follow the steps below.

STEPS

Looking Up Values Using a Lookup Table

1. Input the values which will serve as your lookup table and use **AutoFormat** to format the lookup table.
2. Name this range *Database*.
3. Select your **Lookup I/O Range**.
4. Select a cell in your I/O range to be used to input the search value.
5. Name this cell *InputCell* and apply a unique format to this cell.
6. Select the first cell which will return a value.

7. Use the **Function Wizard** to insert a **VLOOKUP()** function.
8. Use the range *InputCell* for the **search_value** argument, and the range *Database* for the **table_array** argument. Set appropriate values for the other arguments, to return the results you seek.
9. Add an appropriate label in an adjacent cell.
10. Repeat steps 6 through 9, if you wish to have more than one cell return a value. Combine the **VLOOKUP()** function with other operators and functions within your formula to get the desired results.
11. Test your lookup table by inputting various values into *InputCell*, and observing the results.

Approximate Matches

If the *col_index_num* is set to **False**, or omitted, then VLOOKUP() performs an exact match for the search value. Although this is often the behavior you want, there are times when you want to do a 'fuzzy' search, or find an approximate match.

Building upon the previous example, what if the weight of the package being sent was not 1, 5, 25, or 100 pounds? Common sense tells you that if the package weighs more than one, but less than five pounds, the rate will be be $5.00. Table 6.6 summarizes these 'weight ranges,' and their respective shipping costs. If you tried typing a value such as 4 into the value range, and the *col_index_num* is set to **False**, as in the above example, a **#NA** error would be returned.

If the *col_index_num* is set to **True**, then VLOOKUP() will find the greatest value less than the search value. For this functionality to work, there are two rules which you must follow:

- The search range must be the first column of the list, as is the case with all situations using **VLOOKUP()**.
- The compare values must be sorted in ascending order.

The compare values must be in ascending order because Excel finds the first value which is greater than the search value, and then moves back (up) one cell. Thus, if the cells are not in ascending order, an incorrect

TABLE 6.6
Weight Ranges

Weight	Cost (per lb.)	Shipping Code
1 to <5	$5.00	Blue
5 to <24	$3.00	Red
25 to <99	$1.50	White
100 +	$0.75	Green

value might be returned, with no message to indicate that an error occurred. If the two **VLOOKUP()** functions in the previous example were modified to change *col_index_num* from **False** to **True**, the example illustrated in Figure 6.9 would be the result.

What If Your Compare Values Are Not in the First Column?

If your compare values are not in your first column, there are three alternative functions available:

- **HLOOKUP()**
- **LOOKUP()**
- **MATCH()**
- **INDEX()**

HLOOKUP()

For lists with a horizontal orientation, rather than a vertical orientation, you can use the **HLOOKUP()** function. If your compare values are in the first row of a list which has been 'rotated' 90° from a list's 'normal' orientation, the **HLOOKUP()** function has the same syntax and behaves logically, ex-

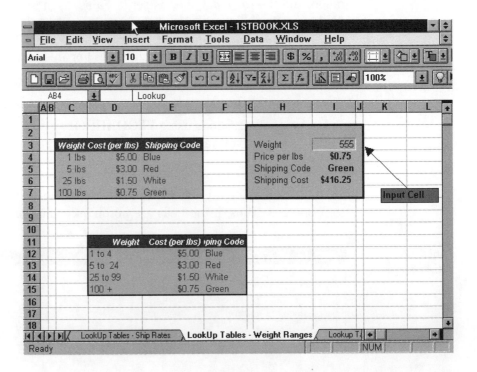

FIGURE 6.9
LookUp tables—
Weight Ranges.

actly the same as **VLOOKUP()**. **HLOOKUP()** searches column by column for the search value, but instead of having a *col_index_num*, **HLOOKUP()** uses a *row_num_index*. The syntax for **HLOOKUP()** is

HLOOKUP(*lookup_value,table_array,col_index_num,range_lookup*)

where:

- *lookup_value* is the search value, or the value that you want to match.
- *table_array* is the range which contains the list you wish to search.
- *row_index_num* is the index number, of the row whose value you seek. The *row_index_num* for the first row (the match column) is zero, and increases incrementally by one for each row down.
- *range_lookup* is a logical value, which specifies whether an exact match must be made, or whether an approximate match can be made.

If the *row_index_num* is less than one, a **#VALUE! Error** is returned. If the *row_index_num* is greater than the number of columns in the list, a **#REF! Error** is returned.

LOOKUP()

Although there are many situations where your compare value will be in the first row (or column), or you can arrange your data to artificially create this situation, there will be many times when the compare value will be in another row (or column). For these situations, you can use the vector version of the **LOOKUP()** function. A **vector** is an array which contains only one row or one column. The vector version of **LOOKUP()** behaves like the **HLOOKUP()** and **VLOOKUP()** functions that have their *range_lookup* argument set to **TRUE**, even though there is no suchi argument for **LOOKUP()**. In other words, the search range is not limited to exact matches (nor can you limit it). This means that the compare values must be in ascending order, as discussed earlier in the **VLOOKUP()** section. The vector form of the **LOOKUP()** function has the syntax:

LOOKUP(*lookup_value,lookup_vector,result_vector*)

where:

- *lookup_value* is the search value, or the value that you want to match.

- *lookup_vector* is the range which contains the list you wish to search. This range must be a vector!
- *result_vector* is the range which contains the value you are seeking. This range must also be a vector!

When a match is made, Excel notes the 'index position' in the *lookup_vector*, and then moves to the position with the same index in the *result_vector*, and then returns the value. As such, these two vectors do not even have to be of the same orientation, although this function is most useful when the two vectors are 'parallel.'

Examine Figure 6.10. In this worksheet, the previous examples' database has been slimmed down, and split into two ranges, and then the **Cost** range was transposed. **WeightVector** is the range C7:C10. **CostVector** is the range C14:F14. Cell I7 (which returns the price per pound value) contains the formula:

$$= \text{LOOKUP}(\textit{InputCell}, \textit{WeightVector}, \textit{CostVector})$$

MATCH()

The **MATCH()** function is used to 'manually' identify the relative position, or index, of an item in an array. Examine the data illustrated in Table 6.7.

The cell which contains the text **Feb**, would have an index of two (2),

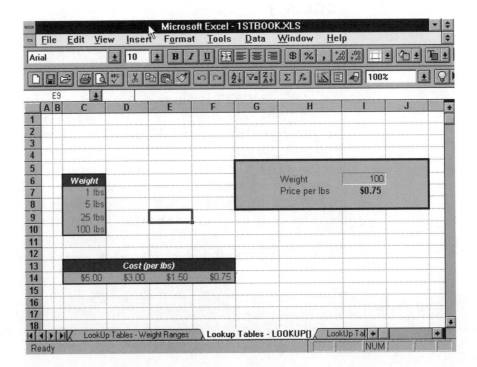

FIGURE 6.10
Lookup Tables—
LOOKUP().

because it is the second cell from the top. Likewise, the cell which contains the text **Mar** would have an index of three (3), and the cell which contains the text **Jan** would have an index of one (1).

The **MATCH()** function has the following syntax:

$$= \text{MATCH}(lookup\_value, lookup\_array, match\_type)$$

where:

- *lookup_value* is the search value, or the value that you want to match.
- *lookup_array* is a contiguous range of cells containing possible lookup values. It can be an array or an array reference.
- *match_type* is an optional argument, which determines how Excel matches the value of *lookup_value*, with the values in *lookup_array*. Table 6.8 summarizes each of the three options. If *match_type* is omitted, it defaults to one (1).

If **MATCH()** is not successful in finding a match, an **#NA Error** value is returned.

Examine the data in Figure 6.11. Cell I4 contains the formula:

$$= \text{MATCH}(InputCell, C4:C7, 1)$$

If you use the value 25 (as in this example), this formula will return

TABLE 6.7

Jan
Feb
Mar

TABLE 6.8
Match_type Values

match_type value	MATCH will find:
1	The largest value which is less than or equal to *lookup_value*. *Lookup_array* must be in ascending order.
0	The first value which is exactly equal to *lookup_value*. *Lookup_array* can be in any order.
−1	The smallest value which is greater than or equal to *lookup_value*. *Lookup_array* must be in descending order.

CHAPTER 6

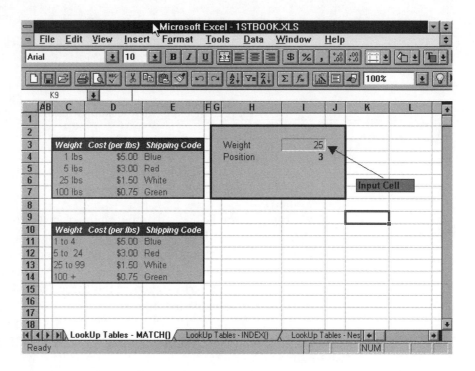

FIGURE 6.11

the value three (3), because the third cell in the range (be careful not to include the column heading! in your *lookup_array range*) contains the value 25. Notice that the values in *lookup_array* are in ascending order. Although the example uses an exact match, this formula will work with any value, because the *match_type* is set to one (1).

HINT If the *match_type* is zero, and the *lookup_value* is text (or a reference to a range which contains text), you can use wildcard characters in your search value.

INDEX()

The array form of the **INDEX()** function is used to get the value of an item in array, whose relative position (or index!) you know. Examine the data illustrated in Table 6.9.

If you want to know the value in the cell which is the second element of this array, you would simply scan the array, until you found the second element. You would then see that the cell contained the text value **Feb**.

TABLE 6.9
INDEX() Data

Jan
Feb
Mar

This is the same way in which the **INDEX()** function works. The **INDEX()** function has the following syntax:

$$= \text{INDEX}(array, row\_num, column\_num)$$

where:

- **array** is an array of cells, or a reference to a range which contains an array of cells.
- *row_num* is the row index, or the relative (to the beginning of the array) number of the row you want to return a value for. If *col_num* is omitted, this is a required argument.
- *col_num* is the column index, or the relative number of the column you want to return a value for. If *row_num* is omitted, this is a required argument.

In other words, the **INDEX()** function must have either a *row_num* argument, or a *col_num* argument, as a minimum requirement. To see the **INDEX()** function in action, examine Figure 6.12. Cell I4 contains the formula:

$$= \text{INDEX}(C4:C7, InputCell)$$

This allows you to change the *row_num* argument. If you input the value three (3) (as is illustrated), this function will return the value of the third cell from the range C4:C7, which is 25. Remember that the cell which you are requesting the value of has a special number format to display the abbreviation for pounds.

Combining MATCH() and INDEX()

The real power for working with lookup tables comes when you nest the **MATCH()** function within the **INDEX** function. Examine Figure 6.13. The formula in cell I4 which in previous examples had used **VLOOKUP()**, has been replaced with the formula:

$$= \text{INDEX}(C3:E7, \text{MATCH}(InputCell, C3:C7, 1), 3)$$

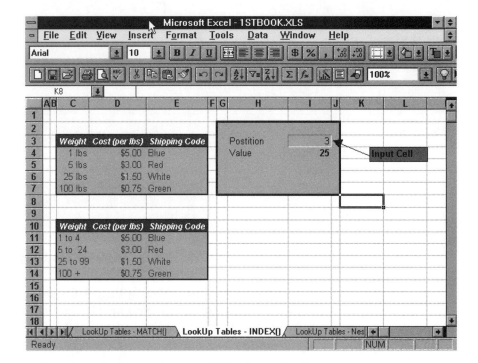

FIGURE 6.12

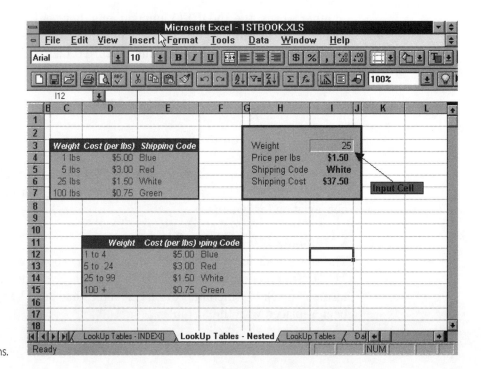

FIGURE 6.13
Lookup tables—
Nested caption:
Nesting the
MATCH() and
INDEX() functions.

TABLE 6.10 Nested INDEX() and MATCH() Functions to Calculate Shipping

Cell	Formula
I5	=INDEX(C3:E7,MATCH(InputCell,C3:C7,1),3)
I6	=INDEX(C3:E7,MATCH(InputCell,C3:C7,1),2)*InputCell

In this formula, the **MATCH()** function is being used to identify the 'index' position of the item whose value you want (*InputCell*), and the **INDEX()** function returns the value of the cell which was located by the position indicated by **MATCH()**. In addition, cells I8 and I9 have been updated with the formulas illustrated in Table 6.10. Although it is probably quicker to input just the **VLOOKUP** function, nesting these two functions gives you greater flexibility.

Summary

In this chapter you have learned:

- A **data table** is a special kind of list, used for what-if analysis.
- **One-input data tables** are used to input values for one variable, and to see the effect on one or more formulas.
- **Two-input data tables** are used to input values for two variables, and to see the effect on one formula.
- One-input tables consist of four components: an **Input Cell**, **List Range**, **Data Table Formula Cell**, and **Output Range**.
- You can easily add additional formulas and/or input values to a one-input data table.
- Each **Data Table Formula Cell** must directly or indirectly reference the input cell and must be located to the right of existing data table formula cells if they are arranged horizontally (in a row), or below existing data table formula cells if they are arranged vertically (in a column).
- Two-input data tables consist of six components: a **Row Input Cell**, **Column Input Cell**, **Row List Range**, **Column List Range**, **Data Table Formula Cell**, and **Output Range**.
- You can set worksheet calculation to **Automatic Except Tables**.
- Pressing **SHIFT+F9** forces calculation of the active worksheet.
- Pressing **F9** forces calculation of all worksheets in all open workbooks.
- A **lookup table** is a special list, in which you use one value, which you know, to find another value, which you don't know.

- The **VLOOKUP()** function is used to search through a vertically oriented list, find a value in its leftmost column, and then return the value of another cell in the same row.
- The **HLOOKUP()** function is used to search through a horizontally oriented list, find a value in its topmost row, and then return the value of another cell in the same column.
- The vector form of the **LOOKUP()** function is used to lookup the value of an element in a vector, and to return the value of the element which has the same index position in another vector.
- The **MATCH()** function is used to identify the relative position, or index, of an item in an array.
- The array form of the **INDEX()** function is used to get the value of an item in array, whose relative position (or index!) you know.
- By nesting the **MATCH()** function within the **INDEX** function, you can simulate the effect of combining the functionality of **LOOKUP()** with either **VLOOKUP()** or **HLOOKUP()**.

CHAPTER 7
Reading and Writing Other Data Formats

Introduction

This chapter will discuss how to use and create data not originally stored as Excel 5.0 worksheets. The focus of this chapter is importing and using databases and lists contained in non-Excel files. Often you will need to send information to, or receive information from, others in your enterprise who are using other spreadsheets, databases, or applications. In this chapter you will learn:

- Which file formats Excel can directly read and write.
- How to import data into Excel.
- How to use TextWizard.
- How to export from Excel.
- How to combine data from multiple files.
- What to watch for when importing or exporting.

Importing Data

It is often necessary to include data from other sources in order to perform an analysis. The process of getting such data into your spreadsheet is called **importing**. Reasons to import data include:

- Updates to the source data are not required, or allowed.
- You want to use a snapshot of the data.
- Security restrictions prevent direct access to the source system.

- The source data does not support ODBC (e.g., FOCUS).
- You do not have the proper ODBC driver for the data source.
- Importing can be faster than attaching to external data.

There are also several reasons not to import data. These include:

- The data is dynamic—using a snapshot would be misleading.
- Updates to the source data are required.
- Data is available in client/server environment.
- The data has more records (rows) than can be read into an Excel worksheet.
- Excel cannot directly read the data source's file format.

Microsoft Excel can directly read several formats including:

- Previous versions of Excel charts, macros, or worksheets
- Text files
- Lotus 1-2-3 files
- Xbase files
- Borland Quattro Pro for DOS files
- Microsoft Works files
- Symbolic Link (SYLK or Multiplan format)
- DIF (Data Interchange Format), as originally defined for Visicalc.

Files are imported using the **Open** command. Each file opened is assigned a new workbook. The workbook name is the actual file name and extension that you opened. The worksheet is given just the file name. When you save an imported file, Excel saves it back in its original format, by default, although you will be warned that this is happening. If you want to keep the data in an Excel 5.0 workbook, you must save it as such.

Text Files

Text files can be either delimited or fixed width. **Delimited** text has a special character, called a delimiter, which separates each column of data. The delimiter must not appear in the data itself, or the data will be split into additional columns. Each row in the text file may vary in length. Common delimiters are spaces, commas, and tabs.

In **fixed width** text, each column uses a fixed (for that column) number of characters. In other words, the column width (or length) is fixed. Each of the columns within a row may be a different width, but all rows are the same length, and each column must be the same width in each row.

HINT *Each row of text must be terminated with a carriage return/line feed combination (ASCII 0x13h/0x10h). This is best done when the file is created by the source system. However, you can edit your file in Notepad or Write and insert the carriage return/line feed manually. This is done by pressing the **Enter** at the point where a new row should start.*

There are two ways to import text into an Excel worksheet:

- The TextWizard
- The **TextToColumns** method in Visual Basic for Applications.

You may also have textual data in an existing spreadsheet that you need to convert to columnar data. You can start the TextWizard by selecting **Data→Text to Columns...**. This will start the TextWizard, which is described in the next two examples. This will only be useful if you have text in a single column that can be split into several columns. This will most likely occur with data resulting from a query to an attached external database, or with spreadsheets which have these types on columns.

TextWizard

The TextWizard is a tool that walks you through the process of either opening text files as Excel worksheets or converting textual data in a single column into several columns. This process is a three step process:

- Identifying the file type (delimited versus fixed width).
- Dividing the text into columns.
- Selecting the format of each column.

Step One: Identifying the File Type

The first step that the TextWizard walks you through is identifying the file type. Figure 7.1 illustrates the first screen of the TextWizard. This screen has the following major components:

- **Original Data Type** option group
- Starting **Import** at spinner control
- **File Origin** drop-down list box
- **File Preview** window.

Original Data Type option group is used to identify whether the source file is delimited or fixed width. By increasing the value of the **Start Import at Row** spinner control, you can skip header information that may be at the top of your text file. The **File Origin** drop-down list box allows

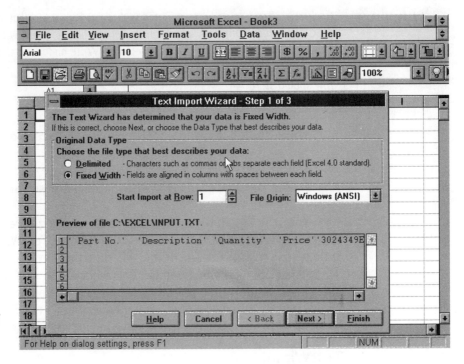

FIGURE 7.1
TextImport Wizard—Step 1 of 3 (Delimited text data.

you to see whether the file was created in the Windows, Macintosh or OS/2 environments. Most ASCII files will work best with the default Windows (ANSI) value. The **File Preview** window displays the first six rows of the text file (or column chosen) when the TextWizard started.

Step Two: Dividing the Text into Columns

Depending on whether you selected delimited or fixed width in Step 1 of TextWizard, you will see one of two different screens here. If you selected delimited text, you will need to choose the delimiters in your data. If you selected fixed width text, you will need to tell TextWizard where each column starts and ends.

Delimited Text If you selected delimited text, you will see the screen illustrated in Figure 7.2 as the second screen of the TextWizard. This screen has the following major components:

- **Delimiters** check boxes
- **Treat consecutive delimiters as one** check box
- **Text Qualifier** list box
- **Data Preview** window.

The **Delimiters** check boxes are used to select the character(s) that

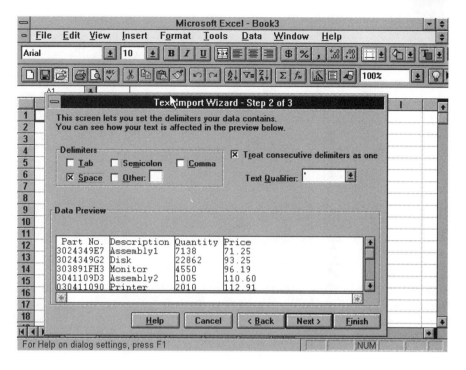

FIGURE 7.2
TextImport Wizard—Step 2 of 3 for delimited text data.

will act as delimiters to divide the input text into columns. You can choose from **Tab**, **Semicolon**, **Comma**, **Space**, or **Other**. If you select **Other**, you can input a character as a delimiter into the adjacent edit box. If the **Treat consecutive delimiters as one** check box is checked, multiple delimiters will be treated as one. If your delimiter is space, then multiple spaces will be interpreted as only a single space. The **Text Qualifier** drop-down list box allows you to set the text qualifier if some columns are text and are enclosed in quotes. If some columns are text and enclosed in quotes, then the text qualifier must be set, or the quotes will be imported into Excel. This is a common requirement to correctly import PRN files, originally designed to be imported into Lotus 1-2-3. The **Data Preview** window displays a preview of the effect the choices made on this panel have on the text being imported. Text should look correct in this panel before proceeding to the last step.

Fixed Width Text If you selected fixed width text in Step 1, you will see the screen illustrated in Figure 7.3 as the second screen of the TextWizard. This screen allows you to set the field widths for each column in your text file. To create a new line, click anywhere in the **Data Preview**. To move an existing line, point to the line you want to move, click and drag it to its new location. To delete a line, double-click on the line you want to delete.

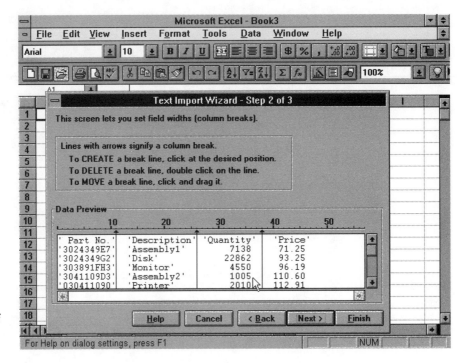

FIGURE 7.3
TextImport Wizard—Step 2 of 3 for fixed width text.

Step Three: Selecting the Format of Each Column

Regardless of whether you choose delimited or fixed width text in Step 1, Step 3 uses the screen illustrated in Figure 7.4. In this final step, you must select the format for each column. The format for each column is shown in the **Data Preview** window, as well as the effect of choosing that format. To change a column format, click on the column you want to change, and select the proper format from the **Column Data Format** option group. You may also choose to skip a particular column if it is not needed. You may choose one of the following formats for each column:

- **General**
- **Text**
- **Date**
- **Do Not Import Column (Skip)**.

The **General** format will provide an automatic conversion, and will be fine for most applications. However, there are instances where this automatic conversion will not produce the desired results. In this case, you must change the column format in this step. In the **Things To Watch For** section below, this example will be used to demonstrate this issue. This conversion issue is the reason the format of the first column was changed to **Text**,

Reading and Writing Other Data Formats

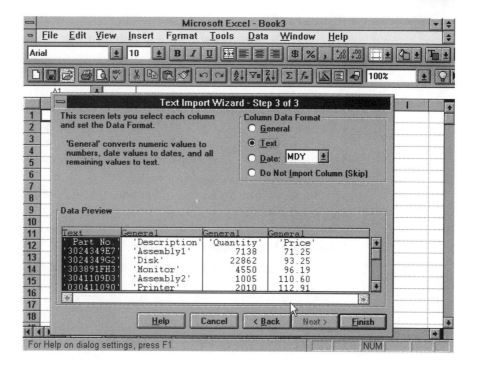

FIGURE 7.4
TextImport Wizard—Step 3 of 3.

which forces the column to be treated as text. **Date** forces the column to be treated as dates and allows you to pick the date format as well. The **Do Not Import Column (Skip)** skips the column. This is handy when you want to import some, but not all, of the columns in a file.

Importing Delimited Text Files

Two commonly used delimited file formats are **CSV** and **PRN**. **CSV** stands for **comma-separated values**. CSV files use the comma as the delimiter. **PRN** files were originally created as a means of importing and exporting data from Lotus 1-2-3. These are space-delimited files, with text enclosed in quotes. To import delimited text file, follow the steps below.

STEPS Importing Delimited Text Data

1. Select **File→Open**.
2. Select the type of text file you want to import from the **List Files of Type** drop-down list.
3. Select the drive where the input file is located from the **Drives** list box.
4. Select the directory of the input file in **Directories** list box.
5. Select the file from the **File Name** list box.

6. Select **OK**. Step one of the TextImportWizard will be displayed.
7. Select the **Delimited** option button from the **Original Data Type** option group.
8. Set the other properties, if the default values do not work well with your data.
9. Select **Next>**. Step two of the TextImportWizard will be displayed.
10. Select the delimiter(s) and other properties as appropriate, so that your data looks correct in the **Data Preview** window.
11. Select **Next>**. The Step three of the TextImportWizard will be displayed.
12. Set your **Column Data Formats** as appropriate for your data.
13. Select **Finish**.

Importing Fixed width Text Files

To import a fixed width text file, follow the steps below.

STEPS   Importing Fixed Width Text Data

1. Select **File→Open**.
2. Select the type of text file you want to import from the **List Files of Type** drop-down list.
3. Select the drive where the input file is located from the **Drives** list box.
4. Select the directory of the input file in **Directories** list box.
5. Select the file from the **File Name** list box.
6. Select **OK**. Step one of the TextImportWizard will be displayed.
7. Select the **Fixed Width** option button from the **Original Data Type** option group.
8. Set the other properties, if the default values do not work well with your data.
9. Select **Next>**. Step two of the TextImportWizard will be displayed.
10. Select the delimiter(s) and other properties as appropriate, so that your data looks correct in the **Data Preview** window.
11. Select **Next>**. Step three of the TextImportWizard will be displayed.
12. Set your **Column Data Formats** as appropriate for your data.
13. Select **Finish**.

Each text file will be imported into its own workbook. Note that in this case, you could not remove the quotes which act as text qualifiers. The facility to remove text qualifiers is only available with delimited text. This example also illustrates that the same file could be imported in different ways.

Xbase Data Files

When Xbase files are opened, index files are ignored. The database is opened and converted into Excel format. Field names are inserted into the first row automatically. Excel also creates the range name *Database*, which encompasses all of the imported data. If the Xbase file contains more than 16,384 rows, only the first 16,384 rows are imported. The rest are ignored. Excel supports dBASE II, III, and IV files, as well as dBASE compatible files such as Microsoft FoxPro. Several dBASE files are shipped with Excel 5.0 and are located in the **\WINDOWS\MSAPPS\MSQUERY** directory.

STEPS Importing Xbase Data

1. Select **File→Open**.
2. Select **dBASE Files (*.DBF)** from the **List Files of Type** drop-down list.
3. Select the drive where the input file is located from the **Drives** list box.
4. Select the directory of the input file in **Directories** list box.
5. Select the file from the **File Name** list box.
6. Select **OK**. The file will be opened.

Lotus 1-2-3 Spreadsheet Files

When a 1-2-3 spreadsheet is opened in Excel, any database in the spreadsheet is automatically converted so it can be used in Excel. Specifically, the range specified with **/ Data Query Input** is converted into the Excel name *Database*. The 1-2-3 criteria range specified with **/ Data Query Criteria** is named *Criteria* when the spreadsheet is opened in Excel, and the range identified by **/ Data Query Output** is named *Extract*. Formatting information is stored in a separate file.

STEPS Importing Lotus 1-2-3 Spreadsheet Data

1. Select **File→Open**.
2. Select **Lotus 1-2-3 Files (*.WK*)** from the **List Files of Type** drop-down list.
3. Select the drive where the input file is located from the **Drives** list box.

4. Select the directory of the input file in **Directories** list box.
5. Select the file from the **File Name** list box.
6. Select **OK**. The file will be opened.

Borland Quattro Pro for DOS Files

Excel can import (and export) files from Borland's Quattro Pro for DOS spreadsheet. Excel cannot directly import or export Quattro Pro for Windows spreadsheets. To import a Quattro Pro for DOS file, follow the steps below.

STEPS

Importing Borland Quattro Pro for DOS Spreadsheet Data

1. Select **File→Open**.
2. Select **Quattro Pro/DOS Files (*.wq*)** from the **List Files of Type** drop-down list.
3. Select the drive where the input file is located from the **Drives** list box.
4. Select the directory of the input file in **Directories** list box.
5. Select the file from the **File Name** list box.
6. Select **OK**. The file will be opened.

Microsoft Works Files

STEPS

Importing Microsoft Works Files

1. Select **File→Open**.
2. Select **Microsoft Works Files (*.wks)** from the **List Files of Type** drop-down list.
3. Select the drive where the input file is located from the **Drives** list box.
4. Select the directory of the input file in **Directories** list box.
5. Select the file from the **File Name** list box.
6. Select **OK**. The file will be opened.

Symbolic Link (SYLK or Multiplan Format)

STEPS **Importing SYLK Files**

1. Select **File→Open**.
2. Select **SYLK Files (*.slk)** from the **List Files of Type** drop-down list.
3. Select the drive where the input file is located from the **Drives** list box.
4. Select the directory of the input file in **Directories** list box.
5. Select the file from the **File Name** list box.
6. Select **OK**. The file will be opened.

DIF (Data Interchange Format)

STEPS **Importing DIF files**

1. Select **File→Open**.
2. Select **Data Interchange Format (*.dif)** from the **List Files of Type** drop-down list.
3. Select the drive where the input file is located from the **Drives** list box.
4. Select the directory of the input file in **Directories** list box.
5. Select the file from the **File Name** list box.
6. Select **OK**. The file will be opened.

Exporting Data

In order to share information with others in your enterprise, it is often necessary to translate data to a format other than Excel. The process of translating to another format is called exporting. Excel supports the following formats for exporting data:

- Formatted Text (Space delimited, DOS, Macintosh, or OS/2)
- Delimited Text (Tab delimited (DOS, Macintosh, or OS/2), or CSV (Comma delimited, DOS, Macintosh, or OS/2))
- Previous versions of Excel
- Lotus 1-2-3 Versions 1, 2, or 3, including format information
- Quattro Pro for DOS
- Xbase (dBASE II, III, and IV files, as well as dBASE compatible files such as Microsoft FoxPro)
- Symbolic Link (SYLK or Multiplan format)

- DIF (Data Interchange Format), as originally defined for Visicalc.

You export Excel worksheets to other data formats via the **File→Save As** command. You select the data format from the **Save File as Type** in the **Save As** dialog box. The default format to save in is the original format of the file. You may choose to save your file in any of the supported formats. When data is exported, only the Excel 4.0 workbook and the 1-2-3 Version 3 format saves the entire workbook. All other export formats save only the current sheet. To export the other sheets in your workbook, you must switch to each one in turn and export it. When you try to save a workbook to a file format that does not support multiple dimensions the message box illustrated in Figure 7.5 will remind you that only the current sheet is being saved.

Also, it is important to remember that Excel does not update Xbase indices when the file is saved. This could result in errors in applications that rely on indices that may have become invalid as a result of reordering rows or truncating the file in Excel.

Text

Formatted Text

In many ways, saving data as formatted text will create the equivalent of a PRN file for 1-2-3. However, PRN files require that text columns be enclosed in quotation marks. Saving a file as formatted text does not do this. To save a worksheet as formatted text, follow the steps below.

STEPS: Saving an Excel Worksheet as Formatted Text

1. Select **File→Save As...**.
2. Select **Formatted Text (Space Delimited)** from the **Save File as Type** drop-down list.
3. Select the drive where you want to save the file from the **Drives** list box.

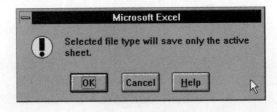

FIGURE 7.5
Selected file type will save only the active sheet message box.

4. Select the directory where you want to save the file from the **Directories** list box.
5. Type a file name in the **File Name** edit box.
6. Select **OK**. The message box which indicates you can save only the active sheet will be displayed.
7. Select **OK**.

The file is now converted and saved.

Delimited Text

Using this format you may save an Excel spreadsheet as one of two common delimited formats:

- CSV
- Text.

    CSV files use commas as their column delimiter. In previous versions of Excel, these were called *comma-separated values* files. The commonly used file extension for CSV files is CSV. **Text** files use the **TAB** character as the column delimiter. The commonly used extension for text files with tab as the column delimiter is TXT. To save an Excel worksheet as a delimited text file, follow the steps below.

STEPS

Saving an Excel Worksheet as a Comma Delimited Text File

1. Select **File→Save As…**.
2. Select the drive where you want to save the file from the **Drives** list box.
3. Select the directory where you want to save the file from the **Directories** list box.
4. Type a file name in the **File Name** edit box.
5. Select **CSV (Comma delimited)** from the **Save File as Type** drop-down list.
6. Select **OK**. The message box which indicates you can only save the active sheet will be displayed.
7. Select **OK**.

STEPS

Saving an Excel Worksheet as a Tab Delimited Text File

1. Select **File→Save As...**.
2. Select the drive where you want to save the file from the **Drives** list box.
3. Select the directory where you want to save the file from the **Directories** list box.
4. Type a file name in the **File Name** edit box.
5. Select **Text (Tab delimited)** from the **Save File as Type** drop-down list.
6. Select **OK**.

Previous Versions of Microsoft Excel

By nature of the fact that you are reading this book, it can be assumed that you are using Excel 5.0. But, what if there are other people in your organization whom you need to exchange data with, but they do not yet have Excel 5.0? Another situation might be that you need to interface with an application that can read Excel 4.0 files, but has not been updated to read Excel 5.0 files. Table 7.1 lists the Excel versions that you can export to. To export a worksheet to a previous version of Excel, follow the steps below.

STEPS

Exporting an Excel 5.0 Worksheet to a Previous Version of Excel

1. Select **File→Save As...**.
2. Select one of the valid Excel file formats listed in Table 7.1, from the **Save File as Type** drop-down list.
3. Select the drive where you want to save the file from the **Drives** list box.
4. Select the directory where you want to save the file from the **Directories** list box.
5. Type a file name in the **File Name** edit box.

TABLE 7.1 Supported Excel Export Formats

Version/Type
Microsoft Excel 4.0 Worksheet
Microsoft Excel 3.0 Worksheet
Microsoft Excel 2.1 Worksheet
Microsoft Excel 4.0 Workbook

6. Select **OK**. The message box which indicates you can only save the active sheet will be displayed. Select **OK** again.

The file is now converted and saved.

1-2-3 Files

To export a database in an Excel worksheet to Lotus 1-2-3, your worksheet must have unique field names in the first row of the database. Table 7.2 lists all of the Lotus 1-2-3 file formats that Excel can export to. To export a worksheet to a Lotus 1-2-3 for DOS file, follow the steps below.

STEPS

Exporting to a Lotus 1-2-3 for DOS File

1. Make sure that you have a range named *Database*, which has unique field names in the first row.
2. Select **File→Save As...**.
3. Select the drive where you want to save the file from the **Drives** list box.
4. Select the directory where you want to save the file from the **Directories** list box.
5. Type a file name in the **File Name** edit box.
6. Select one of the valid Lotus 1-2-3 file formats listed in table 7.2, from the **Save File as Type** drop-down list.
7. Select **OK**. The message box which indicates you can only save the active sheet will be displayed.
8. Select **OK** again.

The file is now converted and saved.

TABLE 7.2
Supported Lotus 1-2-3 Export Formats

File Extension/Type
WK3, FMT (1-2-3)
WK3 (1-2-3)
WK1, FMT (1-2-3)
WK1, ALL (1-2-3)
WK1 (1-2-3)
WKS (1-2-3)

Quattro Pro for DOS

To export a database in an Excel spreadsheet to Quattro Pro, your spreadsheet must have unique field names in the first row of the database. Note that Quattro Pro for Windows is not supported. To export an Excel worksheet to Quattro Pro for DOS, follow the steps below.

> **STEPS**

Exporting Data to Quattro Pro

1. Make sure that you have a range named *Database*, which has unique field names in the first row.
2. Select **File→Save As...**.
3. Select the drive where you want to save the file from the **Drives** list box.
4. Select the directory where you want to save the file from the **Directories** list box.
5. Type a file name in the **File Name** edit box.
6. Select **WQ1(QuattroPro/DOS)** from the **Save File as Type** drop-down list.
7. Select **OK**. The message box which indicates you can only save the active sheet will be displayed.
8. Select **OK** again.

The file is now converted and saved.

Xbase Files

It is important to note that Xbase files are databases alone. There is no facility to store formulas, indexes, or formatting information. When Excel saves a worksheet into DBF format, it saves only the range named *Database*. The first row of the range *Database* is taken to be the field names. These are converted to upper case and written to the database. If you do not have a *Database* range, Excel will attempt to save your current list. Please refer to the chapter on lists for more information. Excel does not create or maintain any indices associated with an Xbase file. To export a worksheet to an Xbase file, follow these steps:

Reading and Writing Other Data Formats

STEPS

Exporting to an Xbase File

1. Select **File→Save As...**.
2. Select the drive where you want to save the file from the **Drives** list box.
3. Select the directory where you want to save the file from the **Directories** list box.
4. Type a file name in the **File Name** edit box.
5. Select **DBF 4 (dBASE IV)**, **DBF 3 (dBASE III)**, or **DBF 2 (dBASE II)** from the **Save File as Type** drop-down list.
6. Select **OK**. The message box which indicates you can only save the active sheet will be displayed.
7. Select **OK** again.

The file is now converted and saved.

Symbolic Link Files

Symbolic link files are used to export data to Microsoft Multiplan. To export a worksheet to a SYLK file, follow the steps below.

STEPS

Exporting to an Symbolic Link File

1. Select **File→Save As...**.
2. Select the drive where you want to save the file from the **Drives** list box.
3. Select the directory where you want to save the file from the **Directories** list box.
4. Type a file name in the **File Name** edit box.
5. Select **SYLK (Symbolic Link)** from the **Save File as Type** drop down list.
6. Select **OK**. The message box which indicates you can only save the active sheet will be displayed.
7. Select **OK** again.

The file is now converted and saved.

Data Interchange Format Files

Data Interchange Format (DIF) was originally defined for use with Visicalc. Some older applications still use this file format. It is not broadly used today. To export a worksheet to a DIF file, follow the steps below.

STEPS

Exporting to a DIF File

1. Select **File→Save As....**
2. Select the drive where you want to save the file from the **Drives** list box.
3. Select the directory where you want to save the file from the **Directories** list box.
4. Type a file name in the **File Name** edit box.
5. Select **DIF (Data Interchange Format)** from the **Save File as Type** drop-down list.
6. Select **OK**. The message box which indicates you can only save the active sheet will be displayed.
7. Select **OK** again.

The file is now converted and saved.

Combining Data from Multiple Files into a Single File

One issue that often arises is the ability to consolidate data from multiple files into a single workbook. In Lotus 1-2-3, this capability is invoked through the **/ File Combine Copy Entire-file** menu choice.

Excel provides a very similar capability which is more flexible and useful. While Lotus 1-2-3 allows only other 1-2-3 spreadsheets to be used in this manner, Excel's method allows any of the file types available in the **Open** dialog box to be used (see above). If you also include all of the data formats available via MS Query and ODBC, you will be hard-pressed to come up with a data source which you cannot incorporate. Follow the steps below to combine data from several files.

STEPS

Combining Data from Multiple, Heterogeneous Files

1. Open or create the file you will merge information into (the target file).
2. Open the file you will merge information from (the source file), using the methods detailed earlier in this chapter. Be sure to pick the proper file type from the list box.

3. Select the entire area you want to merge into your target file.
4. Select **Edit→Copy** to copy this selection to the Windows clipboard.
5. Close the source file. Do not save the changes.
6. Select the area in your target file to merge the data into. Note that it should be the same shape (i.e., the same number of rows and columns) as the source.
7. Select **Edit→Paste**.

> **HINT** *Instead of selecting the whole range, you can select the cell in the upper left hand corner of the target range. Make sure that the target area is clear.*

8. Repeat steps 2–7 for all files from which you will be merging data.
9. Save and close the target file.

If you want to overlay the target area, select **Edit→Paste**. To combine information into the target area, select **Edit→Paste Special...**. Figure 7.6 illustrates the dialog box you use to determine how the information will be merged. Here you must choose whether you merge all aspects of the source (formulas or values, formats, and notes) or only one of these. The only option available in 1-2-3 is **Values**. You can also choose to have the values consolidated using a mathematical operation from the second column. 1-2-3 allows addition or subtraction only.

Things to Watch For

There are two major areas of concern when bringing external information into Excel via text files:

- File format
- Text interpretation

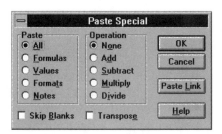

FIGURE 7.6
Paste Special dialog box.

File Formats

The first area of concern has to do with the format of the text file. Each row in the text file must start on a new line (usually indicated by a carriage return / line feed combination). Occasionally, files created as downloads from mainframe systems are not formatted this way and require reformatting before they can be used in Excel. Formatting information in this way is easiest to do in the initial extraction process. See Chapter 10, **Visual Basic for Applications**, for an example of a VBA subroutine that reads in a file that has no carriage return / line feed combinations and writes it out to a new file that does.

Text Interpretation

The second major issue in importing text files into Excel has to do with how Excel interprets text. In other spreadsheets, textual data has traditionally been enclosed in quotes and always treated as text. Excel provides more flexibility which requires the user to be aware of what is happening. When you type an entry into a cell, Excel uses rules to determine whether the entry you made was date, numeric, or text. Any entry that could be interpreted as a date (e.g. 1/1/94 or Jan 1) is entered as a date with an appropriate format. If the entry could be interpreted as a number, Excel converts it into a number (e.g. 123, or 145E09, in scientific notation). All other entries are stored as text. This is the set of rules Excel uses when you specify a column is to be **General** format in the TextWizard.

In the TextWizard example above, the first column was changed to be **Text** format, rather than the default **General** format in order to avoid this misinterpretation. Figure 7.7 illustrates what would have happened if the default **Text** format was used.

In this example, row two has a part number of **3.02E+13**. This is how Excel interpreted the original text **3024349E7**, which is a valid number in scientific notation. Row six was also misinterpreted.

Figure 7.8 illustrates the effect of using **Text** format for the first column.

Summary

In this chapter you have learned:

- How to import data into Excel.
- When not to import data.
- How to export data from Excel.
- How to combine data from multiple data files and sources.
- What to look out for during importing and exporting.

READING AND WRITING OTHER DATA FORMATS

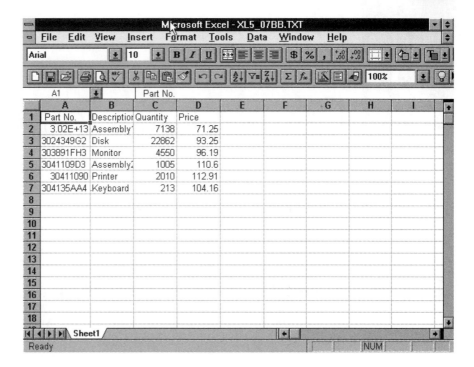

FIGURE 7.7
Incorrect use of General column format in TextWizard.

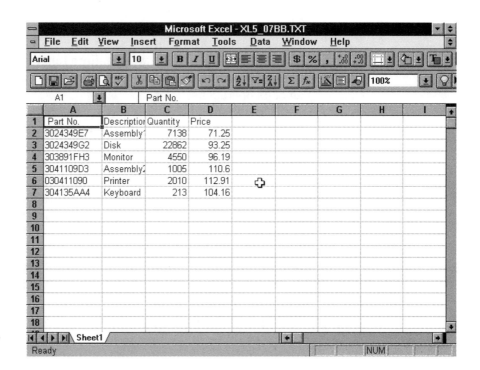

FIGURE 7.8
Correct use of "Text" column format for proper results.

CHAPTER 8

Custom Data Forms

Using VBA to Create a Custom Data Form

Using Visual Basic for Applications, and a dialog sheet, you can create a custom data form instead of creating a data form that looks like a standard data form. The finished form is illustrated in Figure 8.1. This section will discuss the creation of a form that looks similar to, but not exactly like, an Access form. This form has the following requirements:

- The form is only for browsing. A user cannot edit any data in the database using this form.
- The code behind the form will identify a range named *Database* on the worksheet it was called from. This is the range it will use for all of its operations.
- It will have four VCR style buttons to navigate through the database: **Fast Forward** (Last record in the database), **Fast Rewind** (First record in the database), **Next** (Next record in the database), and **Previous** (Previous record in the database).
- If you try to scroll past the first record, a message box indicating that you are on the first record will be displayed.
- If you try to scroll past the last record, a message box indicating that you are on the last record will be displayed.
- A record indicator tells how many records there are and what the current record number is.
- A **Cancel** button which closes the form without saving any changes, if any of the fields have been edited.
- An **OK** button, which will close the form when the user is done working with it.

Custom Data Forms

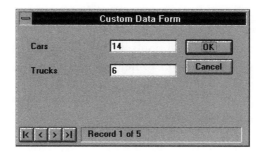

FIGURE 8.1
Custom Data Form dialog box.

Three additional features which are not included here, but should give you food for thought are:

- The ability to edit, add, and delete records from this form.
- An **Undo** button which will 'undo' any changes made to the current record. This button will not be visible/available unless one of the fields has been edited.
- A **Cancel** button which closes the form without saving any changes, if any of the fields have been edited.

In a macro sense, there are two steps to building this custom form:

- Create the form on a **Dialog Sheet**.
- Write all of the VBA code to support all of the objects on the form.

Creating the Form on a Dialog Sheet

Similar to the dialog editor, which came as a separate application with previous versions of Excel, Excel 5.0 sports an integrated form editor which allows you to create dialog sheets, using a graphic environment. Since the focus of this book is not on building custom applications, there will be only a quick overview of what you need to do to build the form, as well as to write the code to make it work.

The first thing that you need to do is to add a new dialog sheet to your workbook. To add a new dialog sheet, follow the steps below.

STEPS Creating a New Dialog Sheet

1. Select **Insert→Macro→Dialog**. A new dialog sheet will be inserted.

You build your dialog sheet by drawing controls on the dialog. Tools to draw these controls are available on the **Forms** toolbar. If this toolbar is not displayed, invoke the toolbar shortcut menu, and select **Forms**.

Figure 8.2 illustrates the AccessForm in design mode. Excluding the lines which are used to simulate a 3-D panel around the record indicator, there are eleven controls on this form. Their names and descriptions are listed in Table 8.1 to help you create a similar form.

You name form objects the same way you name worksheet ranges. While the object is selected, you type a new name in the **Name Box**, and then press **Enter**.

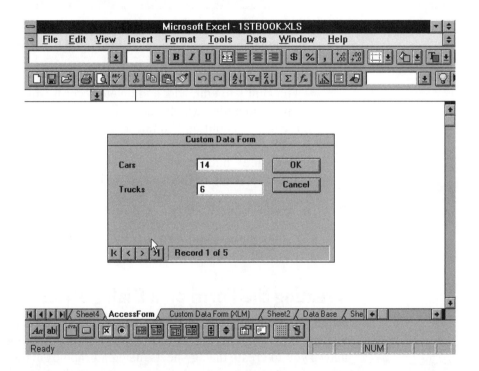

FIGURE 8.2
AccessForm in design mode.

TABLE 8.1
Controls on the AccessForm

Control Name	Description
lblOne	Label for first edit box
txtOne	First edit box
lblTwo	Label for second edit box
txtTwo	Second edit box
cmdOK	OK button
cmdCancel	Cancel button
cmdFirstRecord	GoTo First Row button
cmdPreviousRow	GoTo Previous Row button
cmdNextRow	GoTo Next Row button
cmdLastRow	GoTo Last Row button
lblRecordID	Label that will display the record number

What is VBA

In addition to the XLM macro language which has previously been Excel's only macro/development language, Excel 5.0 also ships with Visual Basic, Applications Edition (VBA). VBA is a special version of Microsoft Visual Basic, which, instead of 'living' in its own development environment, is 'hosted' within an application. Although some VBA code is discussed in Chapter 10, VBA is well beyond the scope of this book. As such, the code in the following sections has been included so that when you take the time to investigate VBA, you will have a jump start on how to use it to work with databases.

Setting Global Variables

Before you can utilize a variable across multiple procedures, you must define all module wide variables. By default, when you use or define a variable in a procedure, its scope is the length of that procedure. In other words, a variable holds its value, only within the procedure it was created in. Thus, you can have several procedures, all within the same module, which use the same variable name. If you want to pass the value of a variable from one procedure to another, its scope must be module wide.

The life of a variable is called its scope. When a variable is defined within a procedure, its scope is said to be local. If you would like several procedures with a single module to share a variable, then you must declare it in the module's global section. By explicitly declaring a variable in the global section, its scope is said to be module wide. The code from the declarations section of the module is listed below.

```
'This Module is Used to Create A Custom Data Form
'
'Author: John S. Dranchak
'Created January 9, 1993
'Last Updated January 9, 1993

Dim FirstRow
Dim FirstColumn
Dim FirstLabel
Dim SecondLabel
Dim FirstCell
Dim SecondCell
Dim FieldOne
Dim FieldTwo
Dim CurrentRecord As Integer
```

Initializing the Data Form

Now that the variables are defined, there are several steps which must be performed to initialize the custom data form:

- Identify the range named *Database* and make sure it exists.
- Determine how many rows long and how many columns wide the database is.
- Determine the row number of the first cell of the database.
- Identify the column headings, step through each one, and read its value into a variable.
- Initialize a variable which will keep track of the cursor position (what the current row is).
- Call a sub-routine which will correctly display the form with all of the correct field labels and edit boxes.

The listing below contains all of the required code for the **Initialize_Data_Form** procedure, with comments before each section.

```
Sub Initialize Data Form()
   Range (``Database´´)
   FirstRow = Range(``Database´´).Row
   FirstColumn = Range(``Database´´).Column

   'Sets up the Field Labels
   FirstLabel  =  Range(Cells(FirstRow,  FirstColumn),
Cells(FirstRow, FirstColumn)).Value
   SecondLabel = Range(Cells(FirstRow, FirstColumn + 1),
Cells(FirstRow, FirstColumn + 1)).Value

   'Finds the value of the first Record
   FieldOne = Range(Cells(FirstRow + 1, FirstColumn),
Cells(FirstRow + 1, FirstColumn)).Value
   FieldTwo = Range(Cells(FirstRow + 1, FirstColumn + 1),
Cells(FirstRow + 1, FirstColumn + 1)).Value

   'Initialize CurrentRecord Cursor—Set it to 1!
   CurrentRecord = 1

   'Run the sub to display the form
   Display Data Form
End Sub
```

Display_Data_Form Procedure

The **Display_Data_Form** procedure must:

- Set the text property of each of the field labels to the text of the corresponding column heading.
- Set the text property of each of the edit boxes that corresponds to a field to the value of the first row (Record).
- Set the text property of the Record ID label to identify what record the cursor is on, and how many records there are in the database.
- Display the dialog sheet, **Access_Form**, defined earlier in this chapter.

The list below contains all of the required code, for the **Display_Data_Form()** procedure.

```
Sub Display Data Form()
'Create the Data Field Labels
  With DialogSheets(``AccessForm´´)
    .Labels(``lblOne´´).Text = FirstLabel
    Labels(``lblTwo´´).Text = SecondLabel
    .EditBoxes(``txtOne´´).Text = FieldOne
    EditBoxes(``txtTwo´´).Text = FieldTwo
    Labels(``lblRecordID´´).Text = ``Record´´ &
CurrentRecord & `` of ´´ & Range(``Database´´).
Rows.Count—1

  End With

DialogSheets(``AccessForm´´).Show `Displays the form

End Sub
```

Move_To_Next Procedure

The **Move_To_Next()** procedure must:

- Increment the **CurrentRecord** counter by one.
- Read the values of the new **CurrentRecord** into their respective memory variables.
- Update the edit boxes on the dialog sheet to reflect values of the new record.

If the current record number is equal to the last record, display a message box that says *Last Record*, and does not increment the **CurrentRecord** counter.

The listing below contains all of the required code for the **Move_To_Next()** procedure.

```
Sub Move To Next()
If CurrentRecord + 1 < Range(``Database´´).Rows.Count
Then
    CurrentRecord = CurrentRecord + 1
  ElseIf CurrentRecord + 1 =
Range(``Database´´).Rows.Count Then
  MsgBox ``Last Record in Database!´´, vbOKOnly +
vbExclamation, ``Database Error´´
End If

'Update the variables which hold the values of the fields
FieldOne = Range(Cells(FirstRow + CurrentRecord,
FirstColumn), Cells(FirstRow + CurrentRecord,
FirstColumn)).Value
FieldTwo = Range(Cells(FirstRow + CurrentRecord,
FirstColumn + 1), Cells(FirstRow + CurrentRecord,
FirstColumn + 1)).Value

'Update the edit boxes on the dialog sheet that correspond
to the database´s fields
  With DialogSheets(``AccessForm´´)
    .EditBoxes(``txtOne´´).Text = FieldOne
    .EditBoxes(``txtTwo´´).Text = FieldTwo
    .Labels(``lblRecordID´´).Text = ``Record´´ &
CurrentRecord & `` of ´´ &
Range(``Database´´).Rows.Count—1
  End With
End Sub
```

Previous_Row Procedure

The **Previous_Row()** procedure must:

- Decrement the **CurrentRecord** counter by one.
- Read the values of the new **CurrentRecord** into their respective memory variables.

- Update the edit boxes on the dialog sheet to reflect values of the new record.

If the current record number is equal to the first record, display a message box that says *First Record*, and does not decrement the **CurrentRecord** counter.

The listing below contains all of the required code for the **Previous_Row()** procedure.

```
Sub Previous Row()
If (CurrentRecord + 1 <=
Range(``Database´´).Rows.Count) Then
   If CurrentRecord = 1 Then
     MsgBox ``You are already on the first record!´´,
vbOKOnly + vbExclamation, ``Database Error´´
   Else
     CurrentRecord = CurrentRecord-1
   End If
End If

'Updates Field Variables
FieldOne = Range(Cells(FirstRow + CurrentRecord,
FirstColumn), Cells(FirstRow + CurrentRecord,
FirstColumn)).Value
FieldTwo = Range(Cells(FirstRow + CurrentRecord,
FirstColumn + 1), Cells(FirstRow + CurrentRecord,
FirstColumn + 1)).Value

'Updates edit boxes on the dialog sheet
   With DialogSheets(``AccessForm´´)
     .EditBoxes(``txtOne´´).Text = FieldOne
     .EditBoxes(``txtTwo´´).Text = FieldTwo
     .Labels(``lblRecordID´´).Text = ``Record´´ &
CurrentRecord & `` of ´´ &
Range(``Database´´).Rows.Count-1
   End With
End Sub
```

First_Row Procedure

The **First_Row()** procedure must:

- Set the **CurrentRecord=1**.
- Read the values of the new **CurrentRecord** into their respective memory variables.

- Update the edit boxes on the dialog sheet to reflect values of the new record.

If the current record number is equal to the first record, display a message box that says *First Record*, and does not decrement the **CurrentRecord** counter.

The listing below contains all of the required code for the **First_Row()** procedure.

```
Sub First Row()
  If CurrentRecord > 1 Then
    CurrentRecord = 1
  ElseIf CurrentRecord = 1 Then
    MsgBox ``You are already on the first record!´´, vbOKOnly + vbExclamation, ``Database Error´´
  Else CurrentRecord = 1 ´ In case you accidentally scroll past the first record
  End If

'Update the variables which hold the values of the fields
FieldOne = Range(Cells(FirstRow + CurrentRecord, FirstColumn), Cells(FirstRow + CurrentRecord, FirstColumn)).Value
FieldTwo = Range(Cells(FirstRow + CurrentRecord, FirstColumn + 1), Cells(FirstRow + CurrentRecord, FirstColumn + 1)).Value

'Update the edit boxes on the dialog sheet that correspond to the database´s fields
  With DialogSheets(``AccessForm´´)
    .EditBoxes(``txtOne´´).Text = FieldOne
    .EditBoxes(``txtTwo´´).Text = FieldTwo
    .Labels(``lblRecordID´´).Text = ``Record´´ & CurrentRecord & `` of ´´ & Range(``Database´´).Rows.Count-1
  End With
End Sub
```

Last_Row Procedure

The **Last_Row()** procedure must:

- Set the **CurrentRecord** = the number of the last record.
- Read the values of the new **CurrentRecord** into their respective memory variables.

- Update the edit boxes on the dialog sheet to reflect values of the new record.

If the current record number is equal to the last record, display a message box that says *Last Record*, and does not increment the **CurrentRecord** counter.

The listing below contains all of the required code for the **Last_Row()** procedure.

```
Sub Last_Row()
  If CurrentRecord + 1 <
Range(``Database´´).Rows.Count Then
     CurrentRecord = Range(``Database´´).Rows.Count—1
  ElseIf CurrentRecord + 1 =
Range(``Database´´).Rows.Count Then
     MsgBox ``You are already on the last record!´´,
vbOKOnly + vbExclamation, ``Database Error´´
  End If

'Update the variables which hold the values of the fields
FieldOne = Range(Cells(FirstRow + CurrentRecord,
FirstColumn), Cells(FirstRow + CurrentRecord,
FirstColumn)).Value
FieldTwo = Range(Cells(FirstRow + CurrentRecord,
FirstColumn + 1), Cells(FirstRow + CurrentRecord,
FirstColumn + 1)).Value

'Update the edit boxes on the dialog sheet that correspond
to the database's fields
  With DialogSheets(``AccessForm´´)
    .EditBoxes(``txtOne´´).Text = FieldOne
   .EditBoxes(``txtTwo´´).Text = FieldTwo
   .Labels(``lblRecordID´´).Text = ``Record´´ &
CurrentRecord & `` of ´´ &
Range(``Database´´).Rows.Count—1
  End With
End Sub
```

Adding a Command Button to the Worksheet that Contains the Database

To make life easier on yourself, you should add a command button to the worksheet that contains the database, to invoke the AccessForm.

STEPS

Adding a Command Button to the Worksheet that Contains the Database

1. Select the worksheet with the database.
2. Display the **Toolbar** shortcut menu by clicking with the right mouse button in any grey area on any other toolbar.
3. Select **Drawing** (if it is not already selected).
4. Select the **Create Button** command button. Your cursor changes to a cross-hair.
5. Click and drag anywhere on your worksheet that you want the button to appear. The **Assign Macro** dialog box will be displayed.
6. Select **Initialize_Data_Form** from the **Macro Name/Reference** combo box.
7. Select **OK**.

Assigning Macros/Modules to the Command Buttons

Table 8.2 lists all of the objects on AccessForm, that have sub-procedures attached to them, and what those procedures are. To make the AccessForm work, you must assign the correct sub-procedures to these objects. To assign a macro to a command button, follow the steps below.

STEPS

Assigning a Sub-Procedure to a Command Button

1. Select the command button you would like to bind the sub-procedure to.
2. Select **Tools→Assign Macro...**. The **Assign Macro** dialog box will be displayed.

TABLE 8.2 Dialog Sheet Objects, and the Sub-Procedures Assigned to Them

Button	Sub Procedure
cmdFirstRecord	'1STBOOK.XLS'!First_Row
cmdPreviousRow	'1STBOOK.XLS'!Previous_Row
cmdNextRow	'1STBOOK.XLS'!Move_To_Next
cmdLastRow	'1STBOOK.XLS'!Last_Row
cmdOK	
cmdCancel	
lblRecordID	

3. Select the name of the sub-procedure from the **Macro Name/Reference** combo box.
4. Select **OK**.

Excel 4.0 Style Dialogs

Although you can still create and use XLM style dialog boxes, this book will not cover this subject. One reason for this is that the old dialog editor is not included with Excel 5.0, which makes creating XLM style dialogs a most annoying procedure. A note of advice is before you install Excel 5.0—copy your Excel 4.0 dialog editor to a safe place, and then continue to use it, if you like this format. The following section will cover how to integrate an existing Excel 4.0 custom data form (read—dialog box) into an Excel 5.0 workbook.

Using Existing Excel 4.0 Custom Data Forms

If you created a database and custom data form in Excel 4.0 (or earlier), you can utilize all of the work which you have already done. To use an Excel 4.0 worksheet that contained a custom data form, follow these steps:

STEPS

Using an Excel 4.0 Custom Data Form

1. Open the Excel 4.0 worksheet which contains the database and custom data form.
2. Save the worksheet as an Excel 5.0 workbook
3. Select **Data→Form**. The custom data form will be displayed.

In versions of Excel prior to 5.0, you had to keep the dialog range for a custom data form on the same worksheet as the database. You could not keep the dialog range for the custom data form on a macro sheet, as you would expect. Because of Excel 5.0's new multi-dimensional workbook model, it is now possible, and advisable, to keep your custom data form dialog range on a macro sheet, separate from the worksheet which contains the database. To move a custom data form's dialog range from the worksheet which contains the database to a new macro sheet, follow these steps:

STEPS

Moving a Custom Data Form's Dialog Range to a New Macro Sheet

1. Select the range named *Data_form*, on the worksheet which contains the database.
2. Select **Edit→Cut**.
3. Insert a new macro sheet.
4. Select your destination cell(s).
5. Select **Edit→Copy**.

That's it! When you select **Data→Form...**, the custom dialog box should be correctly invoked.

CHAPTER 9

Pivot Tables

What a Pivot Table Is

A **Pivot Table** is a special kind of list, which allows you to quickly summarize large amounts of data and easily change your view of the data.

Pivot tables have five major components (Figure 9.1):

- Row Field
- Column Field
- Page Field
- Items
- Summarized data from the data field.

The **Row Field** is used to identify what items will be used for row labels. The **Column Field** is used to identify what items will be used as labels for the column headings. The **Page Field** is used to identify which items will be viewed, one 'page' at a time. The **Items Summarized data from the data field** shows summarized data. An **Item** is a subcategory of a pivot table field. Items can appear as a row label, column label, or page label.

Query and Pivot Toolbar

The default **Query and Pivot** toolbar, which is illustrated in Figure 9.2, contains nine tools:

- PivotTable Wizard
- PivotTable Field

CHAPTER 9

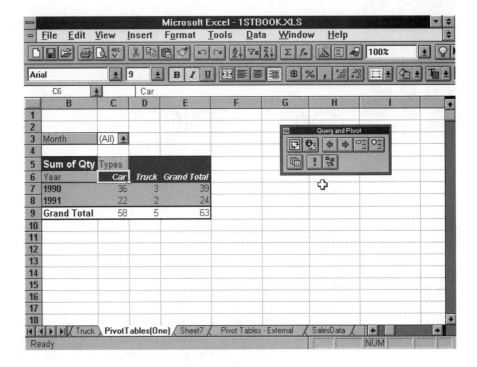

FIGURE 9.1
Pivot table components.

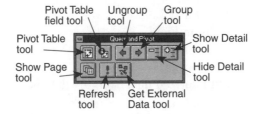

FIGURE 9.2
Query and Pivot toolbar.

- Ungroup
- Group
- Hide Detail
- Unhide Detail
- Show Pages
- Refresh
- Get External Data.

The **PivotTable Wizard** tool invokes the PivotTable Wizard. The **Pivot Table Field** tool displays the dialog box which allows you to define the summary functions which will be applied to the selected field. The **Ungroup** tool separates combined items. The **Group** tool groups items by category to form a single item from multiple items. The **Hide Detail** tool hides the detail items by collapsing the outer item in a field. The **Unhide**

Pivot Tables

Detail tool displays detail items by expanding a field that has been collapsed using the Hide Detail tool. The **Show Pages** tool displays a dialog box that allows you to copy each page of the current pivot table to a new worksheet in the current workbook. The **Refresh** tool queries the data source and updates the pivot table with the most recent data. The **Get External Data** tool is used to invoke MS Query to attach to an external data source. This tool only appears on the toolbar if you have installed the MS Query add-in. To display the **Data and Pivot** toolbar, follow the steps below.

> **HINT**
>
> *If you hold down* **Shift** *while selecting the Ungroup tool, it will behave like the Group tool. If you hold down* **Shift** *while selecting the Group tool, it will behave like the Ungroup tool.*

> **STEPS**

Displaying the Data and Pivot Toolbar Using the Toolbar Shortcut Menu

1. Click with the right mouse button on the grey area of any visible toolbar. The toolbar shortcut menu will be displayed.
2. Select **Toolbars...**. The dialog box illustrated in Figure 9.3 will be displayed.
3. Select the **Query and Pivot** check box.
4. Select **OK**.

> **STEPS**

Displaying the Data and Pivot Toolbar, Using the Toolbars Command

1. Select **View→Toolbars...**. The dialog box illustrated in Figure 9.3 will be displayed.
2. Select the **Query and Pivot** check box.
3. Select **OK**.

Pivot Table Shortcut Menu

Pivot tables also have a special shortcut menu. The pivot table shortcut menu, illustrated in Figure 9.4, contains the following commands:

- Cut
- Copy
- Paste

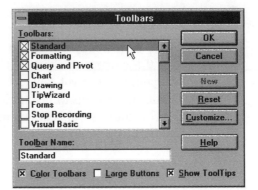

FIGURE 9.3
Toolbars dialog box.

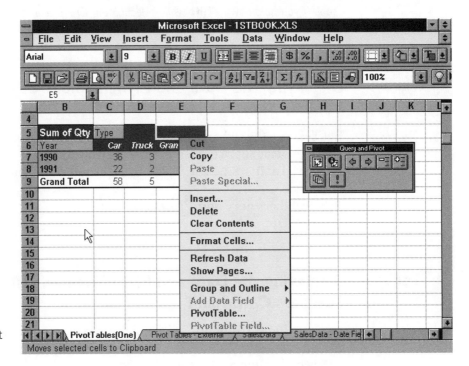

FIGURE 9.4
Pivot table shortcut menu.

- Paste Special
- Insert
- Delete
- Clear Contents
- Format Cells...
- Refresh Data
- Show Pages...
- Group and Outline
- Add Data Field

- PivotTable...
- PivotTable Field....

Cut will delete the contents of the current selection, and copy it to the Windows clipboard. **Copy** will copy the contents of the current selection to the Windows clipboard, leaving the original in place. **Paste** will copy the contents of the Windows clipboard to the current selection. **Paste Special** allows you to copy selected parts (only formatting, only values, etc.) of the contents of the Windows clipboard to the current selection. **Insert** will insert a range of cells. **Delete** will delete a range of cells. **Clear Contents** will clear the contents of the current selection, while leaving formatting and cell notes in place. **Format Cells...** displays the format dialog box, which allows you to change the formatting of the the cells in the current selection. **Refresh Data** queries the data source and updates the pivot table with the most recent data. **Show Pages...** displays a dialog box which allows you to copy each page of the current pivot table to a new worksheet in the current workbook. **Group and Outline** allows you to use Excel's outlining capabilities. **Add Data Field** adds a data field to the pivot table. The submenu contains the names of all of the column headings which are available from your specified data source. **PivotTable...** invokes the **PivotTable Wizard**. **PivotTable Field...** displays the dialog box which allows you to define the summary functions which will be applied to the selected field. To invoke the pivot table shortcut menu, follow the steps below.

STEPS

Invoking the Pivot Table Shortcut Menu, and Selecting a Command

1. Select any cell in the pivot table.
2. Click the right mouse button. The pivot table shortcut menu will be displayed.
3. Select the command you wish to use.

Creating a Pivot Table

Pivot tables can contain data from (any one of) four different sources:

- An Excel range which contains column headings (a list or database).
- An external data source, such as a file or table accessible through ODBC.

- Multiple Excel consolidation ranges.
- Another pivot table, either in the same workbook, or a different workbook.

Regardless of the type of data source you select, you need four basic steps to create a pivot table.

- Select the type of source which holds your data.
- Select the actual data source.
- Place the fields in the proper positions and set their aggregate functions.
- Select the destination location for the pivot table, as well as the table's name and general display and storage options.

There are two ways to create a pivot table:

- PivotTable Wizard
- PivotTableWizard method in a VBA module.

The **PivotTable Wizard** walks you through each of these steps, making a very complex feature very easy to use. For each of the four data sources listed above, the details that the PivotTable Wizard will prompt you for will vary slightly. The **PivotTableWizard method** allows you programatically to create Pivot Tables, with no interaction from the user. This is useful for building custom applications. This chapter will focus on using the PivotTable Wizard. Using the PivotTableWizard method is covered in Chapter 11, Macros/VBA.

Creating a Pivot Table from Internal Data

If the data you would like to build your pivot table from exists either in the workbook you want the pivot table in or as a database or a list (except for a pivot table), the data source is considered to be **internal** to Excel. If the data exists in another Excel workbook, this is also considered **internal data**. To create a pivot table from internal Excel data, follow these steps:

PIVOT TABLES

NOTE When Excel creates and updates pivot tables, if the data source is internal, it ignores any filters on the list or database.

STEPS

Creating a Pivot Table from Internal Data

1. Select **Data→PivotTable...**. The dialog box illustrated in Figure 9.5 will be displayed.
2. Select the **Microsoft Excel List or Database** option button (It is selected by default).
3. Select **Next>**. The dialog illustrated in Figure 9.6 will be displayed. If you have a range named *Database* in your current worksheet, or workbook, Excel fills the name *Database* into the text box and selects the range on the worksheet by placing a 'blinking marquee' around it.
4. In the **Range** edit box, type range name or address which contains the data you would like to use as the source for your pivot table.

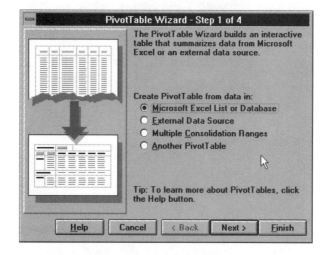

FIGURE 9.5
PivotTable Wizard Step 1 of 4 for an internal database.

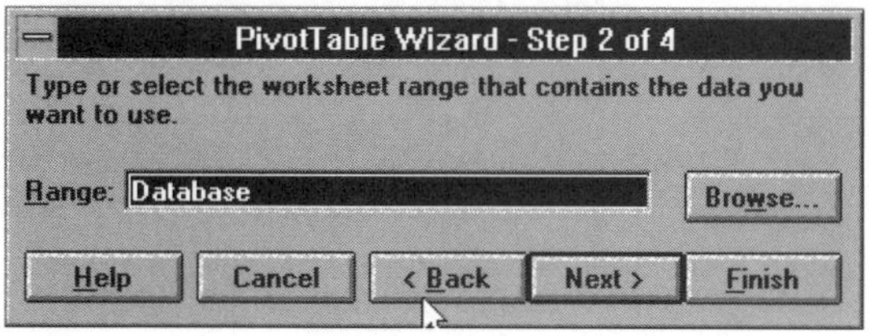

FIGURE 9.6
PivotTable Wizard Step 2 of 4 for an internal database.

X-REF

The **PivotTable Wizard Step 2 of 4** dialog box is modeless, just like the **Define Name** dialog box, described in Chapter 1. You may interact with the Excel workspace as described in **Selecting a Range While the Define Name Dialog Box Is Open** section of Chapter 1 and applying the same technique.

5. Select **Next>**. The **PivotTable Wizard** changes as illustrated in Figure 9.7. Note that the buttons on the right hand side are created from the column headings in your data source.
6. Drag the **Field** buttons on the right side of the dialog to the area of the pivot table where you would like them to appear.
7. Select **Next>**. The Wizard changes as illustrated in Figure 9.8.
8. In the **PivotTable Starting Cell** text box enter the range where you would like the pivot table to start. This can be the same worksheet, a different worksheet, or even a different workbook.

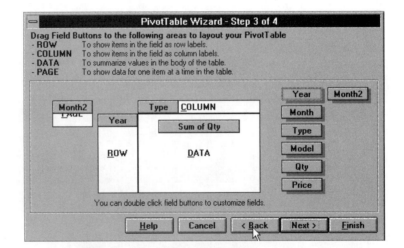

FIGURE 9.7
PivotTable Wizard Step 3 of 4 for an internal database.

FIGURE 9.8
PivotTable Wizard Step 4 of 4 for an internal database.

> **X-REF**
>
> The **PivotTable Wizard Step 4 of 4** dialog box is modeless, just like the **Define Name** dialog box, described in Chapter 1. You may interact with the Excel workspace as described in **Selecting a Range While the Define Name Dialog Box Is Open** section of Chapter 1, and applying the same technique

9. If you do not want to use the default name, type a new name in the **Pivot Table Name** text box.
10. Select or de-select any **Pivot Table Options** that you wish to change. Each of these options will be covered in more detail later in this chapter.
11. Select **Finish**.

Referring to a Data Range in Another Workbook

When specifying the source data range, if you would like to refer to a range that is in a different workbook, you can enter the name of the workbook, the worksheet, and the range name by using the following syntax:

'[WorkbookName]WorksheetName'!Range

Where:

- The square brackets are required delimiters.
- The single quotes are required delimiters.
- *WorkbookName* is the name of the workbook you wish to use. It is optional, but recommended that you include the full path, if the file has already been saved.
- *Worksheet* is the name of the worksheet.
- The exclamation (!) is a required delimiter.
- **Range** is a reference to the range which contains the data. Note that the range must contain column headings or field names.

An example of a valid range would be:

'[1STBOOK.XLS]SalesData'!$D$1:$D$25.

If you are not sure what the name of the workbook is, you can use the **Browse** button in the step 2 dialog box of the PivotTable Wizard. When you select this button, the dialog box illustrated in Figure 9.9 will be displayed. You can navigate through all of the storage resources you have available, browsing until you find the file that contains the data you want to use. When you select the file, and then select **OK**, the name of the file is automatically entered in the **Range** edit box, although the sheet name and range name are not. At this point, you must manually enter the sheet name and the range name.

If you try to finish building the pivot table without dragging a field to the data region, then try to leave **Step 3**, the message box illustrated in Figure 9.10 will be displayed. Select **OK**, and correct the situation by adding at least one field to the data area.

Changing a Field's Aggregate Function

When you add a field to the **Data** section by dragging it, notice that if the field contains numeric data, the button changes to **Sum of Field1**. If on the other hand, the field does not contain numeric data, the button changes to **Count of Field1**. If you would like to override this default behavior while working in the PivotTable Wizard, double-click on the button after it has been dragged into the data area. The dialog box illustrated in Figure 9.11 will be displayed. This option will be detailed later in this chapter.

Creating a Pivot Table from External Data

Chapter seven covered directly importing files into Excel. If you import another file format into Excel, and save it as part of an Excel 5.0 workbook, it becomes internal data. To use it as a data source for a pivot table, you would follow the steps in the previous section, **Creating a Pivot Table**

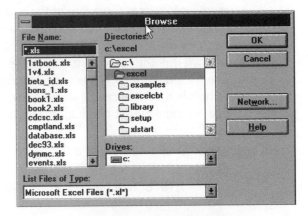

FIGURE 9.9
Browse
dialog box.

FIGURE 9.10
Specify a data field
message box.

Pivot Tables

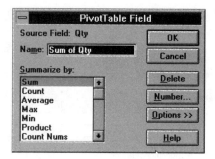

FIGURE 9.11
PivotTable Field dialog box.

from Internal Data. If on the other hand, the data you would like to build your pivot table from exists in a file or DBMS outside of Excel, and you don't want to import it, the data is said to be **external** to Excel.. As such, you must use Microsoft Query (which is included with Excel 5.0) to access and attach your data sources. An example of an external data source might be a dBASE file which exists on your department's file server, or the tables in a SQL Server database, which reside on a divisional database server. To create a pivot table from an external data source, follow the steps below.

> **X-REF**
> For more information on external data and using Microsoft Query, see Chapter 11, *An Overview of Using External Data*.

> **STEPS**
> ### Creating a Pivot Table from External Data
>
> 1. Select **Data→PivotTable…**. The dialog box will be displayed.
> 2. Select the **External Data Source** option button.
> 3. Select **Next>**. The dialog box illustrated in Figure 9.12 will be displayed. Notice the text next to the **Get Data…** button: *No Data Retrieved*.
> 4. Select **Get Data…**. Microsoft Query will be started, and the dialog box in Figure 9.13 will be displayed. At this point, you should build your query.

> **X-REF**
> Building a query using Microsoft Query is covered in Chapter 12, **MS Query as a Standalone Application**. When your query is complete, proceed to the next step (Step 5).

> 5. Select **File→Return Data to Microsoft Excel**. You are returned to the **PivotTable Wizard Step 2 of 4**. Notice that the text next to the the **Get Data…** button has changed to **Data Retrieved**.

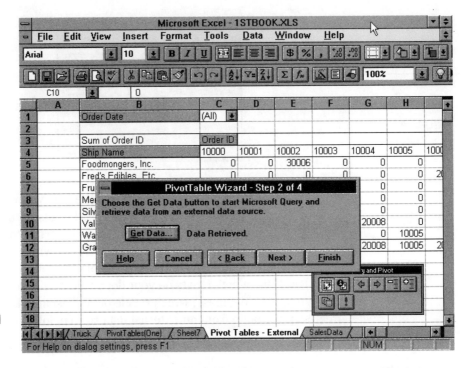

FIGURE 9.12
PivotTable Wizard Step 2 of 4 for an external database.

6. Select **Next>**. The **PivotTable Wizard** changes as illustrated in Figure 9.14. *The field buttons on the right hand side are created from the column headings in your data source.*
7. Drag the **Field** buttons on the right side of the dialog box to the area of the pivot table where you would like them to appear. Note that each one can appear only once on the pivot table.
8. Select **Next>**. The box illustrated in Figure 9.15 appears.
9. In the **Pivot Table Starting Cell** text box, enter the range where you would like the pivot table to start. This can be in the same worksheet, a different worksheet, or even a different workbook.

The **PivotTable Wizard Step 4 of 4** dialog box is modeless, just like the **Define Name** dialog box, described in Chapter 1. You may interact with the Excel workspace as described in **Selecting a Range While the Define Name Dialog Box Is Open** section of Chapter 1 apply the same technique.

10. If you do not want to use the default name, type a new name in the **Pivot Table Name** text box.
11. Select or de-select any **Pivot Table Options** that you wish to change. Each of these options will be covered in more detail later in this chapter.

PIVOT TABLES   163

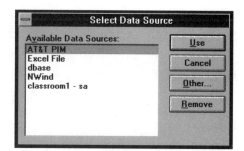

FIGURE 9.13
Select Data Source dialog box in MS Query.

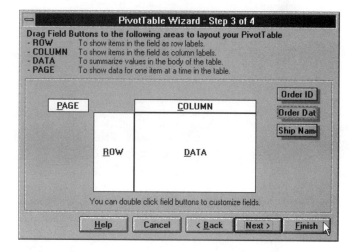

FIGURE 9.14
PivotTable Wizard Step 3 of 4 for an external database.

12. Select **Finish.**

Creating a Pivot Table from Consolidated Data from Multiple Ranges

Although it is not discussed in depth in this book, Excel has the ability to easily consolidate similar data from multiple ranges, into the same or separate worksheets. You can even consolidate similar data from multiple ranges into multiple workbooks.

Examine the data illustrated in Figures 9.16–9.19. Each of these ranges represents the number of vehicles sold, broken down by model and month, for the first quarter of four consecutive years. Notice that they all have the same column headings, but that the number and content of the row headings (the model name) changes. Each of these is stored in a worksheet (**1990 Sales**, **1991 Sales**, etc.) in a single workbook. What if you wanted to combine this data, and use **PivotTables Wizard**'s powerful features to manipulate the data to find trends? The process is very simple, as

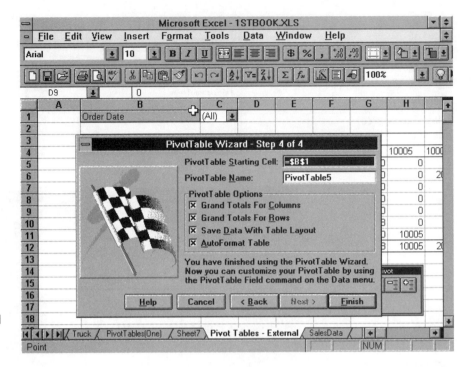

FIGURE 9.15
PivotTable Wizard Step 4 of 4 for an external database.

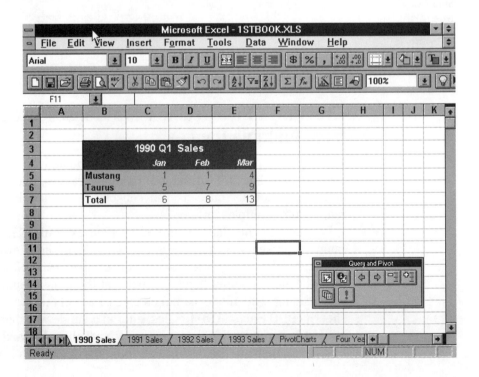

FIGURE 9.16
1990 Q1 Sales.

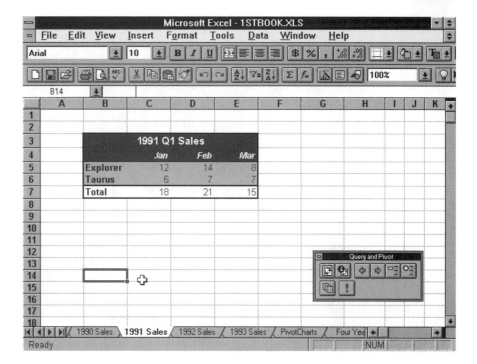

FIGURE 9.17
1991 Q1 Sales.

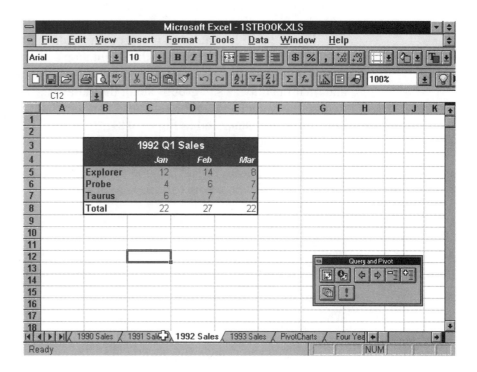

FIGURE 9.18
1992 Q1 Sales.

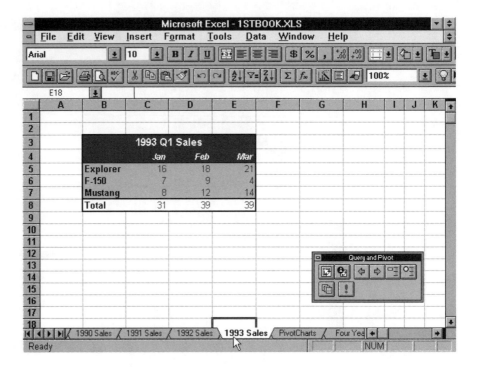

FIGURE 9.19
1993 Q1 Sales.

long as your source data is set up correctly. For more information on how to set up your data to work well with Excel's consolidation features, see your documentation.

Figure 9.20 illustrates the result of consolidating these ranges into a pivot table. If you want to change the orientation and grouping of the table so that you list each month along the vertical axis, and then list the models and their quantity as sub-groups along the same axis, all you have to do is to drag the Model field to the row headings section of the pivot table. The result of this is illustrated in Figure 9.21.

The PivotTable Wizard offers you two ways to create page fields:

- Automatically create a single page field.
- Manually create up to four page fields.

Although these methods are similar, the **PivotTable Wizard** will change slighlty depending on which method you choose. Although each method is covered separately in the following sections, 90% of the process is really the same.

Having Excel Create the Page Field

When you have Excel automatically create a single page field for you, you save a few steps, but you sacrifice the ability to refer to your pages by name. Although you can change the page field's label (the text on the **Page** but-

PIVOT TABLES   167

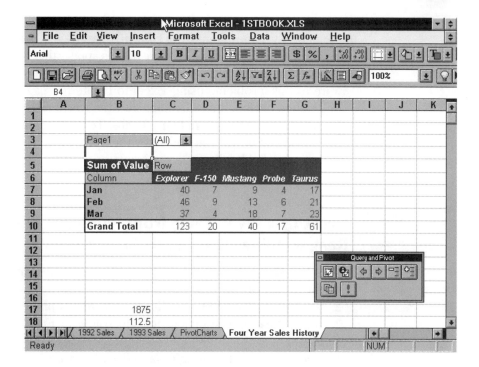

FIGURE 9.20
Consolidated four year sales table.

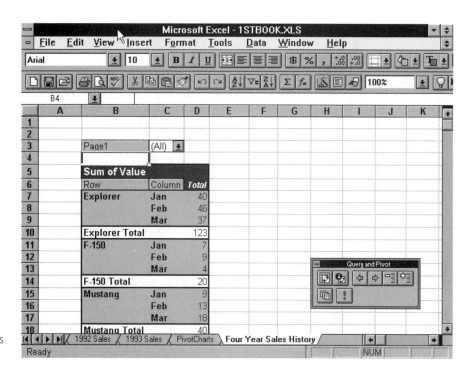

FIGURE 9.21
Consolidated four year sales table, months and models along vertical axis.

ton), you cannot change the labels on the individual page items. Excel automatically names them **Item1**, **Item2**, **Item3**, etc. When a user displays the page field's drop-down list, page names appear that have no relationship to their application. 'Meaningless labels' are generated. Provided you are aware of this 'problem,' using Excel to create the page field for you is a good way to become more familiar with the workings of pivot tables, without getting bogged down in extra details. To create a pivot table from multiple consolidation ranges and have the PivotTable Wizard automatically create a page field, follow the steps below.

STEPS

Creating a Pivot Table from Multiple Consolidation Ranges, Allowing Excel to Create the Page Field

1. Select **Data→PivotTable...**. The dialog box illustrated in Figure 9.22 will be displayed.
2. Select the **Multiple Consolidation Ranges** option button.
3. Select **Next>**. The dialog box illustrated in Figure 9.23 will be displayed.
4. Select the **Create a single page field for me** option button.
5. Select **Next>**.
6. In the **Range** edit box, type range name or address which contains the data you would like to use as the source for your pivot table.

WARNING

If your source range contains totals, do not include them. The default behavior for pivot tables is to automatically create grand totals. If you include your source range totals, your results will be off, because the 'subtotal' will be included in your grand total. Displaying and hiding total is covered later in this chapter.

X-REF

*The **Pivot Table Wizard Step 2b of 4** (Figure 9.24) dialog box is modeless, just like the **Define Name** dialog box, described in Chapter 1. You may interact with the Excel workspace as described in **Selecting a Range While the Define Name Dialog Box Is Open** section of Chapter 1, applying the same technique.*

7. Select **Add**. Notice that the reference is added to the **All Ranges** list box.
8. Repeat Steps 6 through 7 until all of the ranges you would like to consolidate have been added.
9. Select **Next>**. The PivotTable Wizard changes as illustrated in Figure

PIVOT TABLES

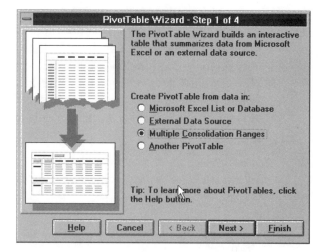

FIGURE 9.22
PivotTable Wizard
Step 1 of 4 for a
consolidated source.

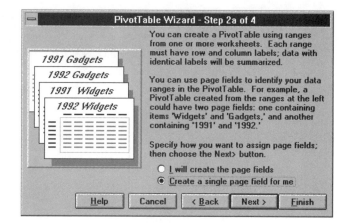

FIGURE 9.23
PivotTable Wizard
Step 2a of 4 for a
consolidated source.

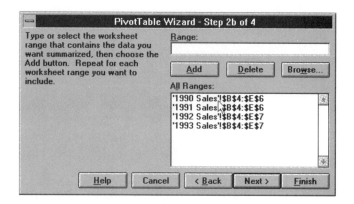

FIGURE 9.24
Pivot TableWizard
Step 2b of 4 for a
consolidated source.

9.25. Notice that unlike the field buttons created using other data sources, the field buttons on the right hand side simply indicate **Row**, **Column**, **Page**, and **Value**, and that they have automatically been placed for you on the pivot table.

10. If you would like to change the initial layout of the pivot table, drag the **Field** buttons to the area of the pivot table where you would like them to appear. Note that each one can only appear once on the pivot table.

> **HINT**
>
> *You can change the text that appears on the button to correspond to your field names at this point by double-clicking on it and typing a new name in the **Name** edit box.*

11. Select **Next>**. The PivotTable Wizard changes as illustrated in Figure 9.26.
12. In the **PivotTable Starting Cell** text box enter the range where you

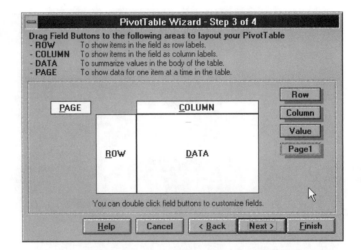

FIGURE 9.25
PivotTable Wizard Step 3 of 4 for a consolidated source.

FIGURE 9.26
PivotTable Wizard Step 4 of 4 for a consolidated source.

would like the pivot table to start. This can be in the same worksheet, a different worksheet, or even a different workbook.

> **X-REF**
>
> The **Pivot Table Wizard Step 4 of 4** dialog box is modeless, just like the **Define Name** dialog box, described in Chapter 1. You may interact with the Excel workspace as described in **Selecting a Range While the Define Name Dialog Box Is Open** section of Chapter 1, and apply the same technique.

13. If you do not want to use the default name, type a new name in the **Pivot Table Name** text box.
14. Select or de-select any **Pivot Table Options** that you wish to change. Each of these options will be covered in more detail later in this chapter.
15. Select **Finish**.

Manually Creating Page Fields

If you would like to create your own labels for each item, and/or use more than one page field, you must manually create the page fields. When you build your pivot table, you can include up to four page fields. Why would you ever want to use more than one page field? Building on the car sales example, if you had the data available, you could have a separate range for each quarter of each year, and then use the pivot table's functionality to create 'page views' that freely allow you to choose the year and the quarter, independently. To create a pivot table from multiple consolidation ranges and manually create page fields, follow the steps below.

> **STEPS**
>
> ### Creating a Pivot Table from Multiple Consolidation Ranges and Manually Creating Page Fields
>
> 1. **Select Data→PivotTable....** The Step 1 of the PivotTable Wizard will be displayed.
> 2. Select the **Multiple Consolidation Ranges** option button.
> 3. Select **Next>**. The Step 2a of the PivotTable Wizard will be displayed.
> 4. Select the **I will create the page fields** option button.
> 5. Select **Next>**. The PivotTable Wizard changes as illustrated in Figure 9.27.
> 6. In the **Range** edit box, type range name or address which contains the data you would like to use as the source for your pivot table.

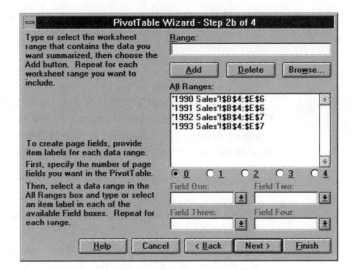

FIGURE 9.27
PivotTable Wizard Step 2b of 4 for a consolidated source).

If your source range contains totals, refer to *Warning*, p. 168.

The **Pivot Table Wizard Step 2b of 4** dialog box is modeless, just like the **Define Name** dialog box described in Chapter 1. You may interact with the Excel workspace as described in **Selecting a Range While the Define Name Dialog Box Is Open** section of Chapter 1, applying the same technique.

7. Select **Add**. Notice that the reference is added to the **All Ranges** list box.
8. Repeat Steps 6 through 7 until all of the ranges you would like to consolidate have been added.
9. Select the **1** number of page fields option buttons (below the **All Ranges** list box). Notice that the **Field One** combo box becomes active. It should be noted that you can create up to four page fields.
10. Select the first range in the **All Ranges** list box.
11. Select the **Field One** combo box. Notice that the range you selected in the previous step stays highlighted.
12. Type in the name that you would like to use for this page.
13. Repeat Steps 10 through 12 until all of your pages have been named.
14. Select **Next>**. The PivotTable Wizard changes. Notice that unlike the field buttons created using other data sources, the field buttons on the right hand side simply indicate **Row**, **Column**, **Page**, and **Value**, and that they have automatically been placed for you on the pivot table.
15. If you would like to change the initial layout of the pivot table, drag the

Field buttons to the area of the pivot table where you would like them to appear. Note that each one can only appear once on the pivot table.

> **HINT**
>
> *You can change the text that appears on the button to correspond to your field names at this point by double-clicking on it and typing a new name in the **Name** edit box.*

16. Select **Next>**. The PivotTable Wizard changes.
17. In the **Pivot Table Starting Cell** text box, enter the range where you would like the pivot table to start. This can be in the same worksheet, a different worksheet, or even a different workbook.

> **X-REF**
>
> *The **Pivot Table Wizard Step 4 of 4** dialog box is modeless, just like the **Define Name** dialog box described in Chapter 1. You may interact with the Excel workspace as described in **Selecting a Range While the Define Name Dialog Box Is Open** section of Chapter 1, applying the same technique.*

18. If you do not want to use the default name, type a new name in the **Pivot Table Name** text box.
19. Select or de-select any **Pivot Table Options** that you wish to change. Each of these options will be covered in more detail later in this chapter.
20. Select **Finish.**

Creating a Pivot Table from Another Pivot Table

When a pivot table is created, no matter what the source is, a hidden copy of the data is placed on the worksheet with the pivot table. This is why you have to manually refresh a pivot table when a change is made to an underlying data source. You can also use an existing pivot table as the data source for another pivot table. This is particularly useful if your source pivot table was created using an external data source. When you create a pivot table and use an existing pivot table as its data source, the new pivot table does not copy the original table's hidden data—it reads it directly. Thus, you have two (or potentially more) pivot tables, but only one data source. When you refresh the source's data, all other pivot tables 'linked' to it are also refreshed, because they all read the same hidden data (which is what you have really updated).

If you have two pivot tables, each based on the same external data source but created independently, when you refresh one, the other will be out of sync. You have to refresh all of the pivot tables at the same time. If you do this manually (or even with VBA code), data anomalies could be created. It should be obvious that by using the original pivot table as the source for additional pivot tables, this problem is eliminated. A single refresh is all that is needed! To create a pivot table from another pivot table, follow the steps below.

One of the cool things that you can do with a pivot table created from another pivot table is to present the user with two different views of the same data, side by side. Changes to the layout of the first table do not impact the layout of additional tables.

STEPS

Creating a Pivot Table from Another Pivot Table

1. Select **Data→PivotTable...**. The PivotTable Wizard will be displayed.
2. Select the **Another Pivot Table** option button.
3. Select **Next>**. The PivotTable Wizard will change as illustrated in Figure 9.28. All of the pivot tables in the active worksheet are listed in the list box.
4. Select the pivot table you want to use as your data source (Figure 9.28).
5. Select **Next>**. The PilotTable Wizard changes.
6. Drag the **Field** buttons on the right side of the dialog box to the area of the pivot table where you would like them to appear. Note that each one can appear only once on the pivot table.
7. Select **Next>**. The PilotTable Wizard changes.
8. In the **Pivot Table Starting Cell** text box, enter the range where you would like the pivot table to start. This can be it the same worksheet, a different worksheet, or even a different workbook.

X-REF

The **Pivot Table Wizard Step 4 of 4** dialog box is modeless, just like the **Define Name** dialog box described in Chapter 1. You may interact with the Excel workspace as described in **Selecting a Range While the Define Name Dialog Box Is Open** section of Chapter 1, applying the same technique.

9. If you do not want to use the default name, type a new name in the **Pivot Table Name** text box.
10. Select or de-select any **Pivot Table Options** that you wish to change. Each of these options will be covered in more detail later in this chapter.
11. Select **Finish**.

FIGURE 9.28
PivotTable Wizard
Step 2 of 4 for
another pivot table.

Using Data From a Pivot Table in Another Workbook

You cannot create a new pivot table from a pivot table in a different workbook. You can only create a new pivot table from a pivot table in the same workbook. This is because pivot tables in different workbooks do not share the same hidden data source, as pivot tables in the same workbook do. If your current workbook does not contain any pivot tables, the **Another Pivot Table** option button in first step of the PivotTable Wizard is greyed out and not available. You can alternatively copy the pivot table to another workbook, although when you paste it in, it will not be a real pivot table—it will just look like one (*sans* the field buttons). You can, however, copy the lookup table's values and formatting to another workbook, and then dynamically link them. Although you cannot manipulate the fields directly as you can in a real pivot table, the linked copy will change as the original changes. So if you change the field page's item in the original pivot table, the linked copy will reflect the change. You can also copy a static version of the pivot table by doing a copy and paste. To create a linked copy of a pivot table, follow the steps below:

STEPS

Creating a Linked Copy of a Pivot Table

1. Select the entire pivot table.
2. Select **Edit→Copy**.
3. Select the workbook and/or worksheet that you wish to place the copy in.
4. Select the cell that will be the upper left hand corner of the pivot table copy.
5. Select **Edit→Paste Special...**. The **Paste Special** dialog box will be displayed.
6. Select **Paste Link**.

Note that your formatting was not copied. If you look at any cell in the copy, you will find an array formula which refers to the workbook, worksheet, and range of the pivot table. You cannot edit this formula.

Refreshing a Pivot Table

Pivot tables are linked statically, not dynamically, to their data sources. This means that if there is a change in the underlying data source, this change is not reflected in the pivot table until you force it to refresh its data. When you refresh a pivot table, four types of changes are reflected:

- Updated items (rows)
- Deleted items (rows)
- Inserted items (rows)
- Deleted fields (columns).

To refresh a pivot table, simply select a cell in the pivot table and use **one** of the three methods below to invoke the refresh.

- Select **Data→Refresh**.
- Select the **Refresh** tool on the **Query and Pivot** toolbar.
- Select **Refresh** on the PivotTable shortcut menu.

Internal Data

When a pivot table created using internal data is refreshed, Excel reads the references which you entered for your source data. If you use actual cell adresses, insert and delete anomalies can occur. This is because Excel does not necessarily know that you have inserted or deleted cells from the range which contains the source data. There are two solutions to this dilemma:

- Every time you add or delete rows from the range which is the data source, go back and modify the pivot table's data source range(s), using the PivotTable Wizard to refelect these changes.
- Use range names, instead of direct cell references.

Although the latter requires an extra step before you set your pivot table up, it can save many repeated steps after the table has been set up, if your data changes frequently. It also is consistent with one of the main conventions of this book, which is to use range names whenever you can.

External Data

When you refresh a pivot table which was created from external data, Excel actually re-queries the source data, using the query definition which you created using Microsoft Query in Step two of the PivotTable Wizard. When you select **Refresh**, you get several status bar messages informing you of the progress being made. It your data source is small, these messages might pass by so fast that you don't even see them. If, on the other hand, your data source is large (and/or includes complicated joins/functions), you might sit staring at your screen for several minutes.

Changing, Adding and Deleting Fields

If you change a column heading (field name) in the underlying data source which is used in the pivot table, you must rebuild your pivot table. Otherwise, when you do a refresh, Excel will not be able to match the field names with the column headings. When this occurs during a refresh, the message box will be displayed. Similarly, although an error will not show up, if you delete or add fields (columns), you should rebuild your pivot table. To change the name of a field, add a field, or delete a field, and rebuild the pivot table, follow the steps below.

STEPS

Changing a Column Heading in the Underlying Data Source, and Rebuilding the Pivot Table

1. In the source range, change the column heading/field name you wish to change.
2. Select a cell in the pivot table.
3. Refresh the table. *The Pivot table was changed during* **Refresh** *operation* message box will be displayed.
4. Select **OK**.
5. Invoke the PivotTable Wizard. Step three, which allows you to place your pivot table fields, will be the active screen. Notice the name change on the field button.
6. Select **Finish**.

CHAPTER 9

STEPS

Adding a Column (Pivot Table Field) in the Underlying Data Source, and Rebuilding the Pivot Table

1. Select the cells where you want the new column.
2. Select **Insert→Cells**. The dialog box illustrated in Figure 9.29 will be displayed.
3. Select the **Shift Cells Right** option button, if it is not already selected.
4. Select **OK**. The cells will be shifted to the right.
5. Add your new field name/column heading and data.
6. Select a cell in the pivot table and refresh the table.
7. Invoke the **PivotTable Wizard**. Step three, which allows you to place your pivot table fields, will be the active screen. Notice that your new field has been added to the buttons on the right side of the screen. Drag the field where you would like it.
8. Select **Finish**.

STEPS

Deleting a Column (Pivot Table Field) in the Underlying Data Source, and Rebuilding the Pivot Table

1. Select the cells of the column you want to delete.
2. Select **Edit→Delete...**. The dialog box illustrated in Figure 9.30 will be displayed.
3. Select the **Shift Cells Left** option button, if it is not already selected.
4. Select **OK**. The cells will be shifted to the left.
5. Select a cell in the pivot table and refresh the table.
6. Invoke the PivotTable Wizard. Step three, which allows you to place your

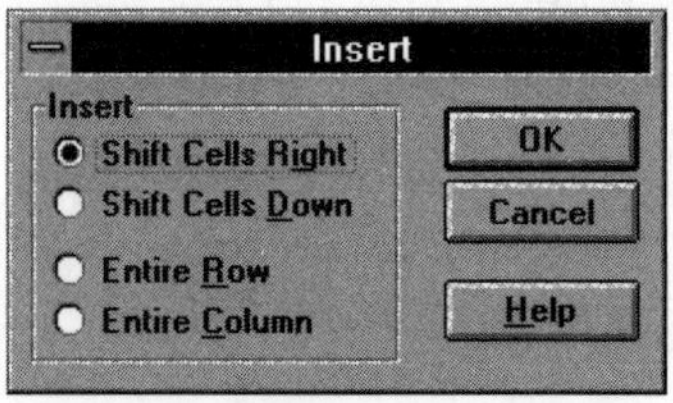

FIGURE 9.29
Insert dialog box.

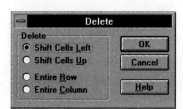

FIGURE 9.30
Delete dialog box.

pivot table fields, will be the active screen. Notice that your field has been deleted from the buttons on the right side of the screen.
7. Select **Finish**.

What Happens to Cell Formatting When Data is Refreshed

When a pivot table is recalculated, reorganized, or refreshed, all cell formatting is removed. If you select the **AutoFormat Table** check box in Step four of the PivotTable Wizard, any formatting which was applied to the pivot table after it was originally created using **AutoFormat** will be recreated. Any formatting which was applied to the pivot table using the **Format→Cells** command will be removed and not restored. If the **AutoFormat Table** check box in Step four of the PivotTable Wizard was not checked, no formatting will be applied to the newly refreshed pivot table.

Creating Charts from Pivot Tables

Creating charts which are linked to pivot tables makes good sense! Pivot tables are a powerful tool because they allow you to quickly change the way you view and consolidate data. When you use a pivot table as the data source for a chart, the chart gains this power, because charts will change dynamically with the underlying pivot table. If, for example, you want to change a chart's orientation would have to select the chart, start the **ChartWizard**, navigate to the second step, change the **Data Series** option, and then select **OK**. You could alternatively manually edit the chart's series formula. Not a task for the light-hearted! If on the other hand, your chart is linked to a pivot table, all you have to do is drag the column field to the row field and the row field to the column field, and you are done. You reduce five steps to two!

Pivot tables also help you to lay out your data, so that it is easier to chart. If you try to create a chart from a database or list, you will find that the ChartWizard is not very good at handling data in this format. After your chart is initally created, you will probably have to do quite a bit of manual tweaking to get your desired results. Examine the data illustrated in Figure 9.31. If you use the Chart Wizard directly on this list, you get the chart illustrated in Figure 9.32. Clearly, this chart will need some manipulation to make it meaningful. On the other hand, the chart illustrated in Figure 9.33 was created from the pivot table in Figure 9.34, which has the original list as its data source. Although this chart can still use a little fine tuning, its initial form is much more comprehensible. Creating a chart from a pivot

CHAPTER 9

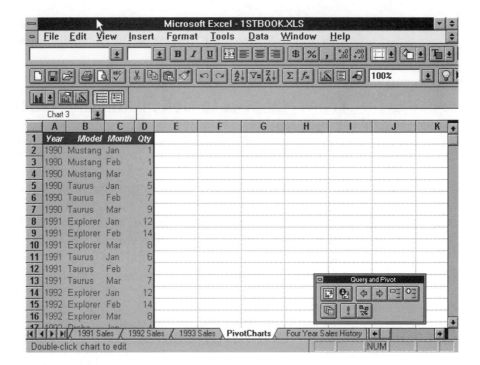

FIGURE 9.31
The original list.

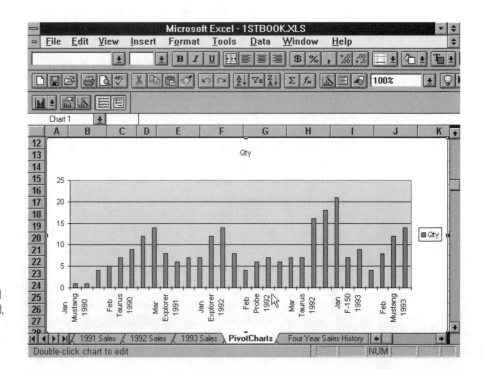

FIGURE 9.32
The chart created with ChartWizard, using the list in Figure 9.31 as its source.

Pivot Tables

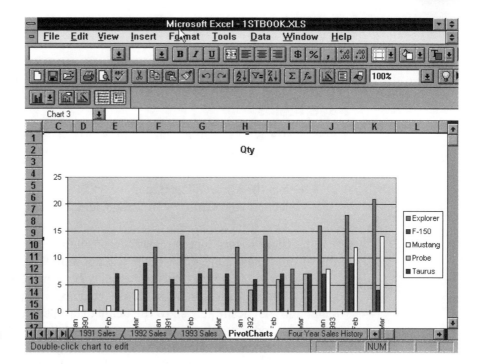

FIGURE 9.33
The chart created using a pivot table as its source.

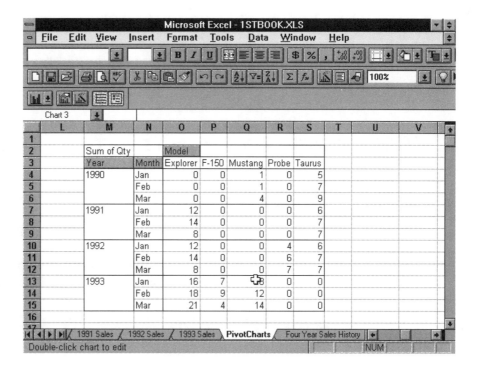

FIGURE 9.34
The pivot table created from the original list.

table also gives you an easy way to quickly create charts from external data sources.

Creating a Chart from a Pivot Table without Page Fields

The easiest way to create a chart from a pivot table is to use the ChartWizard. There are two ways to invoke the ChartWizard:

- Select the **ChartWizard** tool.
- Select **Insert→Chart→On This Sheet...**.

The ChartWizard tool is illustrated in Figure 9.35. When you create a chart from a pivot table, you usually will not want to include grand totals. This is because the grand totals will usually be significantly greater than your detail items, and this would cause your axes to scale in a manner which might not accurately show the detail data. Also, it is common to use stacked bar and area charts to represent grand totals when the chart is created, which replaces the need for including grand totals. To create a chart from a pivot table, using the ChartWizard, follow the steps below.

HINT *Using this method creates a chart object on your worksheet. You can also create a separate chart sheet if you want to separate your chart and worksheet. To create a separate chart sheet, select the entire pivot table (excluding page fields and grand totals), and then press F11. Your new chart will be created.*

STEPS **Creating a Chart from a Pivot Table without Page Fields, Using the ChartWizard**

1. Select the entire pivot table, excluding grand totals.
2. Invoke the **ChartWizard**. Notice that there is a blinking marquee around the selection, and that the cursor has changed to a cross-hair with a chart.
3. Click and drag the cursor on the worksheet to the size and location you would like your chart. When you release the mouse, the dialog

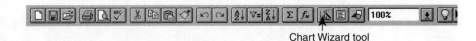

FIGURE 9.35
Standard toolbar.

Chart Wizard tool

illustated in Figure 9.36 will be displayed. Notice that the range you selected has been entered in the **Range** edit box.
4. Select **Next>**. The ChartWizard changes as illustrated in Figure 9.37.
5. Select a **chart type** by selecting the appropriate button.
6. Select **Next>**. The ChartWizard will change as illustrated in Figure 9.38. Note that this step will present different options depending on what type of chart you selected in the previous step.
7. Select a **format** for the chart type you selected by selecting the appropriate button.

FIGURE 9.36
ChartWizard—
Step 1 of 5.

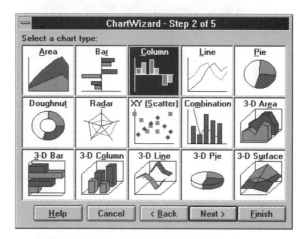

FIGURE 9.37
ChartWizard—
Step 2 of 5.

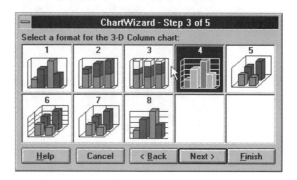

FIGURE 9.38
ChartWizard—
Step 3 of 5.

8. Select **Next>**. The ChartWizard will change as illustrated in Figure 9.39. Notice that a preview of what your chart will look like appears in the **Sample Chart** region of the ChartWizard. Based on the data in your pivot table, Excel takes its best guess at which way you want the chart oriented, and selects whether the data series is in rows or columns.
9. Select either **Data Series in: Rows** or **Columns** to change the orientation of your chart.
10. Select **Next>**. The ChartWizard will change as illustrated in Figure 9.40. Note that this step will present different options depending on what type of chart you selected in the previous step.
11. Type a title for your chart in the **Chart Title** edit box.
12. Type a title for your chart's X axis in the **CATEGORY(X)** edit box.
13. Type a title for your chart's Y axis in the **VALUE(Y)** edit box and Select **Finish**.

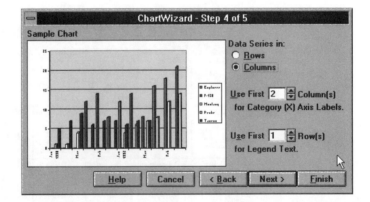

FIGURE 9.39
ChartWizard—
Step 4 of 5.

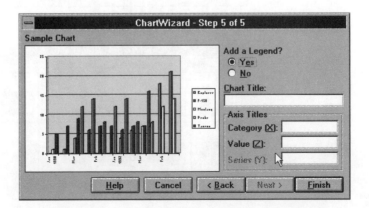

FIGURE 9.40
ChartWizard—
Step 5 of 5.

Creating a Chart from a Pivot Table with Page Fields

To create a chart from a pivot table which has one or more page fields is just as easy as creating a chart from a pivot table which has no page fields. This is because the process is EXACTLY the same. The only difference is what happens when you view the chart and its underlying pivot table. The chart displays only one page at a time. When you switch pages on the pivot table, the chart is automatically updated to reflect the information from the new page's data. To create a chart from a pivot table which contains page fields, follow the steps detailed in the previous section, **Creating a Chart from a Pivot Table Without Page Fields**, paying special attention to make sure that you don't include the page field(s) in the source data range.

CHAPTER 10
Advanced Pivot Tables

Adding and Removing Existing Fields

Once your pivot table has been created, you can easily add and remove fields.

Adding an Existing Row, Column, or Page Field

What if you created a pivot table without specifying a page field and want to add one so that you could look at subsets of your data? If the field already exists in your data source, you can easily add it using the PivotTable Wizard, or **Pivot and Query** shortcut menu. Since **Row**, **Column**, and **Page** fields are all interchangeable, the process for adding all three is exactly the same. The advantage of using the PivotTable Wizard is that it allows you to add several fields (including data fields) in a single step. To add an existing field to your pivot table, follow the steps below.

STEPS — **Adding an Existing Field to a Pivot Table, Using the PivotTable Wizard**

1. Select a cell in the pivot table.
2. Invoke the **PivotTable Wizard**. Step three, which allows you to place your pivot table fields, will be the active screen.
3. Drag the field to the area where you would like it.
4. Select **Finish**.

X-REF *If you would like to add another field to an internal data source and utilize it in your pivot table, see **Changing, Adding, and Deleting Fields**, in Chapter 9.*

If you use the **PivotTable** shortcut menu, there are four different dynamic menu commands that change based on the location of the active cell within the pivot table. The four choices are:

- Add Data Field→
- Add Row Field→
- Add Column Field→
- Add Page Field→

The **Add Row Field**→ command will be available if your active cell is on a row field button. The **Add Column Field**→ command will be available if your active cell is on a column field button. The **Add Page Field**→ command will be available if your active cell is on a page field button. The **Add Data Field**→ command will be available if your active cell is within the data range or in the cell where the row and column headings meet (the leftmost top cell of the pivot table, exclusive of the page field area). When you select one of these choices, you get a submenu which lists all of the fields which are available. When you select the field, and release the mouse, the field will be added to the left of the active cell for row and column fields, below the active cell for page fields, and above the existing fields, if it is a data field.

STEPS

Adding a Data Field to a Pivot Table, Using the PivotTable Shortcut Menu

1. Select a cell in the data area of the pivot table.
2. Select **Add Data Field**→ from the **PivotTable** shortcut menu.

STEPS

Adding a Row Field to a Pivot Table, Using the PivotTable Shortcut Menu

1. Select a cell in the data area of the pivot table.
2. Select **Add Row Field**→ from the **PivotTable** shortcut menu.

STEPS **Adding a Column Field to a Pivot Table, Using the PivotTable Shortcut Menu**

1. Select a cell in the data area of the pivot table.
2. Select **Add Column Field**→ from the **PivotTable shortcut menu.**

STEPS **Adding a Page Field to a Pivot Table, Using the PivotTable Shortcut Menu**

1. Select a cell in the data area of the pivot table.
2. Select **Add Page Field**→ from the **Pivot and Query** shortcut menu.

Removing a Field

If you decide you no longer want a row, column, or page field to be part of your pivot table, you can quickly remove it. To remove a field from a pivot table, drag the field to an area outside of the pivot table, and release it when the cursor changes to a button with a large **X** through it.

HINT *This action can be immediately undone by selecting **Edit→Undo Pivot**.*

Changing the Layout of a Pivot Table

Moving a Field

If you would like to move a field, all you have to do is drag it from one location to another. You can change the orientation of a row or column field, you can move a row or column field to a page field, or you can move a page field to a row or column field.

Examine pivot table in Figure 10.1. What if you wanted the models to be horizontal, and the months to be vertical? This is actually a two-step process. First, drag the column button over the row button. Before you release the mouse, notice how the cursor changes. When you first start to drag the column button, the cursor changes from the arrow to a horizontal array. In addition, there is a position indicator which indicates where the field will end up if you release the mouse button. At the point when you

Advanced Pivot Tables

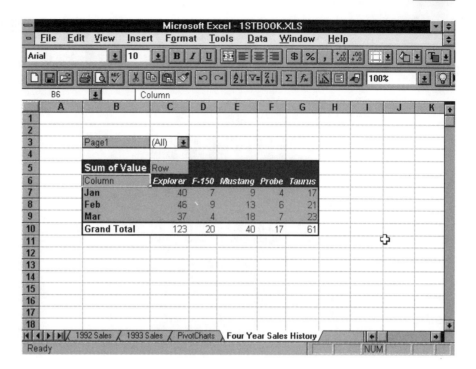

FIGURE 10.1
Months as column fields, models as Row field.

first start to drag, the cursor is a horizontal line, with a small head on each end. As your cursor crosses the horizontal-to-vertical threshold, the cursor becomes a vertical array. Also notice that the position indicator becomes a vertical line with a small head on each end. Last but not least, as you move from side to side over the row button, the position indicator changes. If you release the mouse while the indicator is aligned to the left of the row button's row, the field will be inserted to its left. If you release the mouse while the indicator is aligned to the right of the Row button's row, the field will be inserted to its right. For this example, it really doesn't matter where you place the field, but in others it will. The left-to-right positioning controls the grouping and detail levels. If you drop drop the column button so that it is placed to the row button's left, the pivot table will change as illustrated in Figure 10.2.

You can now drag the row button until its cursor changes to a horizontal array and then release it. The pivot table changes as illustrated in Figure 10.3.

Don't let the description of this process lead you into thinking this process is difficult. It is not! You simply drag and drop your fields where you want them. This example has a page field which allows you to select the year. What if you want to see all of the years' data, and include the actual year in the row heading? All you would have to do is to drag the **Page1** button (which represents the year field) down to where the row

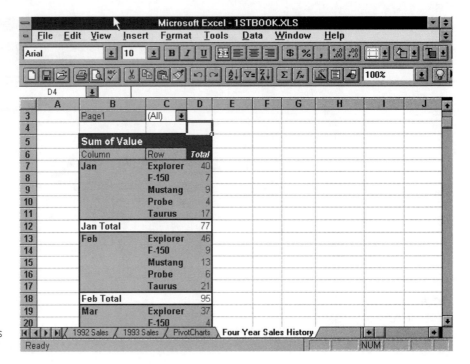

FIGURE 10.2
Months and models as row fields.

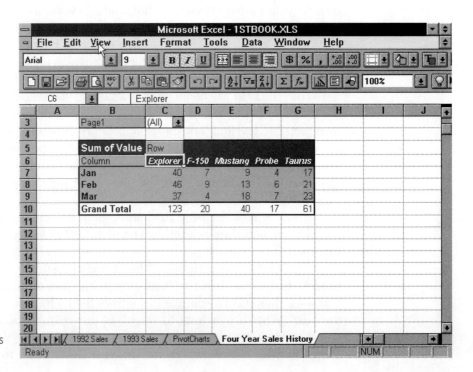

FIGURE 10.3
Months as row fields and models as columns fields.

field is. If you drop it on the right side of the month field (the column button), the year field will be inserted between the month field and the actual data values. Don't worry about not being able to use the page field. Although there is no field there, there is still a 'Page Zone' that you can drop a field onto. Because pivot tables are grouped from left to right, month will be the grouping, and year will be the detail level. This is illustrated in Figure 10.4.

> **X-REF** *Grouping and detail levels are discussed later in this chapter.*

Although this is an interesting way to view the data, it might make more sense to view it grouped by year, with the month as the detail level. In order to do this, drag the **Page1** button (the year field) to the left of the columns button (the month field). Be careful not to drag too far, or else you will delete the field from the table. The result is illustrated in Figure 10.5.

Moving an Item

You can also move an item. What if you decide that you do not like the order of the items in the pivot table? In particular, what if you think that the **F-150** item should be to the left of the **Explorer** item because *F* comes before *E*, alphabetically. To move an item, all you have to do is drag and drop it to its new location. Notice that when you start to drag an item, an outline is placed around the item's complete column. This visual tool is useful for determining where to drop the item. If you want to move several contiguous items, you can select all of them, and then drag them to their new location. You cannot move several discontiguous items in the same step. Figure 10.6 illustrates the result of this action.

Changing the Orientation of Data with Multiple Fields

If you have a single data field, the text which describes the data field and its aggregate function (i.e., **Sum of Quantity**) is displayed in the upper left hand corner of the pivot table, where the row and column fields intersect, as illutrated in Figure 10.7. Notice that it does not appear as a button, like the other fields, even though it appeared as a button in Step three of the PivotTable Wizard.

If you have more than one data field, instead of the 'flat label' you get

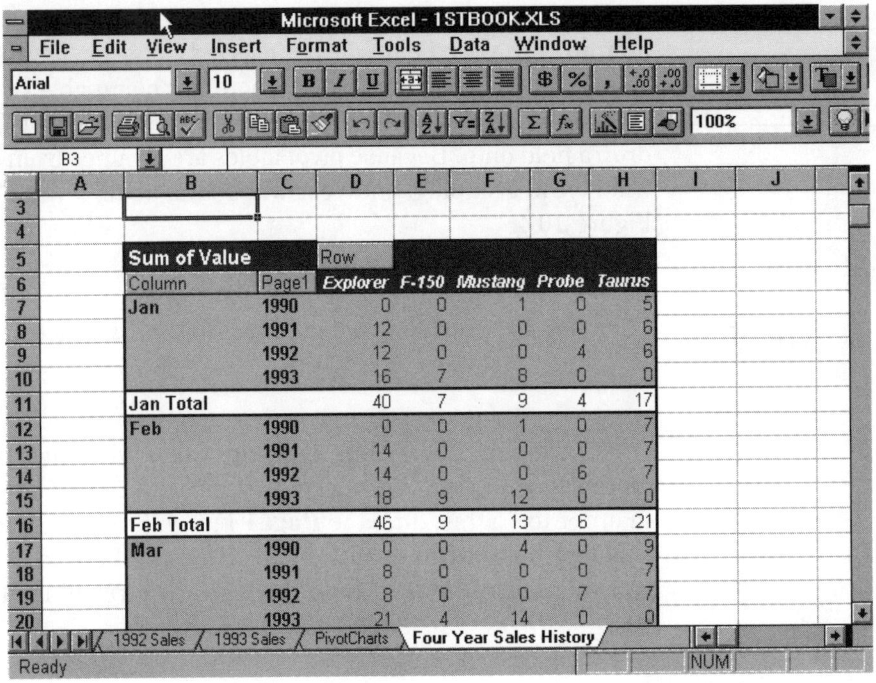

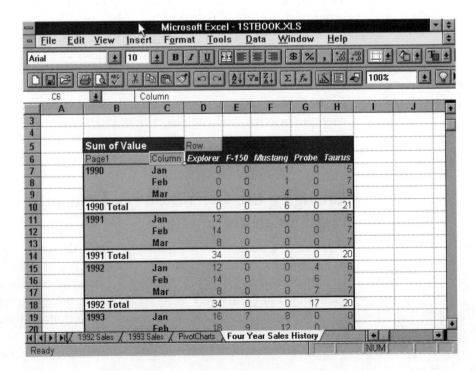

FIGURE 10.4
Months and years as row fields, grouped by month.

FIGURE 10.5
Years and months as row fields, grouped by years.

ADVANCED PIVOT TABLES

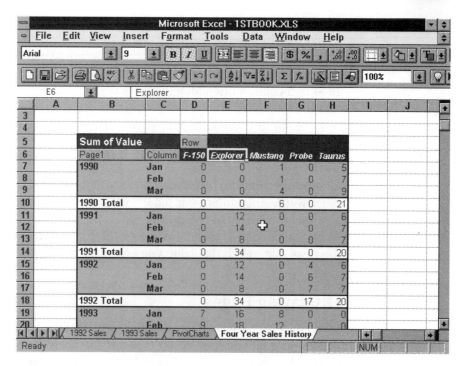

FIGURE 10.6
F-150 and **Explorer** have been moved.

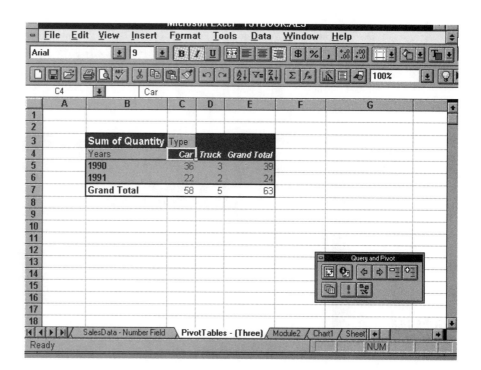

FIGURE 10.7
Pivot table with a single data field.

a button which contains the text **Data**, as illustrated in Figure 10.8. If you would like to change the orientation of your data fields, drag the **Data** button from one orientation to another. Figure 10.9 illustrates the effect of dragging the **Data** button from a row orientation (as illustrated in Figure 10.8) to a column orientation.

Using Page Fields to Change Your View of Data

As described earlier, page fields allow you to view subsets of your data. In other words, they filter your data. If they are properly set up, they provide a powerful and easy-to-use interface for working with your data. Essentially, when you choose a value for a page field, Excel only retrieves the data for the rows that match the value you select for the page field's value.

Displaying Pages

If you have already set up a page field and would like to select which page you display, all you have to do is select the corresponding item from the page field's drop-down list. If you have not built your page field, you can simply drag one of the other fields onto the Page Field.

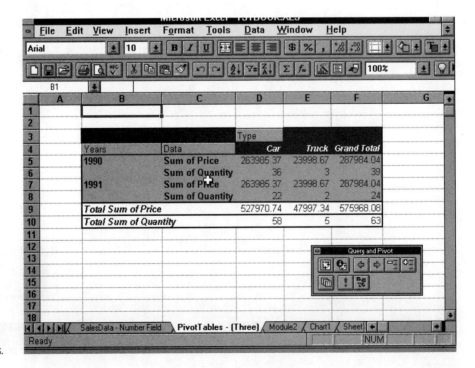

FIGURE 10.8
Pivot table with a multiple data fields.

Advanced Pivot Tables

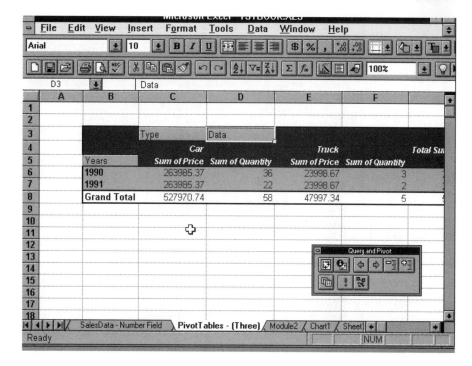

FIGURE 10.9
The pivot table illustrated in Figure 10.8, with its data field orientation changed.

Building on the car example, Figure 10.10 illustrates the page which displays the data for 1990. Notice that for this year, there were only two models sold, Mustang and Taurus. Figure 10.11 illustrates the page which displays the data for 1993. Notice that for 1993, there were three models sold. To select a pivot table page to view, follow the steps below.

STEPS   Selecting a Pivot Table Page to View

1. Click on the down arrow to the right of the page field. A drop-down box with all possible items (pages) will be displayed.
2. Select the item whose page you wish to view.

If you want to view a summary of all of the items available in a page field, select (ALL) from the drop down list. This will combine all of the data and present it in a single page. Using the car example, with all years selected. Notice that there are column field items for **Explorer**, **F-150**, **Mustang**, **Probe**, and **Taurus**. Even though in any given year there were never more than three models (items in the row field—remember that in the

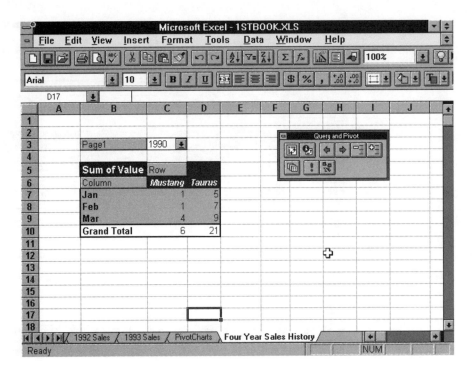

FIGURE 10.10
1990.

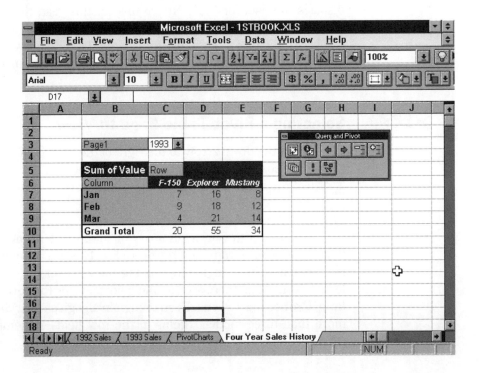

FIGURE 10.11
1993.

Advanced Pivot Tables

original pivot table models were in rows and months were in columns), the combined table has five items.

Using Multiple Page Fields

Using multiple page fields is analogous to using a filter with multiple criteria. Each additional page field that your pivot table contains, will further filter the underlying data source. What if you wanted to interactively look at a single year's worth of data, month by month? You would simply drag the month field to the page field area. You could then select the year from the year page field, and you would then get a filtered list of items in the month page field. In this particular example, all years have the same items listed (months), but if you had chosen a field which had different items in different years (such as model in this example), you would get only the items of model that exist in the year page field which is selected. Figure 10.12 illustrates using two page fields, year and month.

Displaying Pages on Separate Worksheets

Although pages work well when you use them interactively, what happens when you want to view or print more than one page at a time? One option would be to copy and paste each page manually. The shortcoming with this

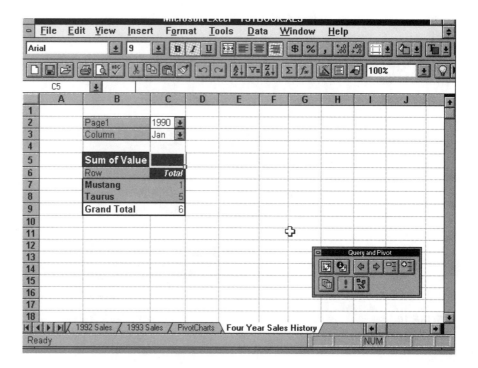

FIGURE 10.12
Two page fields: Year and month.

method is that the copies would not be pivot tables—they would only be static snapshots. You could not use the functionality of pivot tables to change each copy's 'view.' Another solution would be to create a separate pivot table for each page. Even if you linked them all back to the original pivot table, depending on how many items were in the page field, you could spend a long time doing this. Excel has a feature which will automate this process by copying a duplicate pivot table for each page to a new worksheet, and giving the worksheet the same name as the page's item label. To store each page of a pivot table as a separate worksheet, follow the steps below.

STEPS

Storing Each Page of a Worksheet as a Separate Worksheet, Automatically

1. Select any cell in the pivot table.
2. Select **Show Pages...** from the pivottable shortcut menu. The dialog box illustrated in Figure 10.13 will be displayed.

HINT

*You could also select the **Show Pages** tool from the Query and Pivot toolbar.*

3. Select the page field you want to display from the **Show All Pages of** list box.
4. Select **OK**.

WARNING

There is one major drawback to using this method. If your pivot table has more than one page field, you can only select one.

Printing Multiple Pages from a Pivot Table

If you would like to print all of the pages (worksheets) created in the previous section, you could print each one individually, or you could print all of them in one fell swoop. To quickly print each one of these pivot table pages on a separate printed page, follow these steps:

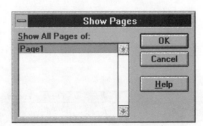

FIGURE 10.13
Show Pages
dialog box.

Advanced Pivot Tables

STEPS

Printing Multiple Pages of a Pivot Table on Separate Physical Pages

1. Select the tab of the worksheet your first pivot table is on.
2. Hold down **Shift** and select the first worksheet that Excel automatically inserted. All of the tabs in between should be highlighted. Notice that Excel's menu bar includes the text **GROUP** after your file name.
3. Select **File→Print**. The dialog box illustrated in Figure 10.14 will be displayed.
4. Select **Selected Sheet(s)** from the **Print What** option group.
5. Select **OK**.

Besides saving time, another advantage of using this method instead of printing each worksheet manually is that each pivot table page will have a consecutive page number in its footer, assuming you use automatic page numbering.

Working with Totals in a Pivot Table

By default, the PivotTable Wizard automatically includes subtotals and grand totals for all pivot tables. **Grand totals** summarize all of the values in all of the rows and columns in a pivot table. This is why it is important not to include totals in the data sources for your pivot tables. Subtotals summarize outer fields when there is more than one row field or column field. When grand totals are calculated, hidden items are excluded. Grand totals do not use subtotal values.

Hiding and Displaying Grand Totals

The only way to hide or display grand totals is by using the PivotTable Wizard. This gives you the option of setting these properties correctly when you first build your pivot table, or using the PivotTable Wizard to modify

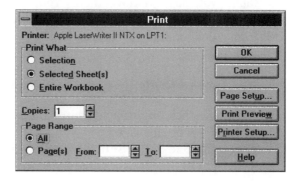

FIGURE 10.14
Print dialog box.

them after the pivot table has been built. Regardless of whether you're creating a new pivot table or modifying one that exists, the row and column grand total properties of a pivot table can only be set from Step 4 of the PivotTable Wizard. To hide or display grand totals, follow the steps below.

> **NOTE** *Technically speaking, the row and column grand total properties of a pivot table are really the rowGrand and columnGrand properties of the PivotTable object.*

STEPS **Hiding Grand Totals**

1. Select any cell in your pivot table.
2. Invoke the PivotTable Wizard.
3. Select **Next>**.
4. Select or clear the **Grand Totals for Columns** check box.
5. Select or clear the **Grand Totals for Rows** check box.
6. Select **Finish**.

If a pivot table contains more than one data field, Excel displays one grand total row or grand total column for each data field. Figure 10.15 illustrates an example that contains both price and quantity data fields. The pivot table includes a separate grand total for each data field.

Hiding and Displaying Subtotals for Row and Column Fields

The PivotTable Wizard automatically includes subtotals for all rows and columns, except the innermost ones, when your pivot table has more than one row or column field. Figure 10.16 illustrates subtotals based on grouping by year. Month has no subtotals because it is the innermost field. If, on the other hand, there is a third row field, as Figure 10.17 illustrates, the second field will also contain subtotals. If you do not want to include subtotals, you must remove them. You can also use functions other than **SUM()**. These will be covered later in this chapter. To remove subtotals from a field, follow the steps below.

STEPS **Removing Subtotals from a Field**

1. Double-click on the field's button. The dialog box illustrated in Figure 10.18 will be displayed.
2. Select **None** in the **Subtotals** option group.
3. Select **OK**.

Advanced Pivot Tables 201

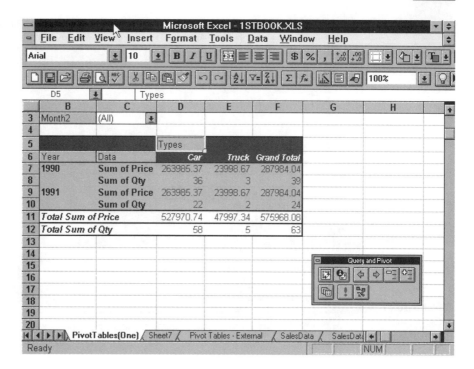

FIGURE 10.15
A pivot table that contains two data fields with a grand total line for each.

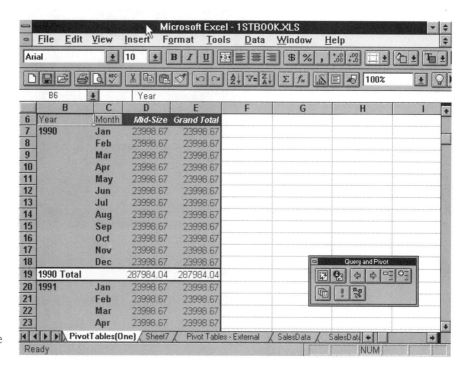

FIGURE 10.16
An example of subtotals on a single row field.

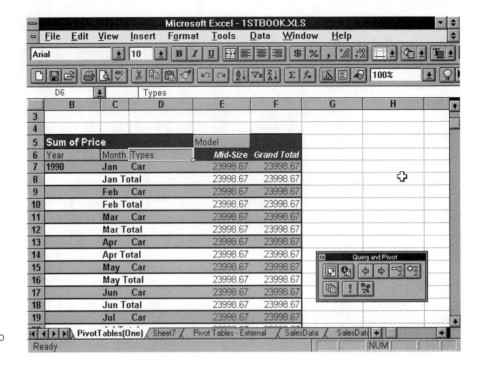

FIGURE 10.17
An example of subtotals on a two row fields.

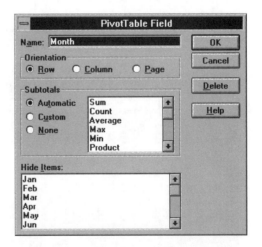

FIGURE 10.18
PivotTable Field dialog box.

STEPS

Adding Subtotals to a Field

1. Double-click on the field's button. The **PivotTable Field** dialog box will be displayed.
2. Select **Automatic** in the **Subtotals** option group.
3. Select **OK**.

Subtotals on Inner Fields

A **block subtotal** is a special kind of subtotal which places a series of total rows or columns above the row grand totals or to the left of the column grand totals. A block subtotal can only be applied to the innermost row or column field when there are two or more fields. Figure 10.19 illustrates a block subtotal applied to the year row field. Notice that for every year, there is a combined subtotal for each of the months, and that it is placed above the **Grand Total** (Note that the full pivot table is not displayed, because a **Split Box** was used to split the window into two panes). To add or remove block subtotals, follow the steps below.

STEPS

Adding a Block Subtotal to a Field

1. Double-click on the field's button. The **PivotTable Field** dialog box will be displayed.
2. Select **Custom** in the **Subtotals** option group.
3. Select **Sum** from the **Subtotals** function listbox.
4. Select **OK**.

STEPS

Removing a Block Subtotal from a Field

1. Double-click on the field's button. The **PivotTable Field** dialog box will be displayed.
2. Select **None** in the **Subtotals** option group.
3. Select **OK**.

You can actually have more than one block total. The function list box allows you to select multiple functions.

Aggregate Functions

By default, if the data that is being totaled is text, Excel automatically uses the **Sum** function to add all values together. If, on the other hand, the data is text, Excel uses the **Count** function to calculate the total number of items. **Sum** and **Count** are two of the eleven functions which Excel supports for working with sets of data in pivot tables. **Sum**, **Avg**, **Min** and **Max** are also available in MS Query. Table 10.1 contains a list of the eleven aggregate functions which can be used in pivot table totals. They are called **aggregate functions** because to calculate their return values, they perform an oper-

CHAPTER 10

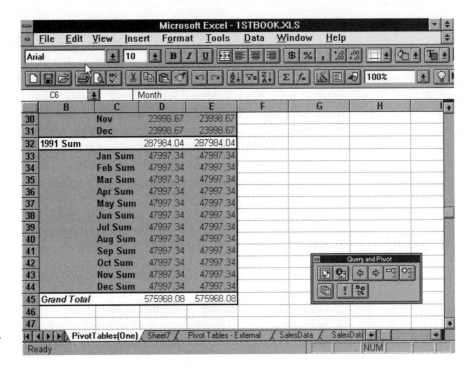

FIGURE 10.19
A block subtotal applied to the year row field.

TABLE 10.1
Aggregate Functions and the Values They Return

Function	Value Returned
Sum	The sum of the values in the underlying data. This is the default summary function for numeric data fields.
Count	The number of selected records or rows in the underlying data. This is the default summary function for data fields that contain something other than numbers.
Average	The arithmetic mean of the values in the underlying data.
Max	The maximum value in the underlying data.
Min	The minimum value in the underlying data.
Product	The product of the underlying data.
Count Nums	The number of selected records or rows that contain numeric data in the underlying data.
StdDev	An estimate of the standard deviation of a population, where the underlying data is a sample of the entire population.
StdDevp	The standard deviation of a population, where the underlying data is the entire population.
Var	An estimate of the variance of a population, where the underlying data is a sample of the entire population.
Varp	The variance of a population, where the underlying data is the entire population.

ation on the **complete set of underlying data**. These functions are sometimes refered to as summary functions, total functions, totals, or subtotals, although the latter two are very misleading.

Aggregate Functions in Subtotals

You can override the default **Sum** and **Count** functions which are used in subtotals, or add additional subtotal lines to your pivot table. Figure 10.20 illustrates a pivot table which has subtotal lines that return the **Sum, Average, Min** and **Max** for each column field for each month. Follow the steps below to change or add aggregate functions to your subtotals.

STEPS Changing the Aggregate Function Used in a Subtotal

1. Double-click on the button for the field you want to change. The **PivotTable Field** dialog box will be displayed.
2. Select the **Custom** option button from the **Subtotals** option group.
3. Select the aggregate function you would like to use from the **Subtotals** list box.
4. Select **OK**.

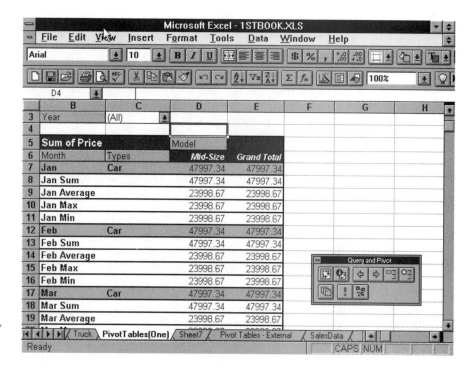

FIGURE 10.20
Sum, Average, Min, and Max subtotals for each month.

STEPS

Adding Additional Aggregate Function Lines to a Subtotal

1. Double-click on the button for the field you want to change. The **PivotTable Field** dialog box (for subtotals) will be displayed.
2. Select the **Custom** option button from the **Subtotals** option group, if it is not already selected.
3. Select the aggregate function(s) you would like to add from the **Subtotals** list box. Note that this is a multiple selection list box.
4. Select **OK**.

Aggregate Functions in Grand Totals

Although the Excel 5.0 documentation explicitly states otherwise, you *can* use functions other than **Sum** and **Count** on grand totals. The label associated with the **Grand Total** will not give you any indication of this, but it works. Examine Figure 10.21, in which the grand totals for 1990 and 1991 are correctly calculated (using SUM()) as 39 and 24. Now examine the data illustrated in Figure 10.22. In this example, the **Grand Total** field was changed from **Sum** to **Max**. As the data shows, this function clearly works! To use an aggregate function on a grand total, follow these steps:

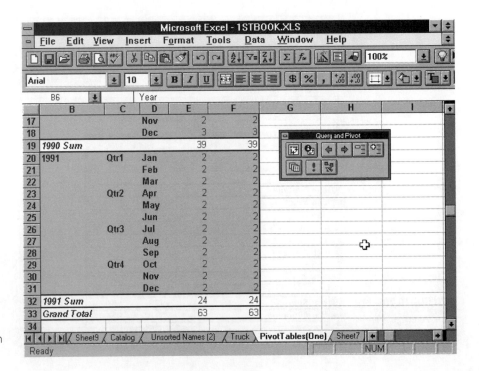

FIGURE 10.21
Grand totals which summarize **Qty**.

Advanced Pivot Tables

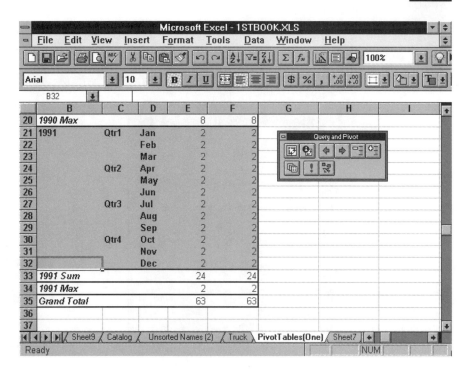

FIGURE 10.22
Grand totals which return the maximum value of **Qty**.

STEPS

Changing the Aggregate Function on a Grand Total Field

1. Select any cell in the **Grand Total** field whose aggregate function you want to change.
2. Select **PivotTable Field...** from the PivotTable shortcut menu. The **PivotTable Field** dialog box (short version) will be displayed.
3. Select **Max** from the **Summarize by** list box.
4. Select **OK**.

Aggregate Functions in Data Fields

You can override the default **Sum** and **Count** functions which are used in calculating the data fields, and/or add data fields for performing additional aggregate functions. Figure 10.23 illustrates a pivot table which has two data fields—one which calculates the minimum **Qty** and one which returns the maximum **Qty**. Follow the steps below to change or add aggregate functions to your data fields.

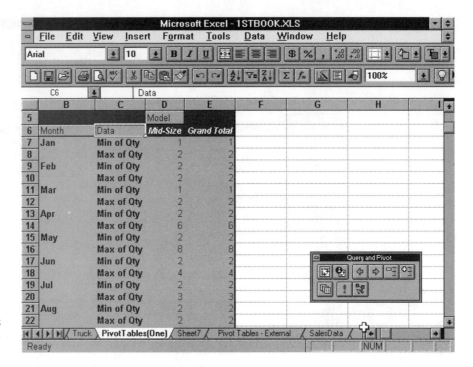

FIGURE 10.23
Min and Max aggregate functions used on the Qty data field.

STEPS Changing the Aggregate Function Used in a Data Field

1. Invoke the PivotTable Wizard.
2. Double-click on the button for the field you want to change. The **PivotTable Field** dialog box (for subtotals) will be displayed.
3. Select the aggregate function you would like to use from the **Summarize by** list box.
4. Select **OK**.

If you would like to use more than one aggregate function on a data field, you need to add an additional instance of the field, and change the new field's aggregate function. The example shown earlier which had both the **Min** and **Max of Qty** was created this way. Figure 10.24 illustrates Step three of the PivotTable Wizard, which is how this was created.

Changing the Calculation Type for a Data Field

If your pivot table contains more than one data field, you can actually define a custom calculation which uses other cells in the data area as part of the calculation. Table 10.2 contains a list of the nine calculation functions which can be used in pivot table data fields.

Advanced Pivot Tables

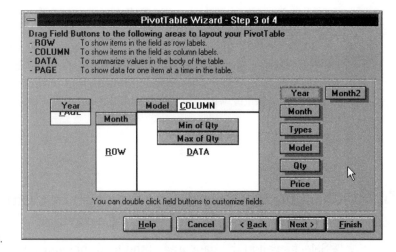

FIGURE 10.24
Multiple occurrences of a single data field, to display different aggregate functions.

TABLE 10.2
Calculation Functions and the Values They Return

Function	Value Returned
Difference From	Displays all the data in the data area as the difference between a Base Field and a Base Item you specify.
% Of	Displays all the data in the data area as a percentage of a Base Field and a Base Item you specify.
% Difference From	Displays all the data in the data area using the same method as the Difference From function, but displays the differerence as a percentage of the Base data.
Running Total In	Displays the data for successive items as a running total. You must select the field whose items will be shown in a running total.
% Of Row	Displays the data in each row as a percentage of the row's total.
% Of Column	Displays all the data in each column as a percentage of the column's total.
% Of Total	Displays the data in the data area as a percentage of the grand total of all the data in the pivot table.
Index	Displays the data using the following algorithm: ((value in cell) × (Grand Total)) / ((Grand Row Total) × (Grand Column Total))

If the custom calculation is required, a **Base Field** is a field in the pivot table, which you would like to serve as the base data for your custom calculation. You can select a base field from the **Base Field** list box. Some calculation functions also require that you specify a **Base Item**, which is the *specific item* within the Base Field that you wish to use as the base data for the calculation. The base item is selected from the **Base Item** list box. Instead of using a single item for your base value, you can choose **(next)** and (**previous**) to use either the following or preceding item, relative to the current item.

Figure 10.25 illustrates an example which shows the total by year (**Sum of Qty2**), and then uses 1990 as the base year for a percentage of comparison. To change the calculation function of a data field, or add additional data fields with different calculation functions, follow the steps below.

STEPS — Changing the Calculation Function of a Data Field, Using the PivotTable Field... Command

1. Select a cell in the data area of the field that you want to change.
2. Select **PivotTable Field...** from the pivot table shortcut menu. The **PivotTable Field** dialog box will be displayed.
3. Select **Options→**. The dialog box will expand. Note that the **Base Field** and **Base** list boxes are greyed out.
4. Select a calculation function from the **Show Data as** drop-down box.
5. Select a base field from the **Base Field** list box, if the calculation function you selected in Step four requires one.

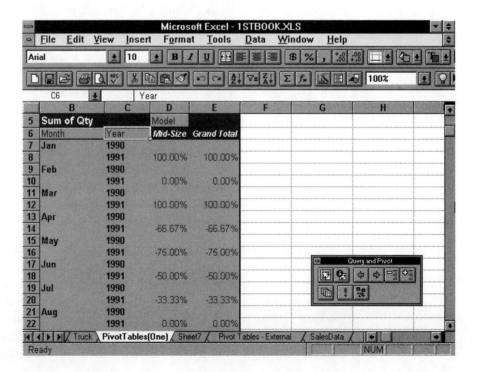

FIGURE 10.25 Percentage of calculation with 1990 as the base year.

Advanced Pivot Tables

6. Select a base item from the **Base Item** list box, if the calculation function you selected in Step five requires one.
7. Select **OK**.

STEPS

Changing the Calculation Function of a Data Field, Using the PivotTable Wizard

1. Select any cell in the pivot table.
2. Invoke the PivotTable Wizard.
3. Double-click on the button of the data field you want to change. The **PivotTable Field** dialog box will be displayed.
4. Select **Options→**. The dialog box will expand. Note that the **Base Field** and **Base** list boxes are greyed out.
5. Select a calculation function from the **Show Data as** drop-down box.
6. Select a base field from the **Base Field** list box, if the calculation function you selected in Step five requires one.
7. Select a base item from the **Base Item** list box, if the calculation function you selected in Step six requires one.
8. Select **OK**.
9. Select **Finish**.

STEPS

Adding an Additional Data Field for Comparison Calculations

1. Select any cell in the pivot table.
2. Invoke the PivotTable Wizard.
3. Drag the field that you want the comparison calculation to be part of onto the data area. (If you already have **Qty**, and want to compare **Qty** to a base item, drag another copy of **Qty** onto the data area.
4. Double-click on the button of the data field you just added.
5. Select **Options→**.
6. Select a calculation function from the **Show Data as** drop-down box.
7. Select a base field from the **Base Field** list box, if the calculation function you selected in Step six requires one.
8. Select a base item from the **Base Item** list box, if the calculation function you selected in Step seven requires one.
9. Select **OK**.
10. Select **Finish**.

Formatting a Pivot Table

Every time you refresh, recalculate, or reorganize a pivot table, any formatting which was applied to the pivot table using the **Format→Cells** command will be removed and not restored. Although this is the case, pivot tables do provide the ability to:

- Apply an **AutoFormat** style every time the table changes.
- Apply a number format to every value cell, which will be retained when the pivot table changes.
- Change field names and still maintain links to your data source.

AutoFormat

When you create a pivot table, Step 4 of the PivotTable Wizard includes a check box labeled **AutoFormat Table**. When this property is set to **True** (when it is checked) when the pivot table is created, an **AutoFormat** will be applied to it. This is its default setting. Subsequently, every time the table is recalculated, reorganized or refreshed, the **AutoFormat** will be re-applied. Additionally, if you apply a different **AutoFormat** style to the pivot table after it has been created, the style you apply will be used every time Excel automatically applies an **AutoFormat** style to the pivot table. To apply an **AutoFormat** style to a pivot table which has already been created, follow the steps below.

> **HINT**
> *If the **AutoFormat Table** check box in Step 4 of the PivotTable Wizard was not checked when you created your pivot table, no formatting will be applied to the new pivot table.*

> **STEPS**
> ### Changing the AutoFormat Property of an Existing Pivot Table
>
> 1. Select any cell in the pivot table.
> 2. Invoke the PivotTable Wizard.
> 3. Select **Next>**.
> 4. Select the **AutoFormat Table** check box to set this property to **True**; Clear the **AutoFormat Table** check box to set this property to **False**.
> 5. Select **OK**.

Advanced Pivot Tables

STEPS

Applying an AutoFormat Style to an Existing Pivot Table

1. Select any cell in the pivot table.
2. Make sure that the **AutoFormat** property is set to **True** (see the steps described above).
3. Select **Format→AutoFormat....** The **AutoFormat** dialog box will be displayed.
4. Select an **AutoFormat** style from the **Table Format** list box. Notice that as you make a selection, the style is previewed in the **Sample** window.
5. Select **OK**.

If the **AutoFormat Table** check box in Step four of the PivotTable Wizard was not checked when you created your pivot table, no formatting will be applied to the new pivot table.

Formatting Numbers in a Pivot Table

By default, Excel uses the number style which is defined in your worksheet's normal style. As discussed above, you can use **AutoFormat** to change the appearance of your pivot table. Unfortunately, **AutoFormat** doesn't offer you much help with number formats. Other than the accounting table formats, all of the formats use the general number format. Excel does, however, offer a viable alternative, the **NumberFormat** property of the **PivotField** object. The **NumberFormat** property allows you to specify/define the number format which will be used for all cells in the value area of your pivot table. To set the **NumberFormat** property, follow the steps below.

STEPS

Formatting Numbers in a Pivot Table

1. Select any cell in the pivot table.
2. Select **PivotTable Field...** from the pivot table shortcut menu.
3. Select **Number....** The dialog box illustrated in Figure 10.26 will be displayed. This is essentially a custom version of the **Format Cells** dialog box, which only allows you to edit number formatting.
4. Select a number category from the **Category** list box.
5. Select a format style from the **Format Codes** list box, or create a custom style by typing in the **Code** edit box.
6. Select **OK**. You will be returned to the **PivotTable Field** dialog box.

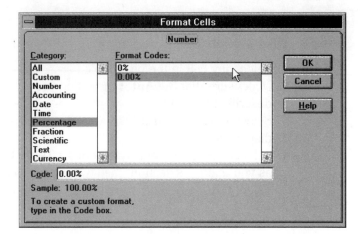

FIGURE 10.26
Format Cells dialog box.

7. Select **OK** again to return to your worksheet.

Now, every time you refresh, recalculate, or reorganize your pivot table, it will retain its number formatting.

Assigning Aliases to Pivot Table Fields

Pivot tables offer the ability to assign *alias*es to field names (sometimes referred to as field labels). An **alias** is an assumed name that you use to refer to your field. Suppose, for example, your pivot table was created from an external data source that has a naming convention that does not support embedded spaces, and you want to use a field named **LastName** in your pivot table. Although this field name is still fairly readable, it would be clearer if you could have Excel display *Last Name* in your pivot table. This is exactly what an alias does. By assigning the alias of *Last Name* to the **LastName** field, all objects linked to **LastName** will always display the text *Last Name*. There are actually three ways you can do this:

- Through the PivotTable Wizard.
- Through the **PivotTable Field** dialog box.
- Directly editing the cell in the pivot table which contains the button.

You can actually use the procedure described below involving the PivotTable Wizard when you first build your pivot table. To assign an alias to a pivot table field, follow these steps:

Advanced Pivot Tables

STEPS

Assigning an Alias to Pivot Table Field Using the PivotTable Field... Command

1. Double-click on the button of the field you want to assign an alias to. The **PivotTable Field** dialog box will be displayed.
2. Type a new name in the **Name** edit box (it is selected by default).
3. Select **OK**.

STEPS

Assigning an Alias to Pivot Table Field, Using the PivotTable Wizard (for an Existing Pivot Table)

1. Select any cell in the pivot table.
2. Invoke the PivotTable Wizard.
3. Double-click on the button of the field you want to assign an alias to. The **PivotTable Field** dialog box will be displayed.
4. Type a new name in the **Name** edit box (it is selected by default).
5. Select **OK**.
6. Repeat Steps three through five for any additional fields you want to add an alias to.
7. Select **Finish**.

STEPS

Assigning an Alias to Pivot Table Field by Directly Editing the Cell

1. Select the button for the field you want to assign an alias to. Notice that the text appears in the formula bar.
2. Place your cursor in the formula bar to switch to *Edit Mode*.
3. Change the text of the field.
4. Select the check box in the formula bar or press **Enter**.

Assigning Aliases to Pivot Table Items

In addition to assigning aliases to field names, you can also assign aliases to item labels, and still maintain your links to the underlying data. In many database systems, numeric values are stored instead of actual text values, and then the databases' end users' application software knows how to interpret these numbers. For instance, if you have an orders table which contains shipper information, instead of storing the text in each record for the shipper, you would store a value that corresponds to a single shipper. This would take up less storage space and allow for faster data retrieval.

WordWide Overnight might have a value of 1, and North American Parcel might have a value of 2. If you were to build a pivot table that used shipper as a field, your items would be all ones and twos. Not very meaningful to the casual observer. By using an alias, you could assign the corresponding shipper's name to the correct item, and make the pivot table much more meaningful. To assign an alias to an item, follow the steps below.

STEPS **Assigning an Alias to Pivot Table Item**

1. Select the cell that contains the item you want to change. Notice that whether you selected a cell or a button, the text appears in the formula bar.
2. Place your cursor in the formula bar to switch to *Edit Mode*.
3. Change the text of the item.
4. Select the check box in the formula bar.

Notice that if the item appears more than once in your pivot table, all have been updated.

Grouping Items in a Pivot Table Field

Pivot tables allow you to:

- Group selected items.
- Group numeric items.
- Group dates and times.
- Create subgroups from groups.

Grouping Selected Items

Grouping selected items is simply a matter of selecting all of the items that you want to be in a group, and then telling Excel that they are a group. You can do this with:

- The **Group** tool, on the Query and Pivot toolbar.
- The **Group** and **Outline→Group...** commands on the pivottable shortcut menu.
- The **Data→Group and Outline→Group...** command.

Examine the data illustrated in Figure 10.27. Because **Year** is the leftmost row field, the row columns are automatically grouped by it. Remember, when you have two or more fields, the data is automatically grouped from left to right. Since there are only two fields, the detail level of **Month** is displayed. What if you want to look at quarterly data? In other words, if you want to provide further grouping by quarter? The underlying database contains separate fields for month and year, but not quarters. If this database just contained a date field, you could actually group by quarter (this is covered in the next section), but it was designed intentionally so that you could not do this. Because there is no quarter field, you cannot automatically have Excel group by quarters. But, with a few mouse clicks, you can easily create a custom grouping! To create a custom grouping from a selection of items, follow the steps below.

STEPS — Creating Custom Grouping from a Selection of Items

1. Display the Query and Pivot toolbar if it is not already displayed.
2. Select the items you wish to group by.
3. Select the **Group** tool.
4. Change the labels for the button and group item, as appropriate.

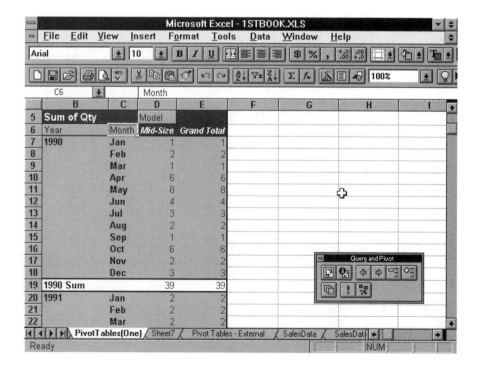

FIGURE 10.27
Default grouping with **Year** and **Month** row fields.

5. Repeat Steps 2 through 4 if you would like to add additional groups to the same field.

The first time you add a group to a field, Excel inserts a duplicate field to the left of the original. Its button has the label **FieldName2**, the new group has the label **Group1**, and every instance in the new field of the group gets this label. Figure 10.28 illustrates this, after creating the grouping for the first quarter. This group was created by selecting the **Jan**, **Feb**, and **Mar** items for the grouping. When you add additional groups, Excel inserts group labels with an incremental suffix (**Group2**, **Group3**, etc.) This is illustrated in Figure 10.29, in which groups for the second, third, and fourth quarters have been added. Finally, you can change all of your labels to accurately describe your groupings. Figure 10.30 illustrates the proper labels for the quarterly grouping.

Removing a Grouping Created from Selected Items

Removing a grouping created from a selection is even easier than applying the grouping in the first place. You can remove either a single group (if your field has more than one group) or all groups. To remove a grouping created from a selection, follow these steps:

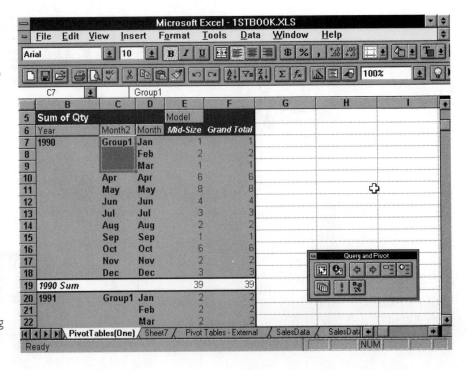

FIGURE 10.28

The result of adding the first group to the pivot table.

ADVANCED PIVOT TABLES

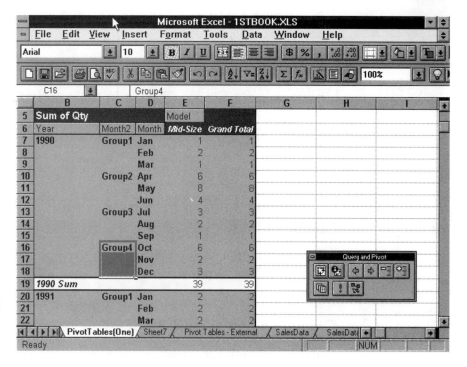

FIGURE 10.29
The result of adding the second, third, and fourth groups to the pivot table.

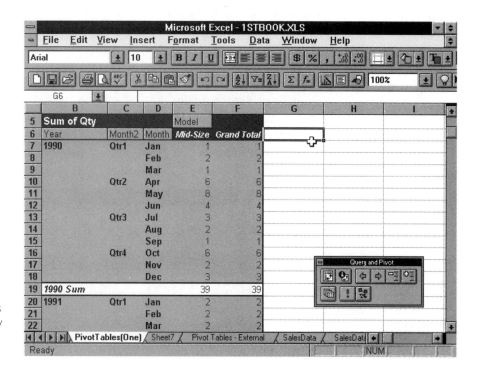

FIGURE 10.30
The result of changing the labels to more accurately describe the grouping.

WARNING — *After you ungroup, there is no corresponding **Undo Action** command available. In other words ungrouping cannot be undone!*

STEPS — **Ungrouping a Single Group in a Row or Column Field**

1. Select the any cell in the grouped item.
2. Select the **Ungroup** tool.

STEPS — **Ungrouping All Grouped Items in a Row or Column Field**

1. Select the button for the field you want to remove all grouping from.
2. Select the **Ungroup** tool.

Grouping Dates and Times

As mentioned in the previous section, if the example data had contained a data field, grouping could have been performed automatically, using one or more of several date and time intervals. When you try to group a field which contains a data or time format that Excel recognizes, the dialog box in Figure 10.31 is displayed. The **Grouping** dialog box allows you to:

- Select the first item you want in your group.
- Determine whether you want the first item selected for you manually or automatically.
- Select the last item in your group.
- Determine whether you want the last item selected for you manually or automatically.

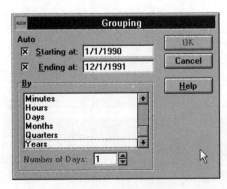

FIGURE 10.31
Date and time **Grouping** dialog box.

ADVANCED PIVOT TABLES

- Select the interval(s) you want to group by.
- Select the number of days you would like in your group, if you select days as one of your groupings.

The **Auto Starting at** check box is used to determine whether you want the first item selected for you manually or automatically. If it is checked, selection of the starting item's value is automatic. This is the default behavior. The **Starting at** edit box is used to change starting item's value. As soon as you make an edit in this control, the corresponding check box will be cleared. The **Auto Ending** at check box is used to determine whether you want the last item selected for you manually or automatically. If it is checked, selection of the last item's value is automatic. This is the default behavior. The **Ending at** edit box is used to change ending item's value. As soon as you make an edit in this control, the corresponding check box will be cleared. The **By** list box allows you to select the interval(s) you would like to group by. Table 10.3 provides a list of all of the intervals which are available. If you select **Days** as an interval, you can actually select the number of days you want in the grouping by using the **Number of days** spinner control. Unless you select **Days** as an interval, this control will be greyed out.

*If you have a multiple selection in the **By** listbox, which includes **Days**, the **Number of days** spinner control will still be greyed out. If you want to have multiple intervals, and include **Days** as one of them, you need to select the **Days** interval first, set the number of days, and then add additional intervals.*

Figure 10.32 shows a variation on the data which has been used for all of the examples where a single data field has been substituted for the separate year and month fields. Figure 10.33 shows a pivot table with this new **Date** field. Figure 10.34 shows the same pivot table after grouping has

TABLE 10.3
Date and Time
Grouping Intervals

Interval
Seconds
Minutes
Hours
Days
Months
Quarters
Years

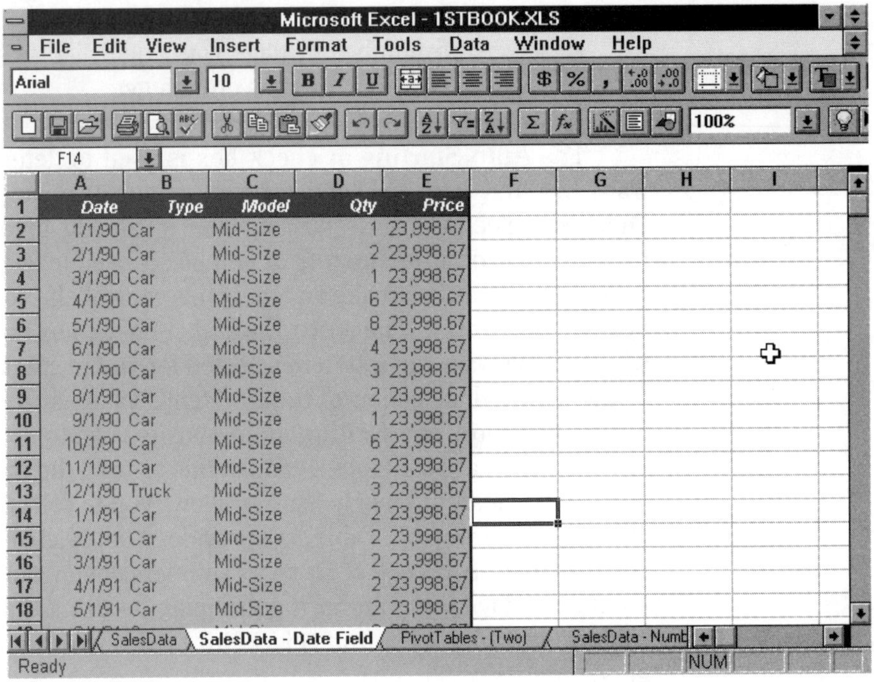

222 CHAPTER 10

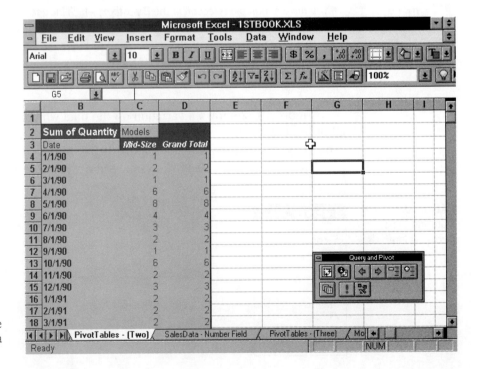

FIGURE 10.32
New data table which substitutes a single **Date** field for the year and month fields.

FIGURE 10.33
Default pivot table with the **Date** as a row field.

ADVANCED PIVOT TABLES

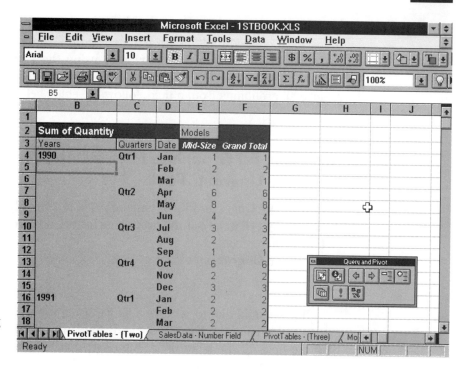

FIGURE 10.34
The result of adding the groups for year, quarter, and month.

been applied for years, quarters and months. It should be noted that this was all done in a single step, including the creation of the appropriate item labels. To group by dates and times, follow the steps below.

STEPS Grouping Dates and Times

1. Display the Query and Pivot toolbar if it is not already displayed.
2. Select any cell in the field you want to group (It must be a valid date or time format).
3. Select the **Group** tool. The **Grouping** dialog box will be displayed.
4. Change the **Starting at** and **Ending at** items if you are not happy with the default selections.
5. Select your interval(s) from the **By** list box. Note that this is a multiple selection list box, so you can select more than one interval in a single step.
6. Select the number of days you want in your group from the **Number of Days** spinner control, if you are grouping on **Days**.
7. Select **OK**.

Ungrouping Items in a Date Field

If you have created multiple groupings from the same date or time field, you cannot remove individual groupings using the **Ungroup** tool. When you use the **Ungroup** tool, you remove all groupings from the field. To remove all groupings from a field, follow the steps below.

STEPS

Removing All Groupings from a Date/Time Field, Using the Ungroup Tool

1. Display the Query and Pivot toolbar if it is not already displayed.
2. Select any cell in any of the groupings for the field you want to remove the grouping from.
3. Select the **Ungroup** tool.

If you would like to remove a single grouping from a data field, you can do so by using the **Group** tool and changing your options, or by dragging the field off the pivot table. Although this requires an extra step or two, it is often quicker than removing all of the groupings and recreating the ones that you want to keep, which is the only other alternative. To remove selected groupings from a date/time field, follow the steps below.

STEPS

Removing Individual Groups from Date/Time Fields, Using the Group Tool

1. Display the **Query and Pivot** toolbar if it is not already displayed.
2. Select any cell in any of the groupings for the field you want to remove the grouping from.
3. Select the **Group** tool. The **Grouping** dialog box will be displayed.
4. De-select the interval(s) you want to remove from the grouping from the **By** list box.
5. Select **OK**.

STEPS

Removing Individual Groups from Date/Time Fields, by Dragging

1. Drag the field button of the field you want to remove, off the pivot table.
2. Release the mouse.

Grouping Numeric Items

When you try to group a field which contains numeric data, the dialog box in Figure 10.35 is displayed. The numeric **Grouping** dialog box allows you to:

- Select the first item you want in your group.
- Determine whether you want the first item selected for you manually or automatically.
- Select the last item in your group.
- Determine whether you want the last item selected for you manually or automatically.
- Select the increment you want to group by.

The **Auto Starting at** check box is used to determine whether you want the first item selected for you manually or automatically. If it is checked, selection of the starting item's value is automatic. This is the default behavior. The **Starting at** edit box is used to change starting item's value. As soon as you make an edit in this control, the corresponding check box will be cleared. The **Auto Ending at** check box is used to determine whether you want the last item selected for you manually or automatically. If it is checked, selection of the last item's value is automatic. This is the default behavior. The **Ending at** edit box is used to change ending item's value. As soon as you make an edit in this control, the corresponding check box will be cleared. The increment **By** list box allows you to select the increment you would like to group by.

Figure 10.36 shows a pivot table with **Quantity** as the row field, **Type** and **Years** as the column fields, and price as the data field. What if you want to group the **Qty** field in groups of five, so that you can look for trends in how many units are sold, and how much revenue is derived from the sale? Figure 10.37 illustrates the results applying a grouping based on a numeric interval of five. In this case, the default starting point (which Excel selected as one, because it is the smallest value in the field), has been manually set to zero, because the first group should represent zero to five, not one to six. This feature is especially useful for grouping product num-

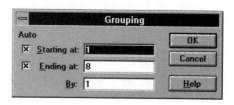

FIGURE 10.35
Numeric **Grouping** dialog box.

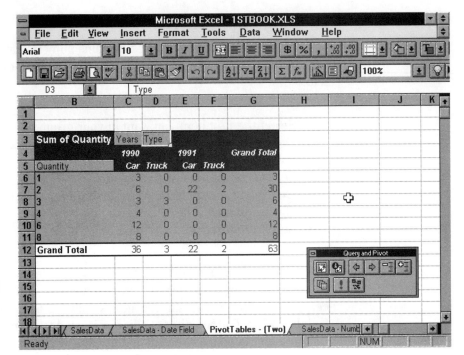

FIGURE 10.36
A pivot table with **Quantity** as the row field, **Type** and **Years** as the column fields, and Quantity as the data field.

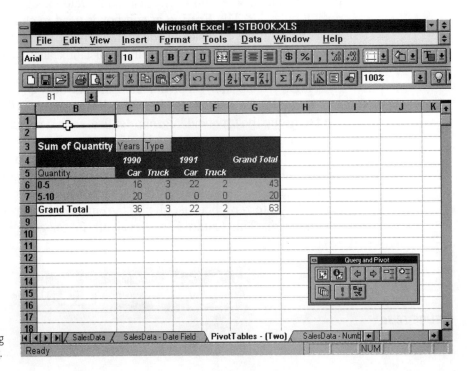

FIGURE 10.37
The result of adding a numeric grouping.

bers (where 100–200 are all cars, 201–300 are trucks, etc.) and zip codes. To group by numeric intervals, follow the steps below.

STEPS

Grouping Numeric Items

1. Display the **Query and Pivot** toolbar if it is not already displayed.
2. Select any cell in the field you want to group.
3. Select the **Group** tool. The numeric **Grouping** dialog box will be displayed.
4. Change the **Starting at** and **Ending at** items if you are not happy with the default selections.
5. Type the increment in the **By** list box.
6. Select **OK**.

Ungrouping Numeric Items

To remove a grouping created from a numeric field, follow the steps below.

STEPS

Removing All Groupings from a Numeric Grouping

1. Display the **Query and Pivot** toolbar if it is not already displayed.
2. Select any cell in any of the grouping for the field you want to remove the grouping from.
3. Select the **Ungroup** tool.

Grouping Items in a Page Field

You cannot directly apply grouping to a page field. If you select a page field's button, and select the Group tool, you will get the message box illustrated in Figure 10.38.

There is however, a way to work around this problem. The solution is to create your grouping(s) on a field while it is a row or column field, and then to drag it into the page field area. Figure 10.39 shows the results

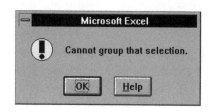

FIGURE 10.38
Cannot group that selection message box.

Chapter 10

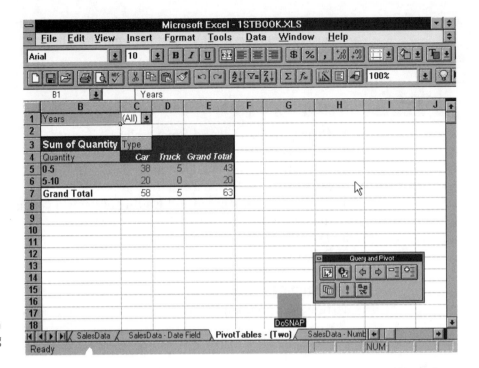

FIGURE 10.39
The **Years** page field, created from the years grouping of the **Date** field.

of doing this with the Years field (which is really derived from the **Date** field). Each year in the date field becomes a page in the new pivot table.

To remove the grouping, drag the page field off the pivot table, or drag it to a row or field column and then remove all or part of the grouping.

Hiding and Showing Detail in a Pivot Table

Pivot tables allow you to hide detail items to display summary data, if your pivot table has more than one row or column field, or if it has grouping. By default, detail information is shown when you create your pivot table. This feature is anlagous to outlining, but is not as structured. A good application of these features is to hide all of the detail information, and present just summary data. By double-clicking on individual summary items, you get a drill-down capability, which is prominent in many EIS (Executive Information Systems), with a minimum amount of work. When finished with the detail information, another double-click will roll the detail back up to the summary level. Although this capability is very usable with standard fields, you will probably use it most frequently in combination with pivot table's grouping capabilities. Pivot tables allow you to:

- Hide the detail for individual items in a field.

- Hide the detail for all items in a field.
- Show the detail for individual items in a field.
- Show the detail for all items in a field.
- Show the detail for the innermost row or column field.
- Display the source data for a cell in the data area in a new worksheet.

Hiding Detail Rows or Columns

You can hide the detail for an individual item by double-clicking on it, or using the **Hide Detail** tool. To hide the detail for a single item in a row or column field, follow the steps below.

STEPS

Hiding the Detail for a Single Item in a Row or Column Field

1. Display the **Query and Pivot** toolbar if it is not already displayed.
2. Select the item.
3. Select the **Show Detail** tool.

STEPS

Hiding the Detail for a Single Item in a Row or Column Field, Using Direct Manipulation

1. Double-click on the item.

Showing Detail Rows or Columns

You can show the detail for an individual item by double-clicking on it, or using the **Show Detail** tool. To show the detail for a single item in a row or column field, follow the steps below.

STEPS

Showing the Detail for a Single Item in a Row or Column Field

1. Display the **Query and Pivot** toolbar if it is not already displayed.
2. Select the item.
3. Select the **Show Detail** tool.

STEPS — **Showing the Detail for a Single Item in a Row or Column Field, Using Direct Manipulation**

1. Double-click on the item.

Showing Detail for All Items in a Row or Column Field

You can show the detail for all items in a field in a single step. To show the detail for all items in a row or column field, follow the steps below.

STEPS — **Showing the Detail for All Items in a Row or Column Field**

1. Display the **Query and Pivot** toolbar if it is not already displayed.
2. Select the field button.
3. Select the **Show Detail** tool.

Hiding Detail for All Items in a Row or Column Field

You can hide the detail for all items in a field in a single step. To hide the detail for all items in a row or column field, follow the steps below.

STEPS — **Hiding the Detail for All Items in a Row or Column Field**

1. Display the **Query and Pivot** toolbar if it is not already displayed.
2. Select the field button.
3. Select the **Hide Detail** tool.

Showing Detail for the Innermost Row or Column

The innermost field always contains detail information, whether visible or not. If you try to double-click on an innermost field, as you would expect, it cannot be expanded to show another level of detail. If the items in the innermost field are visible, you can actually add another field, and have it displayed just for the innermost field's item. At this point, the field is no longer the innermost field because a new (innermost) field has been added, and you can add more fields.

Figure 10.40 shows a pivot table, in which **Date** (which is grouped by month) was the innermost field. An additional field, **Price**, was added for the **Jan** date item. Now, when you double-click on an item in **Date**, the **Price** detail for that month will be displayed, along with a total. To show detail for an innermost field, follow the steps below:

STEPS Showing Detail for the Innermost Row or Column Field, Using Direct Manipulation

1. Make sure that the item information is displayed for the innermost row or column field.
2. Double-click on an item you would like to see detail items for. The dialog box illustrated in Figure 10.41 will be displayed.
3. Double-click on the field which contains the detail you want to show.

If the item information is not displayed for the innermost row or col-

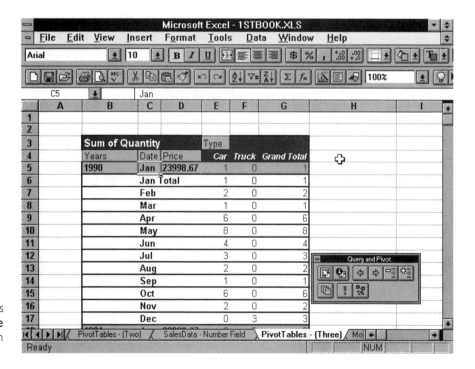

FIGURE 10.40
Price field added as detail data for **Date** (grouped by month field).

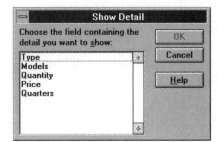

FIGURE 10.41
Show Detail dialog box.

umn field, and you try to double-click on any of the 'blank' cells, you will get the error message displayed in Figure 10.42.

Displaying the Source Data for a Cell in the Data Area

If you would like to see a copy of the source data for a cell in the data area, all you have to do is double-click on it. This will insert a new worksheet, and copy all of the source data to the range starting at R1C1.

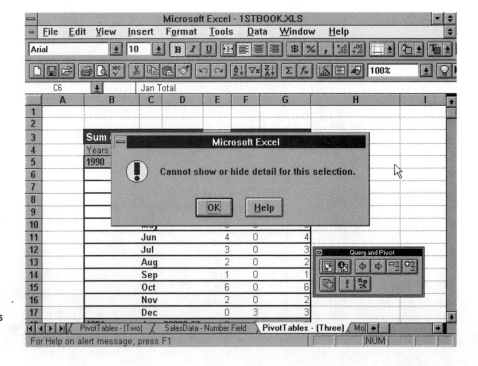

FIGURE 10.42
Cannot show or hide detail for this section message box.

CHAPTER 11
Macros/VBA

Working with Text

TextToColumns Method

Text importing may be performed using a Visual Basic for Applications (VBA) program. The **TextToColumns** method is available to parse cells containing text into columns of data. The **TextToColumns** method syntax is:

> object.**TextToColumns**(*destination, datatype, textqualifier, consecutive delimiter, tab, semicolon, comma, space, other, othercharacter, fieldinfo*)

where:

- **TextToColumns** is the method name.
- **object** is a required range object.
- **destination** is an optional range to place the data.
- **datatype** optionally specifies the text format.
- **textqualifier** optionally specifies the text qualifier.
- **consecutivedelimiter** is a logical variable where **True** indicates that multiple delimiters are treated as one.
- **tab, semicolon, comma, space, or other**—logical variables that indicate whether that character is a delimiter.

- **othercharacter**—if **other** is **True,** this is the other delimiter character.
- **fieldinfo** is an optional array containing parsing information about each column.

Adding a Carriage Return/Line Feed to a Text File

As discussed briefly in Chapter 7, a common problem in dealing with text files created in other environments is that they do not always have the carriage return/line feed combination that is required for importing fixed width text.

The Visual Basic for Applications (VBA) subroutine illustrated below is one way to add a carriage return/line feed to a text file that is lacking end of lines. The source file in the example is Input.txt (the same file used in Chapter 7). Instead of directly manipulating the source, this routine opens the source file, reads in the record (which has a fixed length), and then writes it out to a new file (output.txt), using the **Print #** statement. When the **End of File** (EOF) marker is encountered, the loop ends, and both files are closed. The only variable that needs to be changed here is **46**, which is the length of each row. This could easily be set using an input box, or by passing an argument to the routine.

The following is the code for a subprocedure to add a carriage return/line feed combination:

```
Sub AddCRLF()
   Dim Record As String * 46
   Open ``C:\EXCEL5\Input.Txt´´ For Random Access Read As #1 Len = 46
   Open ``C:\EXCEL5\Output.Txt´´ For Output Access Write As #2
   Do While Not EOF(1)
     Get #1, , Record
     If Not EOF(1) Then Print #2, Record
   Loop
   Close #1
   Close #2
End Sub
```

Using Pivot Table Methods in VBA Code

If you would like to create a pivot table in a custom application on the fly, you can use the **PivotTable Wizard method**. This method can be used on the worksheet object. It creates a pivot table, based on the arguments you pass it, without displaying the screens of the PivotTable Wizard.

The PivotTable Wizard method has the following syntax:

object.**PivotTableWizard**(*sourceType, sourceData, tableDestination, tableName, rowGrand, columnGrand, saveData, hasAutoFormat, autoPage*)

where:

- **Object** is the object that the method will be invoked on. This must be a worksheet object.
- **sourceType** is an optional argument which is used to identify the type of the data source which will be used to populate the pivot table. Table 11.1 lists the possible values for this argument. Notice that they correspond to the four choices in the first step of the PivotTable Wizard dialog box. If you omit this argument, Excel assumes that you wish to use *xlDatabase* as your data source, and that you wish to use a range named *Database* as your date source (more on this argument in a moment). If you do not have a range named *Database* Excel uses the **current region** if the selection is in a range of more than ten cells containing data. If this criteria is not met, the method will fail. If you specify a **SourceType**, you must also specify a value for the **sourceValue** argument. If you do not, the method will fail.
- **sourceData** is an optional argument which is used to identify the data for the pivot table. If the **SourceType** that you specify is *xlDatabase, xlConsolidation,* or *xlPivotTable,* valid values are a range, an array of ranges, or a text constant representing the name of another pivot table. If your *SourceType* is *xlExternal*, this must be a two-element array where the first element is the ODBC con-

TABLE 11.1
Values for SourceType Argument

Value	Type of Data Source
xlDatabase	Microsoft Excel list or database
xlExternal	Data from another application
	Multiple consolidation ranges
xlPivotTable	Same source as another pivot table

nection string, and the second is the SQL query string which will retrieve the data that you want to use in your pivot table. If you specify a **dataSource**, you must also specify a value for the *SourceType* argument. If you do not, the method will fail.

> **X-REF** ODBC is covered in Chapter 12, *An Overview of Using External Data*. SQL is covered in Chapters 14 and 15.

- **TableDestination** is an optional argument which is used to specify the range where the pivot table should be placed. Valid ranges can be on the same worksheet, on a different woksheet within the same workbook, or on a worksheet in a different workbook. Table 11.2 shows an example of each one of these scenarios. If the **TableDestination** contains data, a message box will be displayed. If you wish to overwrite the contents of the active cell, select **OK**. If this argument is omitted, the pivot table is placed at the active cell. If this argument is omitted, and the active cell is within the range referred to by the **dataSource** argument, a new worksheet will be inserted into your workbook, and the pivot table will be placed in cell R1C1.
- **tableName** is an optional argument which specifies the name of the pivot table.
- **rowGrand** is an optional argument which determines whether or not the pivot table shows row grand totals. The value for this argument can be either **True** or **False**. If set to **True**, row grand totals will be shown. If set to **False**, row grand totals will not be shown.
- **columnGrand** is an optional argument which determines whether or not the pivot table shows column grand totals. The value for this argument can be either **True** or **False**. If set to **True**, column grand totals will be shown. If set to **False**, column grand totals will not be shown.
- **saveData** is an optional argument which determines whether or not data is saved with the pivot table. The value for this argument

TABLE 11.2
TableDestination Examples

Source Workheet	Destination Worksheet	Destination Workbook	Table Destination
Sheet1	Sheet1	Book1.xls	"$A$1"
Sheet1	Sheet2	Book1.xls	"Sheet1!$A$1"
Sheet1	Sheet1	Book3.xls	Range("[BOOK3.XLS]Sheet1!$A$1")

can be either **True** or **False**. If set to **True**, data is saved with the pivot table. If set to **False**, data is not saved with the pivot table

- **hasAutoFormat** is an optional argument which determines whether or not the pivot table is automatically formatted whenever it is refreshed or fields are moved. The value for this argument can be either **True** or **False**. If set to **True**, the pivot table is automatically formatted. If set to **False**, the pivot table is not automatically formatted.
- **autoPage** is an optional argument which determines whether or not the pivot table automatically creates a page field for the consolidation. This argument is only applicable if the **sourceType** is *xlConsolidation*. The value for this argument can be either **True** or **False**. If set to **True**, a page field is automatically created for the consolidation when the pivot table is created. If set to **False**, you must manually create the page field(s).

CHAPTER 12
MS Query Overview

External Data

As mentioned in Chapter 7, there are several reasons to attach to external data instead of importing it. These include:

- The data is dynamic—using a snapshot would be misleading.
- Updates to the source data are required.
- Data is available in client/server environment.
- The data has more records (rows) than can be read into an Excel worksheet.
- Excel cannot directly read the data source's file format, although it is supported by ODBC.

Attaching to data is the process of creating a real-time link to a data source, and having it look to you and your application as data native to your application.

What MS Query Is and How It Works with Excel

MS Query is a stand-alone application included with Excel 5.0, which, as its name implies, is used mainly to query data. Although Query can be run as a separate application (see Chapter 13), it is tightly integrated with Excel 5.0. When you want to use external data in Excel, you invoke MS Query from the **Data** menu (you need to have an add-in installed first). After you build your query in MS Query, you return your result set to an Excel workbook. When you do this, you can either end the link to Query (and the underlying data source), or you can keep it, so that you can periodically refresh your data.

MS Query is designed to make building queries easy and intuitive, by implementing features such as drag-and-drop. MS Query connects to a variety of data sources, via ODBC (covered in the next section). Despite the fact that almost all data sources have different syntaxes, Query provides an interface that allows you to deal with all ODBC data sources, with no changes in syntax or how you build your queries. If, for example, you are working with both dBASE files (tables), ad SQL Server data, all of your query operations such as adding tables, fields, sorts, and criteria are exactly the same to you, the user, despite huge implementational issues on how each data source carries out the request you issued.

On the other hand if your data source has special features which are not directly accessible through Query's graphic toolset, you can bypass the interface and send SQL calls directly to your data source through the **Execute SQL** dialog box. For instance, if you want to create SQL Server stored procedures, you have to type the correct SQL code into the **SQL Statement** edit box, since there is no *Create SQL Sever Stored Procedure* button on the toolbar, that will walk you through the process.

Installing MS Query

When you installed Excel 5.0, if you selected **Complete Installation,** then MS Query and all of its standard data source drivers were installed for you. If you performed a **Minimal Installation** MS Query was not installed on your system. If you performed a **Custom Installation**, you may or may not have installed MS Query and/or all of the data access drivers that come standard with it. If Query is installed on your system, there will be an icon for it in the **Microsoft Office** program group in the Windows **Program Manager.** If you have Query installed, you can skip to the next section. If you have to install Query, follow the steps below.

STEPS

Installing MS Query

1. Launch the MS Excel **Setup** program, by double-clicking on it.
2. Select **Add/Remove...**.
3. Double-click on the **Data Access** check box in the **Options** list box.
4. Select all of the check boxes. This will install MS Query, Help, Cue Cards, and all of the standard data access drivers it ships with.
5. Select **Continue**.

6. Select **OK**. You will be prompted for the proper disks.
7. When you are returned to the **Setup** main window, select **Exit Setup**.

Windows Open Services Architecture (WOSA)

Do you remember printing from the DOS environment before you started using Windows? Each individual application provided its own printer drivers. If you were using Lotus 1-2-3, WordPerfect, and dBASE III, you had to install three separate printer drivers, one for each application. If the vendor of an application you were using didn't provide a driver for the printer you were using, you were out of luck. What if, after you installed all of the applications you were using an Epson dot matrix printer, you later decided to upgrade to a Hewlett Packard Laserjet? You installed the new printer once, but then had to install three separate printer drivers, one for each of the applications that you were using. If the Laserjet was a new model, one of the software vendors might not provide a driver immediately so you had to wait, even though your other two applications had the correct drivers available.

This kind of experience is long gone! Although many users take it for granted, Windows revolutionized how applications and printing services interface. In Windows, a printer driver is installed once, and all Windows applications have access to it. If you move from 1-2-3 for Windows, to Excel 5.0 for Windows, you do not have to worry about installing a new printer driver for the additional program. If you get a new printer, you simply install one driver, and all Windows applications share it. Since printer setup is handled through the **Control Panel** and/or **Print Manager**, you get a consistent interface for changing printers and/or printer settings. This has also created a market for third-party printer drivers. If you are not happy with the driver that came with your printer, there are many third-party choices available that address special needs of certain applications. Even though they don't necessarily need to, some software vendors include their own drivers. Although this can sometimes have unpredictable results when used with another vendor's software, it gives you, the user, more choice. Another advantage of this is that applications software vendors can focus their energies on writing better applications, not hardware drivers, which ultimately gives you better applications. All the programmers have to do is write to the Windows API, which handles how applications interface with print services.

Not content with just delivering the capability to print services, Microsoft has decided to provide this plug-and-play capability to other services that Windows users might use, through **Windows Open Services Architecture, WOSA. WOSA** provides three categories of services:

- Common Application Services
- Communication Services
- Vertical Market Services.

ODBC

Open Database Connectivity (ODBC) is an **Applications Programming Interface (API)** which works through **WOSA**, to provide transparent data access from Windows and Macintosh desktops. It is a member of the Common Application Services family. The objective of ODBC is to allow users (and applications) to connect transparently to, and work with, a variety of heterogeneous data sources.

Open Database Connectivity is supported by many database providers. Using ODBC allows an application to connect with a wide variety of database platforms without additional effort on behalf of the developer or user. ODBC acts as a translation layer between an application and the database. In the following section, you will learn to configure ODBC.

ODBC Drivers That Come with Excel 5.0

The following ODBC drivers come standard with Excel 5.0:

- Microsoft FoxPro (versions 2.0 and 2.5)
- Microsoft Access (versions 1.0 and 1.1)
- Borland Paradox (versions 3.0 and 3.5)
- dBASE (versions III and IV)
- Microsoft/Sybase SQL Server (1.1, 4.2 -NT, OS/2 and UNIX)
- Microsoft Excel (versions 3.0, 4.0 and 5.0)
- Btrieve (version 5.1)
- ORACLE Server (Version 6.0)
- ODBC ODS Gateway
- Text.

It should be noted that this list can and probably will change slightly over time. At the time this book was written, Access 2.0 was not a shipping product, and support for it is not listed. It is fairly safe to assume that when Access 2.0 ships, Excel 5.0 will ship it with a driver that can work with its new file format.

Setting Up ODBC Data Sources

Adding a New Data Source

An ODBC **Data source** contains the name of a valid ODBC driver, all of the information that is required to make a connection to it, and a descriptive name. A data source can either be a file-based source, such as FoxPro, where your data source will store the name of a directory that all of your files are in, or a table-based system like SQL Server, where you must specify the server name. You can have several different data sources, all connecting to the same database driver, and even the same database server (or DOS file directory, in the case of file-based systems). To add a new data source, follow the steps below.

STEPS Adding/Defining a Data Source

1. Open the Windows **Control Panel**. This should be in the **Main** program group of the **Program Manager**. Figure 12.1 illustrates **Control Panel**. If no ODBC icon is available, ODBC must be installed. Either run Excel's setup again, as detailed elsewhere in this chapter, or see your information technology support group for help.
2. Double-click the ODBC icon. Figure 12.2 illustrates the **Data Sources** dialog box.
3. If your data source does not appear in the list of Data Sources, select **Add...**. Figure 12.3 illustrates the **Add Data Source** dialog box.

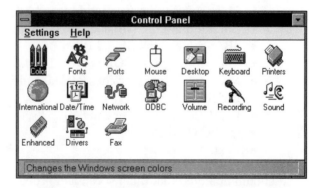

FIGURE 12.1
Windows **Control Panel**.

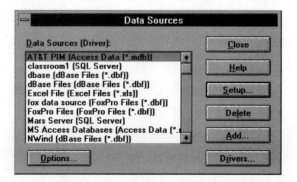

FIGURE 12.2
ODBC **Data Sources** dialog box.

MS QUERY OVERVIEW

4. Select the ODBC driver you would like to use for your new data source from the **Installed ODBC Drivers** list box.
5. Select **OK**. The **ODBC Setup** dialog box, illustrated in Figure 12.4, for the driver you selected will be displayed. This example uses the SQL Server driver including the optional Login and language parameters. The configuration options for each driver will be different. The rest of the steps in this process discuss SQL Server options.
6. Enter a meaningful name that you will use to identify this data source (e.g., Human Resources) in the **Data Source Name** edit box. This is the text that is displayed in the **Data Sources** dialog box.
7. Enter a longer description of your data source in the **Description** edit box (e.g., Salary and performance history).
8. Select the name of the server that you want to connect to from the **Server** combo box. If you do not know which server your information is located on, contact the information technology support group in your enterprise.

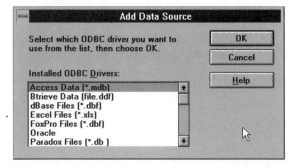

FIGURE 12.3
ODBC **Add Data Source** dialog box.

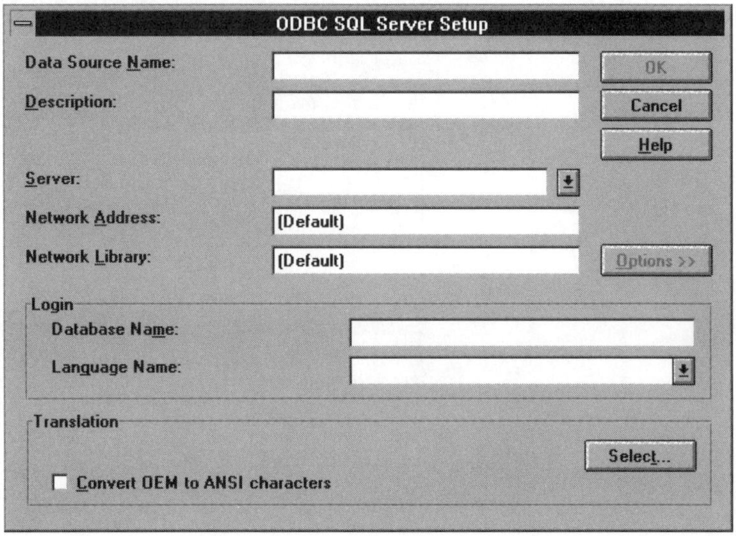

FIGURE 12.4
ODBC SQL Server **Setup** dialog box.

9. Type the name of the database you want to default to in the **Database Name** edit box (*Master* or *pubs* are fairly safe bets). You should not have to change the items marked (**Default**).
10. Select **OK**. You will be returned to the **Data Sources** dialog box. Note that **Human Resources (SQL Server)** is now a valid choice in the **Data Sources** list box.
11. Select **Close**.
12. Close the **Control Panel**.

Adding a New ODBC Driver

After ODBC is installed, you can add new drivers. If, for example, you want to access a database that is not supported by the drivers that come with Excel 5.0, you can purchase ODBC driver packages directly from Microsoft, or from other vendors, such as Q + E Software. To install a new ODBC driver to your system, follow the steps below.

STEPS

Adding an ODBC Driver

1. Select the **ODBC** icon in **Control Panel**. The **Data Sources** dialog box will be displayed.
2. Select **Drivers....** The **Drivers** dialog box, illustrated in Figure 12.5 will be displayed.
3. Select **Add....** The **Add Driver** dialog box, illustrated in Figure 12.6 will be displayed.

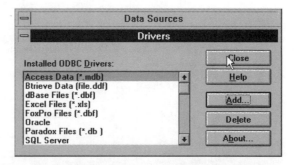

FIGURE 12.5
ODBC **Drivers** dialog box.

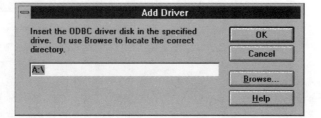

FIGURE 12.6
ODBC **Add Driver** dialog box.

4. Enter the path to the relational database driver you wish to add, or use **Browse...** to navigate through your drive resources.
5. Select **OK**.
6. Select **Close**.
7. Select **Close**.
8. Close the **Control Panel**.

Display Driver Information

Sometimes you will want to know more information about an ODBC driver which you have installed on your system. You can find:

- What data source the driver is for.
- What the driver's file name is.
- A description of the driver.
- What company wrote the driver.
- What its version number is.
- What language is being used.
- When the driver was created.
- How large the driver is.

Figure 12.7 illustrates the ODBC Driver **About** dialog box for Access. To get detailed information about an ODBC driver, follow the steps below.

STEPS Getting Driver Information

1. Select the **ODBC** icon in **Control Panel**. The **Data Sources** dialog box will be displayed.
2. Select **Drivers...**. The **Drivers** dialog box will be displayed.
3. Select the driver that you want information about from the **Installed ODBC Drivers** list box.

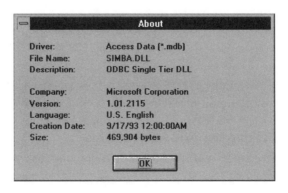

FIGURE 12.7
ODBC Driver **About** dialog box for Access.

4. Select **About...**. The **About** dialog box for the driver you selected will be displayed.
5. Select **OK** to return to the **Drivers** dialog box.
6. Select **Close** to return to the **Data Sources** dialog box.
7. Select **Close** to return to the **Control Panel**.
8. Close the **Control Panel**.

Data Access from an Excel Worksheet

Excel 5.0 comes with three add-ins to help you work with external data:

- XLQUERY.XLA
- QE.XLA
- ODBC.XLA.

XLQUERY.XLA provides functionality to retrieve data from MS Query. First of all, it adds the **Get External Data...** command to the **Data** menu and the **Get External Data** button to the Query and Pivot toolbar. It also changes the way that the **Refresh Data** command and the **Refresh Data** button behave, so that if the data source is external, Query is not displayed when the pivot table is refreshed. Last but not least, it adds command equivalent functions so that you can use macros to retrieve data from Query. **QE.XLA** contains command equivalent functions, so that with very little modification any macros that you used with Q+E will now work with MS Query. Two areas to beware of are to create a data source name that corresponds with your Q+E data source name, and to change all of your DDE initiate calls from

$$=\text{INITIATE(``QE'',``SYSTEM'')}$$

to

$$=\text{INITIATE(``MSQUERY'',``SYSTEM'')}.$$

Finally, ODBC.XLA provides eight macros and one function that allow you to do direct ODBC calls.

Making the Add-Ins Available

If you did not install the add-ins, you will need to re-run Excel's **Setup**. Follow these steps to install the data access add-ins:

MS QUERY OVERVIEW

STEPS

Making Add-Ins Available

1. Select **Tools→Add-Ins...**. The **Add-Ins** dialog box will be displayed.
2. Select the check boxes for the add-in you want. If they don't appear in the list, use **Browse...** to find them.
3. Select **OK**.

Attaching to an External Database and Returning the Query Results to Excel

Once the XLQUERY.XLA add-in has been installed, attcahing to an external database is an easy process.

To start Query from Excel, select **Data→Get External Data...**. Perform your query within Excel, and when the results are correct, select **File→Return Data** to Microsoft Excel. Your results will then be placed in your original spreadsheets. To attach to an external database, follow the steps below.

STEPS

Returning Query Results

1. Select **Data→Get External Data...**. MS Query will be started, and the **Data Sources** dialog box will be displayed.
2. Select a data source from the **Available Data Sources** list box.
3. Select **Use**.
4. Build your query.

X-REF

See Chapter 13, *Microsoft Query as a Stand-Alone Application*, for detailed information on building queries.

5. When you are happy with the results, select **File→Return Data** to Microsoft Excel. Query will close, and the dialog box illustrated in Figure 12.8 will be displayed.
6. Select the options you want.
7. Select **OK**.

NOTE

Keep Query Definition will allow you to update the data at a later time, without re-creating the query. It essentially creates a link to the underlying data source.

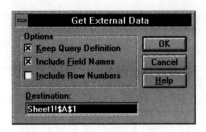

FIGURE 12.8
Get External Data dialog box.

CHAPTER 13

Microsoft Query as a Stand-Alone Application

Starting MS Query

There are two ways to start Microsoft Query:

- As a stand-alone application
- From Excel, **Using the Get External Data** command....

Starting and working with MS Query from Excel was covered in Chapter 12. This chapter will focus on using MS Query as a stand-alone application. To start MS Query from the Windows **Program Manager**, follow the steps below.

STEPS Starting MS Query from the Program Manager

1. Select the Microsoft Office program group in the **Program Manager** (or whatever program group you installed Excel in).
2. Double-click on the Microsoft Query icon.

MS Query's application window, which is illustrated in Figure 13.1, is what you will see when MS Query first starts.

Cue Cards

The first time you start MS Query, a feature called **Cue Cards** is displayed. Cue Cards are an extension of the Help system and provide an interactive mechanism to help you learn about MS Query, by working through ex-

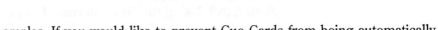

FIGURE 13.1
MS Query application window.

amples. If you would like to prevent Cue Cards from being automatically displayed on start up, select the **Don't display this card on startup** checkbox. To close Cue Cards, double-click on the **Control menu**. To open Cue Cards, select **Help→Cue Cards**.

Parts of the MS Query Workspace

MS Query is a Multiple Document Interface (MDI) Application and, as such, allows multiple windows within its workspace. Each query that you create and use has its own Query window. Depending on whether or not Query windows are open within the workspace, the menus change dynamically, although the toolbar always remains the same. As an MDI application, Query windows can be freely moved around the workspace, as well as iconized. Figure 13.2 illustrates the MS Query workspace and its major components.

MICROSOFT QUERY AS A STAND-ALONE APPLICATION

Menus

Menus When No Queries Are Open

When you first open MS Query, and have not yet opened a query, there are two menus available:

- File
- Help.

The **File** menu, which is illustrated in Figure 13.3, lets you work with queries. It offers a subset of the commands available through the File menu when a query is open. Its commands let you:

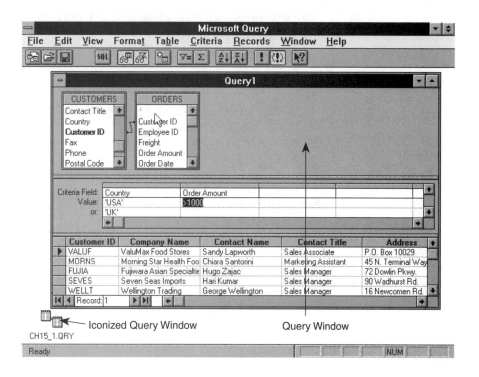

FIGURE 13.2
Query workspace.

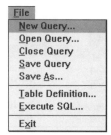

FIGURE 13.3
The **File** menu, with no query open.

- Create, or open, a query.
- Modify table and database structure.
- Create tables and databases.
- Execute SQL code against your datasource.
- Exit Query.

The Help menu, is exactly the same, and is described in the next section.

Menus When Queries Are Open

After you open a query, MS Query's menus change, to reflect many commands that would have no use if a query were not open. MS Query's menu has nine choices that allow you to create, edit, execute, and save your queries.

The **File** menu, which is illustrated in Figure 13.4, lets you work with queries. Its commands let you:

- Create, open or close a query.
- Save the query in the active window.
- Modify table and database structure.
- Create tables and databases.
- Execute SQL code against your datasource.
- Exit Query.

The **Edit** menu, which is illustrated in Figure 13.5, is used to make changes to data and objects in a query. Its commands can:

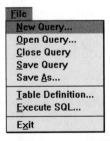

FIGURE 13.4
The File menu.

FIGURE 13.5
The Edit menu.

- Undo an Action.
- Cut, copy and paste data and objects.

The **View** menu, which is illustrated Figure 13.6, is used to display and hide components of the query window, and to modify the query. Its commands can:

- Display or hide the table pane.
- Display or hide the criteria pane.
- Display the Zoom Field box.
- Edit the query's properties.
- Display and edit the SQL code behind the query.

The **Format** menu, which is illustrated in Figure 13.7, allows you to change the appearance of the **Data** pane. You use its commands to

- Set the font type, style and size.
- Set row height.
- Set column width.
- Show and hide columns.

The **Table** menu, which is illustrated in Figure 13.8, is used to work with tables. Its commands can:

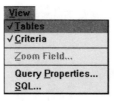

FIGURE 13.6
The **View** menu.

FIGURE 13.7
The **Format** menu.

FIGURE 13.8
The **Table** menu.

- Add tables to the query.
- Remove tables from the query.
- Create joins.
- Edit joins.
- Remove joins.

The **Criteria** menu, which is illustrated in Figure 13.9 is used to add and remove criteria.

The **Records** menu, which is illustrated in Figure 13.10, provides keyboard alternatives for many of the direct manipulation features of Query. You can use its commmands to:

- Add columns to the data pane.
- Remove columns from the data pane.
- Edit columns in the data pane.
- Apply sorting to the query.
- Move to and select a specific record.
- Run the query if the **Automatic Query** property is turned off.
- Toggle **Automatic Query** on or off.

The **W**indow menu, which is illustrated in Figure 13.11, allows you to navigate and arrange query windows. Its commands can:

FIGURE 13.9
The Criteria menu.

FIGURE 13.10
The Records menu.

FIGURE 13.11
The Window menu.

Microsoft Query as a Stand-Alone Application

- Tile all of the open query windows.
- Cascade all of the open query windows.
- Make any open query window the active window.

The **Help** menu, which is illustrated in Figure 13.12, is used to provide access to Query's help system. With its commands you can:

- Display Help's table of contents.
- Search through Help looking for keywords.
- Display **Cue Cards**.
- Display a dialog box which gives information about Query.

Toolbar

MS Query's toolbar is illustrated in Figure 13.13. It gives you quick access to common tasks such as opening queries, applying sorting, and executing a query by clicking on the desired button. Table 13.1 summarizes what each item on the toolbar does.

Query Window

The **query window**, which is illustrated in Figure 13.14, has several standard components which may or may not be visible (or available) at any given time. These components are:

- Criteria pane

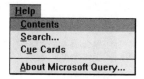

FIGURE 13.12
The **Help** menu.

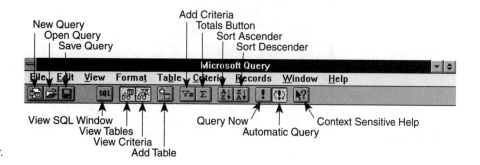

FIGURE 13.13
MS **Query** toolbar.

TABLE 13.1
Toolbar Buttons

Toolbar Item	Description
New Query button	Opens up a new query window.
Open Query button	Opens an existing query.
Save Query button	Saves the current query.
View SQL button	Displays the
View Tables button	Displays or hides the Table pane.
View Criteria button	Displays or hides the Criteria pane.
Add Tables button	Displays a dialog that allows you to add tables to your query.
Add Criteria button	**Applies a criteria which will select records containing the same value as the active cell.
Totals button	**Steps through the six **Total** functions which can be applied to a field.
Sort Ascending button	Sorts records in ascending order.
Sort Descending button	Sorts records in descending order.
Query Now button	Runs a query, when the **Automatic Query** property is turned off.
Automatic Query button	Toggles the ability to run queries automatically every time you make a design change.
Context Sensitive Help button	Changes the cursor to a pointer with a question mark, which enables you to get context sensitive help for anything you click on.

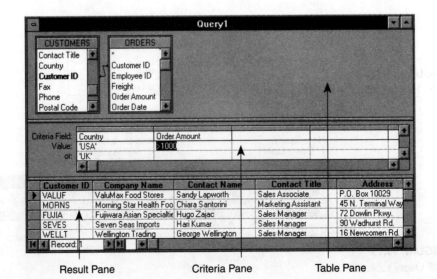

FIGURE 13.14
Query window.

- Data pane
- Table pane
- Record selectors
- Scroll bars
- Sizing buttons
- System menu.

Before beginning a discussion about each of the three panes, it should be noted that you can resize each of the three panes using the mouse. As you move the cursor over the thick line which separates each pane, notice now the cursor changes into a double headed arrow. When it does, you can click and drag the border to resize the pane.

Table Pane

The **Table pane** is where the tables in a query, and their joins, are graphically displayed. For every table that you add to a query, MS Query adds a graphical representaion of it, which contains a field list. Although these field lists cannot be maximized or minimized (and, as such, do not have control menus or sizing buttons), they behave like windows in that they can be moved anywhere in the Table pane by dragging their title bar, and can be resized by dragging their borders.

The fields in field lists are displayed in alphabetical order, not the physical order in which they exist in the underlying table. If there are joins between tables, they will be displayed in this pane. If there are no joins, you can add them to this window so that you have a complete view of the query. If the Table pane is visible, a check appears next to the **View→Table...** command, and the **View Tables** button will be recessed. This pane also contains its own horizontal and vertical scroll bars, so that you can move through this pane, without affecting the view of your other panes. Some queries cannot be represented graphically (such as calling SQL Server Views and Stored Procedure). When this happens, Query will display a message box that informs you of this. Select **OK** and continue. Query will display the correct result set (unless there are GROUP BYS or other SQL extensions which return extra rows).

Criteria Pane

The **Criteria pane** is where a query's criteria are viewed graphically and edited. The criteria pane can be hidden or displayed by selecting **View→Criteria...**, or the **View Criteria** button. If the critera pane is visible, a check appears next to the **View→Criteria...** command, and the **View Criteria** button will be recessed.

The criteria pane consists of a series of rows and columns. Each column represents a field or expression that you would like an expression to. Each column consists of:

- A criteria field
- An equals value
- One or more **OR** values.

This pane also contains its own horizontal and vertical scroll bars, so that you can move through this pane without affecting the view of your other panes.

Data Pane

The **Data pane** is where the result set of your query is displayed. It consists of a series of rows and columns. Each column is a field (or calculated field). Each row is a record in the result set of the query. You can change the display font of all text in this pane. This pane also contains its own horizontal and vertical scroll bars so that you can move through this pane without affecting the view of your other panes. You cannot turn the Data pane off, although some queries you execute (especially procedures on a database server) may not return a dataset (such as a SQL Server **Create Procedure...** command).

The Data pane also contains several controls to help you navigate through your data, and/or provide information about the current record. Figure 13.15 illustrates components of the Data pane.

Record Selectors

The Record Selector is the grey area to the left of every row in the Data pane. Although record selectors have no labels, they are similar in usage, look, and feel to Excel row labels. The record selector of the active row (record) always contains a Record Selector symbol. These symbols and what they mean are given in Table 13.2.

In addition to displaying information about a record, you can use the record selector(s) to select one or more records. This is useful for operations like cutting and pasting data to another application.

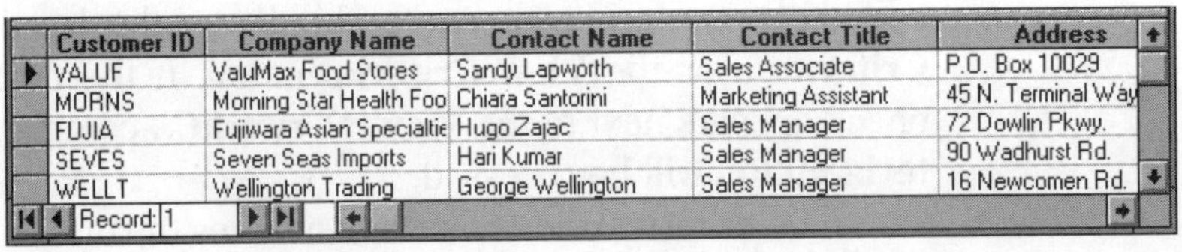

FIGURE 13.15
Data pane components.

Customer ID	Company Name	Contact Name	Contact Title	Address
▶ VALUF	ValuMax Food Stores	Sandy Lapworth	Sales Associate	P.O. Box 10029
MORNS	Morning Star Health Foo	Chiara Santorini	Marketing Assistant	45 N. Terminal Way
FUJIA	Fujiwara Asian Specialtie	Hugo Zajac	Sales Manager	72 Dowlin Pkwy.
SEVES	Seven Seas Imports	Hari Kumar	Sales Manager	90 Wadhurst Rd.
WELLT	Wellington Trading	George Wellington	Sales Manager	16 Newcomen Rd.

Record: 1

MICROSOFT QUERY AS A STAND-ALONE APPLICATION

The Navigation Buttons

The **navigation buttons**, illustrated in Figure 13.16, are used to maneuver throughout your result set, record by record.

The **Move to First Record** button is used to move to the first record in the result set. The **Move to Previous record** button is used to move to the previous record in the result set. The **Record Number box** is used to display the number of the current record. **The Move to Next Record** button is used to move to the next record in the result set. The **Move to Last Record button** is used to move to the last record in the result set.

> **HINT**
>
> *You can move quickly to a specific record by typing the number in the **Record Number** box, and then pressing **Enter**.*

Scroll Bars

Each pane in a query window has its own scroll bars, if they are required. **Scroll bars** are required if a pane cannot fit all of its data/information in the height and width of the pane. There are two kinds of scroll bars:

- Horizontal
- Vertical.

Scroll bars have three components:

- The scroll box
- The scroll area
- The scroll arrows.

TABLE 13.2 Record Selector Symbols

Record Selector Symbol	Identifies
▶	Current Record (not yet edited)
*	New Record
... ✎	Record Edited but not yet saved
⊘	Record locked by another user

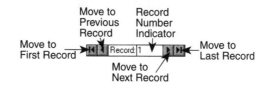

FIGURE 13.16 Navigation buttons.

Table 13.3 lists what action you should take to navigate through your panes.

Sizing Buttons

The sizing buttons are used to:

- Minimize the active window.
- Maximize the active window.
- Restore a window to its last size.

Selecting a sizing button will perform the corresponding action listed in Table 13.4.

Control Menu

The **Control Menu** is used to:

- Resize a window.
- Move a window.
- Close a window.
- Navigate to the next window.

TABLE 13.3 Actions for Navigating Using the Scroll Bars

To	Do this
Scroll up one row	Click the up scroll arrow
Scroll down one row	Click the down scroll arrow
Scroll up one full window	Click above the vertical scroll box
Scroll down one full window	Click below the vertical scroll box
Move to an approximate vertical location	Drag the vertical scroll box
Scroll left one column	Click the up scroll arrow
Scroll right one column	Click the down scroll arrow
Move to an approximate horizontal location	Drag the horizontal scroll box
Scroll up one full window	Click above the horizontal scroll box
Scroll down one full window	Click below the horizontal scroll box

TABLE 13.4 Sizing Buttons

Button	Action
▲	Maximizes the active window
▼	Minimizes the active window
♦	Restores a window to its last size

To invoke the Control menu, click on it. Select any of its commands, just as you would select any menu choice. To quickly close any window, quickly double-click on the Control menu.

Building a Simple Query

What exactly is a query? A **query** is, simply put, a question. When you build a query in MS Query, you are asking the table or tables in your data source, to give you an answer back, in the form of a result set. Since computers do just what they are told, you must be very specific about what question you pose to the data source. The more detailed your question is, the more accurate your answer will be.

To build a query, there are several steps which must completed. You must:

- Open a new query.
- Select a data source.
- Add the table(s) that you want to use.
- Add the fields that you want to use.
- Run the query if you are not in **Auto Query** mode.
- Save the query.

Creating a New Query

The first three steps of building a simple query are for all intents and purposes, one large step—creating a query. This is because whenever you create a new query, MS Query prompts you for a data source by displaying the **Select Data Sources** dialog box. It then prompts you to select one or more tables from that data source. Although you can select **Cancel** at any point during this process, MS Query walks you through this every time. To create a new query, follow the steps below.

STEPS

Creating a New Query

1. If MS Query is not already running, launch it.
2. Select **File→New Query...**. The dialog box illustrated in Figure 13.17 will be displayed.
3. Select your data source from the **Available Data Sources** list box.

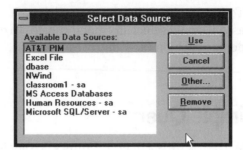

FIGURE 13.17
Select Data Sources dialog box.

 *If you need more information on selecting a data source, how to set up a data source, or ODBC in general, see Chapter 12, **An Overview of Using External Data**.*

4. Select **Use**. A new query window is opened, but moved to the back as the dialog box illustrated in Figure 13.18 is displayed. It should be noted that based on your data source, this dialog box will probably look slightly different. The examples in this chapter use the Nwind data source, which is a set of DBF files that ship with MS Query.
5. Double-click on the table you want to add, in the **Table** list box. Notice that it is added to the query window, even though the **Add Tables** dialog box still has focus. You can add more than one table, but to keep this example straightforward, that process is covered later in this chapter.
6. Select **Close**. You are now in a query window. Notice that there is nothing in the data pane, and that the criteria pane is not visible.

Adding Fields to the Query

There are five ways that you can add fields to your query, once the table which contains the field has been added to the query:

- By dragging the field name(s) from a field list in the Table pane to the Data pane.
- By double-clicking on a field name in the field list, in the Table pane.
- By selecting a field name from the field list combo box, in a blank column's column heading, in the Data pane.
- By typing a valid field name in a blank column's column heading, in the Data pane.
- By using the **Records** menu.

Microsoft Query as a Stand-Alone Application

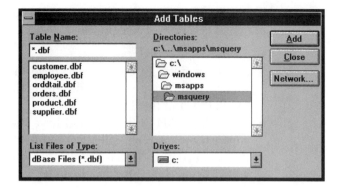

FIGURE 13.18
Add Tables dialog box.

The first two of these methods are called direct manipulation, because using the mouse, you directly interact with and manipulate the object.

HINT

Remember, you are not limited to using only one of these techniques when you are building a query. Since each of these techniques has both drawbacks and advantages, you will find yourself switching between them, based on the query you are building, and how you want your data laid out.

Drag-and-Drop

Query takes full advantage of the drag-and-drop capabilities of the Windows interface by allowing you to drag fields from a field list in the Table pane, to columns in the Data pane. Using this method, you can selectively place the fields in the order you would like to see them, and insert them between other fields. Simply click on the field you want to add, drag it to the location you want, and release the mouse. When you start to drag, if you have a single field selected, the cursor changes to represent a single field. If you have selected multiple fields, the cursor changes to represent multiple fields. When the cursor is released, the fields will be inserted to the left of the column where you release the mouse. To add fields by dragging, follow the steps below.

STEPS

Adding Fields Via Drag-and-Drop

1. Select the field(s) that you want to add.
2. Drag and drop the field(s) over the column which is immediately to the right of where you want them to appear. They will be inserted to the left of the column you dropped them over.

There are also several techniques that allow you to work with more than one field at a time. You can select:

- All of the fields in the list, and have them placed in alphabetical order when they are dropped. This is the order they appear in, in the field list in the Table pane.
- All of the fields in the list, and have them placed in the order in which they are physically ordered in the underlying table when they are dropped. This is usually the order in which the fields were added when the table was created.
- Two or more contiguous fields.
- Two or more discontiguous fields.

Follow the steps below to make multiple field selections.

STEPS — Selecting All of the Fields in a Field List So That They Are Added in Alphabetical Order

1. Double-click on the field list's title bar. All of the fields will be selected.
2. Drag the selection to the Data pane.

STEPS — Selecting All of the Fields in a Field List So That They Are Added in the Physical Order of the Table Structure

1. Select the asterisk in the field list for the table.
2. Drag the asterisk to the Data pane.

STEPS — Selecting Two or More Contiguous Fields

1. Select the first field.
2. Hold down the **Shift** key.
3. Select the second field. All of the fields in between will be selected.
4. Release the **Shift** key.
5. Drag the selection to the Data pane.

Selecting Two or More Discontiguous Fields

STEPS

1. Select the first field.
2. Hold down the **Ctrl** key.
3. Select the second field. All of the fields in between will be selected.
4. Release the **Ctrl** key.
5. Drag the selection to the Data pane.

Double-Clicking

If you would like to add a field to the rightmost column of your query, you can simply double-click on it. You can also double-click on the asterisk to add all of the fields in the table to the query, in the order in which they exist in the underlying table. It should be noted that unless you add all of the fields, this technique can only be used to add single fields. Additionally, you cannot insert fields between other columns. Fields are always added to the right side of a query.

Selecting a Field Name from the Column Heading Box's Field List Combo Box

When you select the column heading box for the blank column which is always the rightmost column in the Data pane, an arrow appears. If you click on this arrow, a drop-down list which contains all of the fields in the table(s) is displayed. Selecting a field from this list adds it to the query. To add a field using the column heading box's drop-down list, follow the steps below.

Adding Fields by Selecting a Field Name from the Column Heading Box's Field List Combo Box

STEPS

1. Select the column heading box for the rightmost column (which is always blank). As soon as you do, an arrow appears in the column heading box.
2. Click on the arrow. A drop-down list of all of the fields will be displayed, as illustrated in Figure 13.19. If your query has more than one table, field names will be preceded by their table names.
3. Select the field that you want to add.

Typing a Field Name Directly into the Column Heading Box

You can also add a field by typing a valid field name in a blank column's heading box . You can also use the asterisk (*) to add all of the fields that are available. If you have more than one table, the field name should be

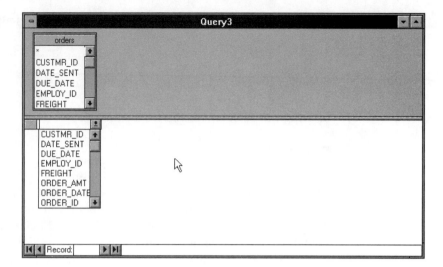

FIGURE 13.19
Drop-down list of field names in a blank column heading box.

preceded by the table name and a period. The period is a required delimiter. This is done so that if two tables have fields with the same name, Query can identify the correct field to retrieve. To add a field by typing its name in a blank column heading, follow the steps below.

STEPS

Adding Fields by Typing the Field Name Directly into the Column Heading Box

1. Move your cursor over the column heading for the rightmost column (which is always blank). Notice that the cursor changes to an I-beam.
2. Click within the column heading box. As soon as you do, an arrow appears in the column header.
3. Type the name of the field you want to add, preceded by the table name and a period, if you have more than one table.
4. Press **Enter**. The field will be added.

The Records Menu

If you do not like using the mouse, then the **Records** menu provides you with an alternative way to add fields, just by using the keyboard. Using the **Records** menu, you can:

- Insert a new column to the left of the current column.
- Add a new column, as the rightmost column in the query.

MICROSOFT QUERY AS A STAND-ALONE APPLICATION

In addition, the dialog box which is used by these two commands allows you to select a field, add an alias for it, and apply an aggregate function to it, all in a single step. To add or insert a field to the query, using the **Records** menu, follow the steps below.

X-REF *Aliases and aggregate functions are covered later in Chapters 9 and 14.*

STEPS

Adding Fields Using the Records→Add Column... Command

1. Make sure that you don't have any columns selected in the Data pane.
2. Select **Records→Add Column...**. The dialog box illustrated in Figure 13.20 will be displayed.
3. Select the field you would like to add from the **Field** drop-down list.
4. Type an alias in the **Column Heading** edit box if you want to use one.
5. Select an aggregate function from the **Total** drop-down list if you wish to apply one.
6. Select **Add**. The column will be added as the rightmost column in the query.
7. Repeat Steps 3 through 6 if you wish to add additional columns.
8. Select **Close**.

STEPS

Inserting Fields Using the Records→Insert Column... Command

1. Select the column which is directly to the right of where you want your new column inserted.
2. Select **Records→Insert Column...**. The dialog box illustrated in Figure 13.21 will be displayed.
3. Select the field you would like to insert from the **Field** drop-down list.

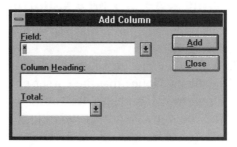

FIGURE 13.20
Add Column dialog box.

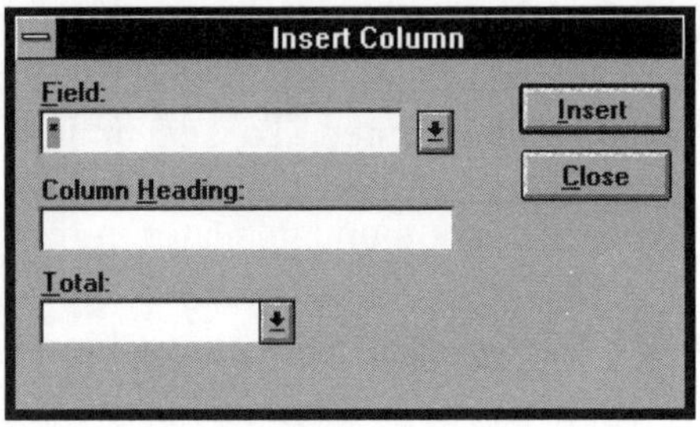

FIGURE 13.21
Insert Column dialog box.

4. Type an alias in the **Column Heading** edit box, if you want to use one.
5. Select an aggregate function from the **Total** drop-down list if you wish to apply one.
6. Select **Insert**. The column will be inserted to the left of the current column.
7. Repeat steps 3 through 6 if you wish to insert additional columns.
8. Select **Close**.

Deleting and Moving Columns

MS Query allows you to quickly and easily delete and move columns from the Data pane. To delete or move columns, follow the steps below.

STEPS   Deleting One or More Columns

1. Select the column(s) that you want to delete by clicking in their column heading.
2. Press **Del**.

STEPS   Moving One or More Columns

1. Select the column(s) that you want to move by clicking in their column heading.
2. While they are highlighted, click on any one of the selected column headings. Notice that the cursor changes to an arrow with a square.
3. Drag the column(s) to their new location. When you release the mouse, the column(s) will be inserted to the left of the column you drop them over.

Microsoft Query as a Stand-Alone Application

Modifying Records

In addition to retrieving the result sets of queries, MS Query allows you to edit the data in an underlying table, provided there is only one table in the query (see section on joins later in this chapter). MS Query allows you to:

- Update existing records.
- Add new records.
- Delete records.

By default, editing is not allowed. You must explicitly turn it on. To allow editing, Select **Records→Allow Editing**. When editing is allowed, a check appears next to the **Allow Editing** menu item, and a new record indicator (an asterisk) appears at the bottom of the record selector. To edit, delete, or add a record, follow the steps below.

STEPS Editing a Record

1. Select **Records→Allow Editing** to make sure that editing is allowed.
2. Place your cursor in the column of the record you want to edit.
3. Type your new value. Notice that as soon as you start typing, the record selector symbol changes to a pencil.
4. When you move the cursor to another record, the change is written to the underlying table.

STEPS Deleting a Record

1. Select **Records→Allow Editing** to make sure that editing is allowed.
2. Select the entire row that you want to delete by clicking in the row's record selector.
3. Press **Delete** or select **Edit→Delete**. The dialog box illustrated in Figure 13.22 will be displayed.

FIGURE 13.22
Delete 1 record(s)?
dialog box.

4. When you move the cursor to another record, the change is written to the underlying table.
5. Select **OK**.

STEPS

Adding a Record

1. Select **Records→Allow Editing** to make sure that editing is allowed.
2. Place your cursor in the first column of the row with the new record symbol (*). Notice that the asterisk changes to the current record indicator.
3. Enter values for each column.
4. After filling in the last column, move to the next new record by pressing either **Tab** or **Enter**.

Saving a Query

Now that you have built your query, you should save it. When you save a query, you don't actually save the data that was retrieved. You only save the query's design. If you are new to databases, this might seem a bit unusual, but it really makes a lot of sense. The next time you or someone else opens the query, it is executed against your data source. As such, your query retrieves the most recent data. To save a query, follow the steps below.

STEPS

Saving a Query

1. Select **File→Save....** Select **Data Source** dialog box. The dialog box illustrated in Figure 13.23 will be displayed.
2. Select **QRY File**.
3. Select **Save**. The dialog box illustrated in Figure 13.24 will be displayed.
4. Select the drive and directory where you want to store the query file.

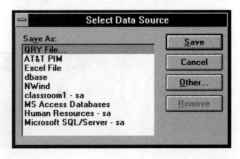

FIGURE 13.23
Data Source
dialog box.

MICROSOFT QUERY AS A STAND-ALONE APPLICATION

5. Type the name you want to use for your query in the **File Name** edit box. Note that Query automatically suggests the name **query1.qry**. If you do not type an extension, Query automatically assigns the **qry** extension.
6. Select **OK**.

Closing a Query

When you are finished working with a query, you can close it. Although you will typically save your queries, there will be times when you know you will never use the same query again. Since it is the norm to save queries, if you try to close a query that has not been saved, or if you make changes to a query that has already been saved, Query will display the dialog box illustrated in Figure 13.25. If you do not want to save the changes, select **No**. To close a query, follow the steps below.

STEPS

Closing a Query

1. Select **File→Close Query**.

At this point you could either exit from MS Query by selecting **File→Exit**, or continue to work within Query.

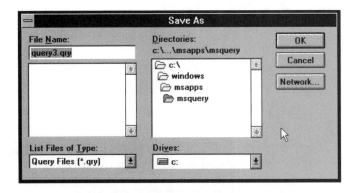

FIGURE 13.24
Save As dialog box.

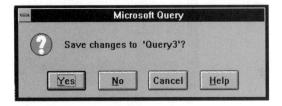

FIGURE 13.25
Save changes message box.

Building Advanced Queries

Now that you understand how to build a simple query, you can build an Advanced Query. To build an advanced query, you need to:

- Open a simple query for modification, or create a new query.
- Add criteria to limit the result set.
- Add sorting to change the order of the data.
- Join additional tables.
- Format the Query window.
- Output your results.

Opening a Query

To use a query which has already been created and saved, you need to open it. In addition to working with its own query files, MS Query can also read query files created with Q+E (formerly Pioneer Software) Software's Q+E. These files have the extention QEF. This capability has been provided to guarantee compatibility for users of prior versions of Excel, which included Q+E as its data access tool. It should also be noted that, as discussed earlier, MS Query is an MDI application, which means you can open more than one query at a time. To open a query, follow the steps below.

STEPS Opening a Query

1. Select **File→Open Query...**. The dialog box illustrated in Figure 13.26 will be displayed.
2. Select the kind of query file that you would like to open from the **List Files of Type** combo box. MS Query files, which have the extention **qry**, are the default.

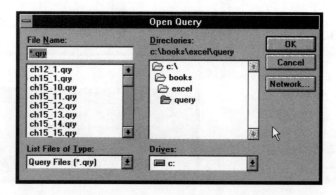

FIGURE 13.26
Open Query dialog box.

3. Select the drive where your query file is saved, from the **Drives** combo-box.
4. Select the directory where your query file is saved, from the **Directories** list box.
5. Select the file from the **File Name** list box.
6. Select **OK**.

Adding Criteria to Limit the Result Set

Suppose that you have an **Orders** table, and you are interested in examining all of the orders where the order amount was greater than $10,000. In essence, you want to 'throw away' all of the records in **Orders** where the **Order Amount** was less than $10,000, and only keep the **Orders** where the **Order Amount** was greater than $10,000. Don't worry about the use of the words 'throw away' and 'keep.' You don't really want to throw anything away. You merely want to restrict the query so that the records you don't care about are not part of your result set. You do this by specifying criteria.

There are three ways in which you can specify criteria in Query:

- Using the **Criteria→Add Criteria...** command.
- Using the **Add Criteria** button.
- Using the Criteria pane.

Whichever method you use, you create criteria which are compared against one or more columns. If the criteria matches, the row that contains the match is returned. The criteria contains one or more values in one or more columns that you wish to search for in your table.

Adding Criteria Using the Add Criteria Button

The easiest way to add criteria to a query is with the **Add Criteria** button. Although this is easy, it is also very limited, although there will be many times when you still find it very useful. The way it works is like this. You look at your 'unfiltered' query, and see a value that interests you. The example uses **CUSTMR_ID** in the **ORDERS** table. You select a cell that contains the value that you want to restrict the query to, and then select the **Add Criteria** button. MS Query restricts the query to only records that match the value in the cell where your cursor was. If you have already specified a criteria, and use the **Add Criteria** button, it is going to add an **OR** to the criteria. In other words, the criteria would read *Select the rows where FieldX = A OR Field X = B*. To add a criteria using the **Add Criteria button**, follow these steps:

STEPS

Adding Criteria Using the Add Criteria Button

1. Select a cell in your query that contains the value you want to match.
2. Select the **Add Criteria** Button.

That's it!

Adding Criteria Using the Criteria→Add Criteria... Command

If you would like to use more complex critera based on operators other than equality, the **Add Criteria** dialog box provides an interface which will help you create your criteria. The **Add Criteria** dialog box, which is illustrated in Figure 13.27 has the following major components:

- **And** option button
- **Or** option button
- **Total** drop-down list
- **Field** combo box
- **Operator** drop-down list
- **Value** edit box
- **Add** command button
- **Close** command button
- **Values...** command button.

The **And** option button is used when you want to add an additonal criteria for a column. In other words, all other criteria **and** the new criteria must be true. The **Or** option button is used when you want the old criteria **or** the new criteria to be true. The **Total** drop-down list is for creating a criteria based on a calculated field. The **Field** combo box is used to select the field that you want the criteria applied against. The **Operator** drop-down list is used to specify which comparison operator you want your criteria to use. The **Value** edit box allows you to type in a value, list of values,

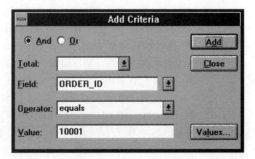

FIGURE 13.27
Add Criteria dialog box.

MICROSOFT QUERY AS A STAND-ALONE APPLICATION

or expression that you wish to use in the criteria. The **Values...** command button displays the dialog box illustrated in Figure 13.28. It queries the table and provides a list of values that you can choose to have added to the **Value** edit box. It should be noted that the **Values** list box allows multiple selections, which means you can copy several values to the **Value** edit box, if it is appropriate for the operator you have selected. (The *is one of* operator is an example of one which allows multiple values.) The **Add** command button adds the criteria to the query, and allows you to add more during the same session. The **Close** command button closes the **Add Criteria** dialog box. To add a criteria, using the **Criteria→Add Criteria...** command, follow the steps below.

HINT *For more information on comparison operators, see Chapter 3, Filtering.*

STEPS

Adding Criteria Using the Criteria→Add Criteria... Command

1. Select **Criteria→Add Criteria...**.
2. Select the proper conjunction operator (**And/Or**).
3. Select an aggregate function from the **Total** drop-down list. This is not required.
4. Select the field you would like to compare from the **Field** combo box.
5. Select the comparison operator you would like to use from the **Operator** drop-down list.
6. Type a value in the **Value** edit box.
7. Select **Add.**
8. Select **Close.**

Adding Criteria Using the Criteria Pane

For your most complex criteria, you should work directly with the **Criteria pane**. Once you understand the components which you need to build criteria, you will probably find that you never use the other two methods. The

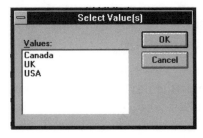

FIGURE 13.28
Select Values dialog box.

interface which MS Query uses for the Criteria pane is known as a **Query By Example (QBE)** grid. This is because you define the comparison criteria by placing examples of what you want to search for on the QBE grid. The QBE grid consists of two parts:

- One row, which defines criteria field.
- One or more rows, which define comparison criteria.

Criteria fields are the fields that you want to search against. The **Values** row(s), which are used to define your **Comparison criteria**, are contained in row(s) below the criteria fields. MS Query allows you to specify only eight rows of comparison criteria. If you need to list more than eight values that you would like to compare for, you need to use a function such as **Like()**. Each cell in the grid which contains comparison criteria contains two components:

- Comparison operator
- Comparison value (or formula).

Using the QBE grid is a two step process:

- Add the field that you want to compare.
- Add the criteria that you want use in the comparison.

There are two ways that you can add a field to the QBE grid:

- Drag a field from the Table pane.
- Select a field one from the drop-down list that appears when you select a criteria field.

To enter a comparison criteria, all you do is type the comparison operator, followed by the comparison value, in a cell below the criteria field you wish to match. To build a comparison criteria using the Criteria pane, follow the steps below.

STEPS

Building a Comparison Criteria Using the Criteria Pane

1. Make sure that the Criteria pane is displayed.
2. Drag the field that you want to use from the Table pane to the criteria field.
3. Type your first operator and value in the Value row.

4. Type your **or** operator and value in the second value row.

Removing Criteria

There are two ways that you can remove criteria:

- Using the **Criteria→Remove All Criteria** command.
- Selecting and then deleting columns in the Criteria pane.

To remove criteria, follow the steps below.

STEPS

Removing All Criteria Using the *Criteria→Remove All Criteria* Command

1. Select **Criteria→Remove All Criteria**.

STEPS

Removing Criteria Using the Criteria Pane

1. Select the column(s) of the criteria you would like to remove.
2. Press **Delete**. The criteria will be deleleted.

Sorting

Sorting allows you to change the order that your data is displayed in. Sorting is applied on a column by column basis. You can apply more than one sort to a query, so that as data is grouped together, subgroups can then be sorted. The order that your columns appears in in the data pane, has no impact on sorting. If you change the order of the columns after you apply sorting, this will have no impact on your sorting. If you do not apply a sort, the data will be sorted in the order in which it physically exists in the underlying table.

In MS Query, there are two kinds of sorts that you can apply to a column:

- Ascending
- Descending.

For more information on ascending and descending sorts, see Chapter 2, Sorting. There are two ways you can apply a sort to a query:

- The **Sort Ascending** and **Sort Descending** buttons
- The **Records→Sort...** command.

Each time you apply a sort to a single column using either method, you can either overwrite all existing sorts, or add an additional sort to the list of existing sorts. The new sort will be performed after all other existing sorts. To add sorts to a query, follow the steps below.

STEPS Sorting a Single Column, Using the Sort Buttons

1. Place your cursor anywhere in the column you want to sort by.
2. Select either the **Sort Ascending** or **Sort Descending** button, as is appropriate for the outcome you seek.

That's it! If you now repeat these steps on another column, the original sort will be replaced by the new sort.

STEPS Sorting a Single Column, Using the Records→Sort... Command

1. Select **Records→Sort...**. The dialog box illustrated in Figure 13.29 will be displayed.
2. Select the column that you want to apply a sort to, from the **Column** drop-down list.
3. Select either the **Ascending** or **Descending** option button, as is appropriate for the outcome you seek.

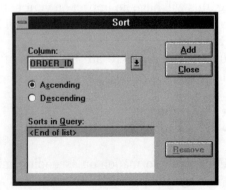

FIGURE 13.29
The **Sort** dialog box.

4. Select **Add**. Note that the sort has been added to the **Sorts in Query** list box.
5. Select **Close**.

STEPS

Sorting Additional Columns, Using the Sort Buttons

1. Place your cursor anywhere in the column you want to sort by.
2. Hold down **Control** while simultaneously selecting either the **Sort Ascending** or **Sort Descending** button, as is appropriate for the outcome you seek.

The sort you just created has been added to the other sorts.

STEPS

Sorting Multiple Columns, in a Single Step, Using the Sort Buttons

1. Arrange the columns that you want to sort, in the order that you want to sort them.
2. Select all of the columns that you want to sort.
3. Select either the **Sort Ascending** or **Sort Descending** button, as is appropriate for the outcome you seek.

The columns will be sorted in a left-to-right order. At this point, you could now re-order your columns, and the query will still retain the sorts in the correct order.

STEPS

Removing a Sort, Using the Records→Sort... Command

1. Select **Records→Sort...**. The **Sort** dialog box will be displayed.
2. Select the sort that you want to remove from the **Sorts in Query** list box.
3. Select **Remove**.
4. Repeat Steps two through three for any additional sorts you want to remove.
5. Select **Close**.

If you have multiple sorts, and would like to change the order they are applied in, you must delete and re-create the sort(s) that you wish to move.

Joining Multiple Tables

Joining is the process of linking two related tables together. In correctly designed relational tables, data is never duplicated within the same table. Take the Nwind database (either the DBF files that ship with MS Query, or the MS Access version). Each customer has a single record in the **Customer** table, and is uniquely identified by a **Customer ID** field. There is a separate **Orders** table which stores information like what the order data is, what the ship date is, and what customer the order is for. Instead of actually placing the customer name in the **Orders** table, you use a **Customer ID**. This is because **Customer ID** is the primary key of the **Customer** table. Why isn't the customer's name in the **Orders** table? Since each customer can have more than one order, this could lead to replicated data. This would take longer to enter, take up more storage space, and be prone to data anamolies. What if a clerk misspells a customer's name when taking an order?

To join two (or more) tables together, you need a common field. This is the **foreign key**. Although the fields do not need to have the same name (although they often will), they do need to have the same datatype. Would you expect a database server to be able match up a field which contains binary objects (such as video clips), with a field that has integers? In some cases, a match is possible if the data in one of the fields is converted to another datatype. If you have a text field that contains values like "*1*", "*2*," and "*3*," there is a very good likelihood that this data could be converted to an integer datatype, and tested for equivalance against a numeric datatype. If Query finds a primary key in one table, and a field with a matching name in another, Query automatically creates a join for you. If your tables do not meet this criteria, you can still manually create the join. When you join tables in a query, the result is a set (or temporary table) that contains data from both tables that you specify.

The question is, how can you view all of the order information, and the customer's name, contact, and phone number? Since both of these tables have a **Customer ID** field, you can use this common field to link them together. When adding the second table to the table window, a **join line** is automatically created for you, as illustrated in Figure 13.30.

MICROSOFT QUERY AS A STAND-ALONE APPLICATION

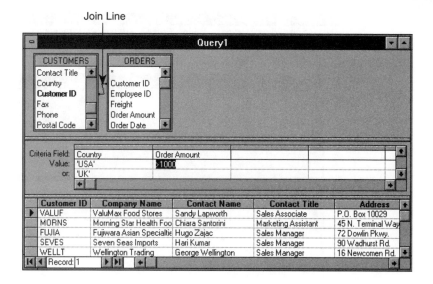

FIGURE 13.30
Equi join based on Customer ID.

> **NOTE** It is important to note that MS Query does not allow you to edit tables in a query that contains multiple tables. In MS Query, this capability is purely for information retrieval purposes. If you try to edit any data in a multiple table query, a message box will be displayed. If you need to edit multiple-table queries, you should consider using Microsoft Access, which has this capability.

In this section, four primary types of **joins** will be covered:

- Equi joins
- Outer joins
- Self joins
- Unrestricted joins.

Equi Joins

An **equi join** is one in which the columns being joined are compared for equality. All columns from both tables are returned in the result set if the columns compared are equal. If the query is modified to exclude the duplicate join column, the query is then called a **natural join**. This form of join effectively combines the information from the two tables. Examine the data illustrated in the table in Figures 13.31 and 13.32. These two simple tables contain a field which is used to uniquely identify the row. When these two tables are joined using an equi join, the data set illustrated in Figure 13.33 results. In a real world situation, you would not include the field where the tables are joined twice. You would only display this natural

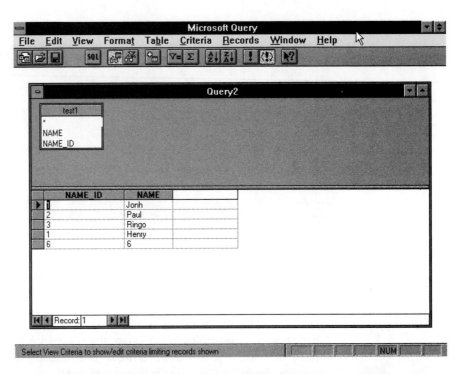

FIGURE 13.31 Test1 table.

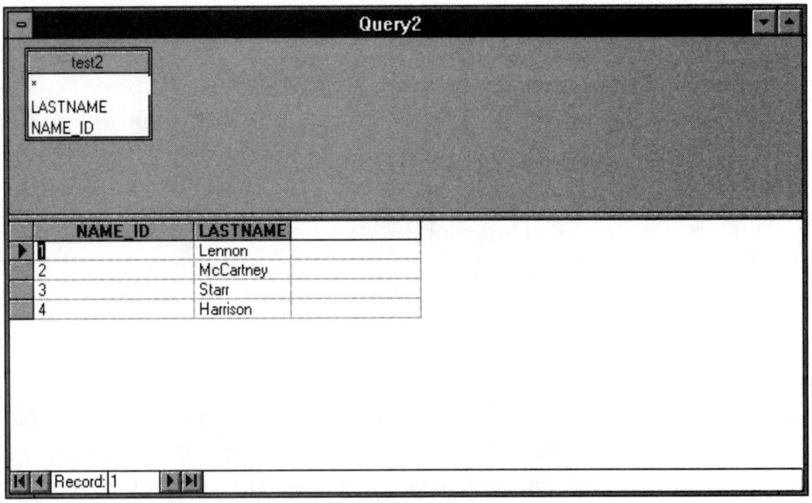

FIGURE 13.32 Test2 table.

join once. The natural join of the previous example is illustrated in Figure 13.34.

Depending on whether or not our table(s) already have keys defined, Query will or will not automatically create joins for you. If one of your tables contains a primary key, and the other table contains a field with the same name, Query will try to create an equi join for you. Sometimes, if the fields

MICROSOFT QUERY AS A STAND-ALONE APPLICATION

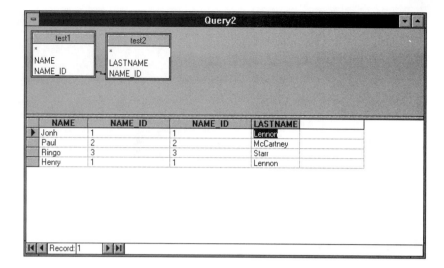

FIGURE 13.33
The result of joining **Test1** and **Test2**, using **NAME_ID** as the common field.

contain different datatypes, and an implicit conversion cannot be performed, the join will not be completed. If Query cannot automatically create the join for you, you can still manually create it. This is what you will need to do when your tables don't have a primary key defined, or if the field names are different (for example, you call a common field **ManagerID** in one table, and **EmployeeID** in another table, even though they both really identify an **Employee ID**).

STEPS Letting Query Build the Joins Automatically

1. Create a new query (this example uses Nwind).
2. Add *orders.dbf* and *customer.dbf*. Notice that as soon as you add the second table, a line is drawn between the two tables.
3. Close the **Add Tables** dialog box.
4. Expand the Table pane.
5. Resize each of the tables' field lists so that you can see all of the fields in each table. Note the line that connects **CUSTMR_ID** in both tables.
6. Add the **ORDER_ID**, **COMPANY**, **DATE_SENT** and **DUE_DATE** fields the Data pane. Note that you don't have to include the joined fields in the query's result set, although you might want to, just to verify that the result set is correct.

If Query doesn't automatically create a join for you (usually because

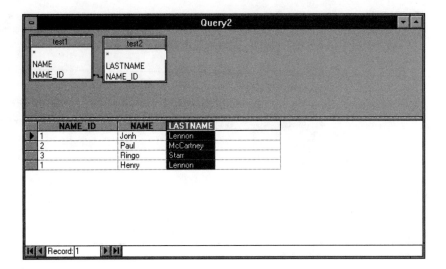

FIGURE 13.34
The result of using a natural join to join Test1 and Test2.

you don't have a primary key defined), there are two ways you can manually create one:

- By dragging the join field from one table to the other.
- By using the **Table→Joins...** command.

The dragging method can only be used to create an equi join by default, although the join can be easily modified after it is created. The **Table→Join...** command also creates an equi join by default, but since you use a dialog box in this process, you can quickly create outer joins, or an inner join based on another operator. This will be detailed later in this chapter. To create an equi join manually, follow the steps below.

STEPS Creating an Equi Join by Dragging

1. Make sure that both of the tables are in the Table pane.
2. Re-size the field lists, or scroll their contents so that you can see the source and target field names.
3. Click on the source field (usually from the left table), and drag it to the target field (usually the right table). Remember that the field name does not have to be identical.
4. Release the mouse. The join line will be drawn. Be careful to drop the source field over the correct target field. It is easy to 'miss,' and drop it on the field that is either above or below the target. This can lead to an unexpected result set.

STEPS

Creating an Equi Join by Using the Table→Join Command

1. Make sure that both of the tables are in the Table pane. If you select a field in one of the tables, it will be the default selection in the **Left** drop-down list, in the **Joins** dialog box.

HINT

*If you select a field in one of the tables before invoking the **Joins** dialog box, it will be the default selection in the **Left** combo box, which determines the "left" side of the join.*

2. Select **Table→Join....** The dialog **Joins** box will be displayed. Note the text in the first (**1**) option of the **Join Includes** option group. This is a verbose description of the join that will be created, based on your selections in the **Left**, **Operator**, and **Right** controls.
3. Select the source table and field from the **Left** combo list.
4. Select the target table and field from the **Right** combo list.
5. Select **Add**.
6. Select **Close**.

The equi joins described above are also known as **inner joins**. Both terms are correct, although technically speaking, an inner join can use a comparison operator other than equal to. You can use any of the comparison operators listed in Table 13.5. If, for example, you choose <>, this would be the same as performing a **Cartesian join**, which is described later in this chapter.

To change the comparison operator in a join, all you have to do is to change the operator in the **Operator** drop-down list, in the **Joins** dialog box. You can do this when you are first using the dialog to create a join, or after a join has been created.

TABLE 13.5
Comparison Operators

Operator	Description
<	Less than
<=	Less than or equal to
>	Greater than
>=	Greater than or equal to
=	Equal
<>	Not equal to

Outer Joins

In equi joins, or normal joins, any rows that do not match the search conditions are excluded from the result set. Often, however, it is useful to see these rows. For example, in the Nwind database, if you want to see a list of customers and their orders, customers that have not placed orders should still be included in the result set. In particular, by using a criteria that looks at a period of time, you can find out which customers haven't placed an order in the past six months. A normal join would exclude any customers without orders. A join which includes all of the records from one of the tables which are joined, even if there are no matches, is called an **Outer join**. There are two kinds of outer joins that Query supports:

- RIGHT OUTER JOINS
- LEFT OUTER JOINS.

In a RIGHT OUTER JOIN, all records from the right table are included, while only matching records from the left table are included. On the other hand, in a LEFT OUTER JOIN, all records from the left table are included, while only matching records from the right table are included.

Figure 13.35 illustrates a RIGHT OUTER JOIN between the Customer table, and the **Orders** table. NULL values are used to fill in the missing

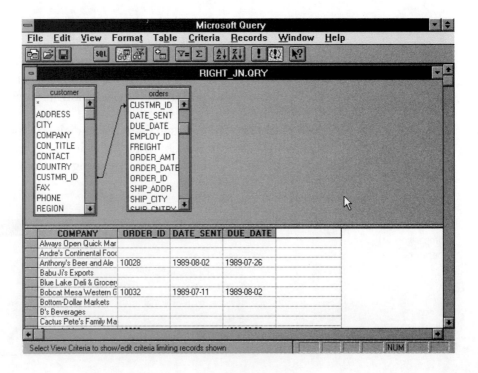

FIGURE 13.35
RIGHT OUTER JOIN.

data. Note that the join line now has a right pointing arrow on its right end. Also note that for those customers with no orders, the **ORDER_ID**, **DATE_SENT**, and **DUE_DATE** columns are NULL (indicated as a blank cell in Query).

Figure 13.36 illustrates a LEFT OUTER JOIN between the **Customer** table, and the **Orders** table. Note that the join line now has a left pointing arrow on its left end. As you expect, all orders are included, even if there is no corresponding company with a matching ID. In Figure 13.37, the order of the columns has been changed slightly to make the data more meaningful.

MS Query makes creating outer joins very easy, by giving you some hints in the **Joins** dialog box. You cannot create an OUTER JOIN by clicking-and-dragging, but you can change an existing join so that it beomes an OUTER JOIN. If you want to create an OUTER JOIN from scratch, apply the methods below to invoke the **Joins** dialog box. It has to be created from the **Joins** dialog box.

To modify a join after it has been created, you have three ways to invoke the **Joins** dialog box:

- Double-click on the join line you want to edit.
- Select the join line you want to edit, and then select **Table→Join...**.

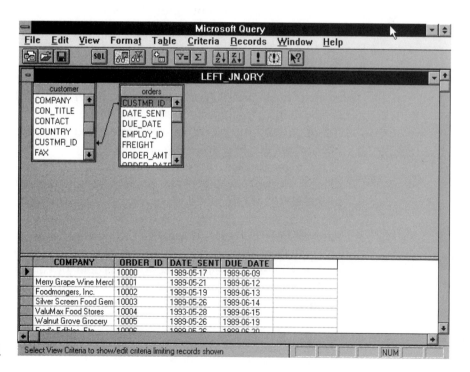

FIGURE 13.36
LEFT OUTER JOIN.

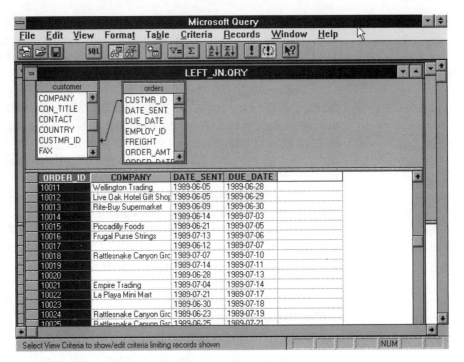

FIGURE 13.37
LEFT OUTER JOIN, columns reorganized.

- Select **Table→Join...**, and then select the query you want to edit from the **Joins in Query** list box.

Self Joins

Self joins allow the linking of a table to itself. While this may seem odd, it is often quite useful. For example, consider the **EMPLOYEE** table in Nwind. It includes fields for both an employee and the employee's manager. Although each record, which is uniquely identified by the **EMPLOY_ID** field, stores the employee's first and last names, it does not store the name of the manager. This is because a single manager can have many subordinates. Because managers are employees, each manager's name is stored in the **EMPLOYEE** table. As such, each record contains a reference to another employee through the **REPORTS_TO** field. This field really contains an **EMPLOY_ID**. What if you want to know the name of an employee's manager? You can find this out by creating a self join, or a join in which a table is linked to itself. In Access, this is done by adding a second instance of the table to your query, and then joining the two fields together. To create a self join, follow these steps:

MICROSOFT QUERY AS A STAND-ALONE APPLICATION

NOTE *Table aliases are described in more detail in Chapters 9 and 14.*

STEPS

Creating a Self Join

1. Create a new query.
2. Add the first instance of the table.
3. Add the second instance of the table. The message box illustrated in Figure 13.38 will be displayed.
4. Select **OK**.
5. Create or modify the join.
6. Add your fields and criteria.

Unrestricted Joins

In an **unrestricted join**, there are no matching values in the field that are used for matching rows in each table. An unrestricted join's result set is the **Cartesian product** of the tables you are joining. If you have two tables, one with ten rows and one with twenty rows, the resulting set would contain two hundred rows (10 * 20). For more information on unrestricted joins, see Chapter 13, Structured Query Language Basics.

Removing a Join

There are two ways to remove a join:

- Direct manipulation
- The **Joins** dialog box.

To directly remove a join, simply click on it, and press **Delete**. To remove a join from the **Joins** dialog box, follow these steps:

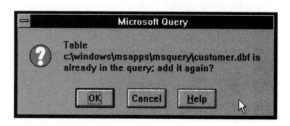

FIGURE 13.38
Table c:\windows\ms apps\msQuery.\customer.dbf is already in the query; add it again? message box.

STEPS

Removing a Join via the Joins Dialog Box

1. Select **Table→Joins....** The **Joins** dialog box will be displayed.
2. Select the join you want to remove, from the **Joins in Query** list box.
3. Select **Remove**.

Formatting Query Windows

You can format the Data pane of your query window to fit the data you are retrieving. You can set:

- The font type.
- The font size.
- The font style.
- The height of all rows.
- The width of individual columns.
- Whether a column is visible or hidden.

Setting the Display Font

By default, all text and data in the Data pane is displayed in an eight point MS Sans Serif font. Although there will be many situations in which you find this default acceptable, there will also be many times when you want to change it. You cannot change the display font of individual cells or columns. All text in the Data pane uses the same display font. To change the font properties, follow the steps below:

STEPS

Setting the Display Font

1. Select **Format→Font....** The dialog box illustrated in Figure 13.39 will be displayed.
2. Select a font from the **Font** combo box. Note that as you make selections in this dialog box, they are previewed in the **Sample** area.
3. Select a style from the **Font Style** combo box.
4. Select a size from the **Size** combo box.
5. Select the **Underline** check box, if you would like the text underlined.
6. Select **OK**.

MICROSOFT QUERY AS A STAND-ALONE APPLICATION

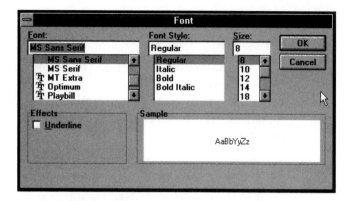

FIGURE 13.39
Font dialog box.

> **NOTE**
> *If the row **Standard Height** property is checked (set to **True**), row height will automatically be adjusted whenever the display font requires it to change.*

Setting Row Height

All columns in the data window have the same height. There are two reasons why you would want to change the height of a row:

- If you want the data in a field to scroll, within the field's cell.
- If you change the font type, style, or size.

By default, rows have a **Standard Height** property which is set to **True**, that automatically changes the height of all rows every time you change the font formatting (if necessary). If you increase the column height and decrease the column width, long data will scroll to additional lines within the field's cell. There are two ways that you can change the height of a row:

- By dragging a row border.
- By using the **Format→Row Height...** command.

To change the height of a row, follow the steps below.

STEPS

Changing Row Height by Dragging

1. Move the cursor to the record selector section of the Data pane. Note that as you move the cursor over the row borders, it changes to a double headed arrow.
2. Click on a row border and drag it to the new height that you want.
3. Release the mouse.

STEPS

Changing the Height of a Row Using the Format→Row Height... Command

1. Select **Format→Row Height...**. The dialog box illustrated in Figure 13.40 will be displayed.
2. Type a new height in the **Row Height** edit box. The row height number is in points, just like font sizes. A point is 1/72 of an inch.
3. Select **OK**.

You can return the **Standard Height** property back to its default state **(on)** by clicking on the **Standard Height** check box in the **Row Height** dialog box.

Setting Column Width

Unlike rows, each column in the Data pane can have its own unique width. There are two basic ways you can set a column's width:

- Direct manipulation
- The **Format→Column Width...** command.

Direct manipulation includes dragging a column's border, as well as double-clicking on it. You can also change the width one column at a time, or by setting several contiguous columns to the same width. To change the width of a column by dragging its border or typing a column width into the **Column Width** dialog box, follow the steps below.

STEPS

Changing the Width of a Single Column by Dragging its Border

1. Move the cursor to the column headings. Notice that as you move over the column borders, the cursor changes to a double-headed arrow.
2. Click and drag on the right border of the column you want to change.
3. Release the mouse when the column is the width you desire.

FIGURE 13.40
Row Height dialog box.

MICROSOFT QUERY AS A STAND-ALONE APPLICATION 293

STEPS

Changing the Width of a Several Columns by Dragging a Single Column's Border

1. Select several contiguous columns by dragging over their column headings.
2. Click and drag on the border of one of the columns you want to change.
3. Release the mouse when the column is the width you desire. All of the columns will be re-sized.

STEPS

Changing the Width of a Single Column Using the Format→Column Width... Command

1. Move the cursor to the column headings. Notice that as you move over the column headings, the cursor changes to a single-headed arrow that points down.
2. Click on the column you want to change.
3. Select **Format→Column Width...**. The dialog box illustrated in Figure 13.41 will be displayed.
4. Type a new width in the **Column Width** edit box. The width is the number of characters you would like the column to display, based on the display font.
5. Select **OK**.

STEPS

Changing the Width of a Several Columns Using the Format→Column Width... Command

1. Select several contiguous columns by dragging over their column headings.
2. Select **Format→Column Width...**. The **Column Width** dialog box illustrated will be displayed.
3. Type a new width in the **Column Width** edit box. This width will be applied to all of the columns in the selection.
4. Select **OK**.

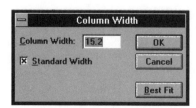

FIGURE 13.41
Column Width dialog box.

Query also has a **best fit** feature which can be used to automatically change the width of a column to accomodate the widest piece of data on the screen. This feature can be invoked by:

- Double-clicking on a column header's border.
- Selecting the **Best Fit** button in the **Column Width** dialog box.

When you use the best fit feature, Query does not look at the whole result set. It only looks at the current screen. As such, as you navigate through your result set, you will probably have to adjust the width of any columns that were sized using best fit. To use best fit to automatically change the width of a column, follow the steps below.

STEPS — Using Best Fit on a Single Column via Double-Clicking

1. Double-click on the right border of the column you want to change.

STEPS — Using Best Fit on Several Columns via Double-Clicking

1. Select several contiguous columns by dragging over their column headings.
2. Double-click on the border of one of the columns you want to change. All of the columns will be re-sized.

STEPS — Using Best Fit on a Single Column via the Format→Column Width... Command

1. Move the cursor to the column headings. Notice that as you move over the column headings, the cursor changes to a single-headed arrow that points down.
2. Click on the column you want to change.
3. Select **Format→Column Width...** The **Column Width** dialog box will be displayed.
4. Select **Best Fit**.

STEPS

Using Best Fit on Several Columns via the Format→Column Width... Command

1. Select several contiguous columns by dragging over their column headings.
2. Select **Format→Column Width...**. The **Column Width** dialog box will be displayed.
3. Select **Best Fit.** This width will be applied to all of the columns in the selection.

You can also set a column's width back to its default size by selecting the **Standard Width** check box, in the **Column Width** dialog box. Whenever you modify the width of a column, this check box is de-selected.

Hiding and Showing Columns

There will be times when you want to hide one or more columns. Perhaps you want to use a column as a basis for a calculation, but do not want to display it in the result set. By selecting two or more contiguous columns, you can hide several columns in a single step. To hide a column, follow the steps below.

STEPS

Hiding a Column

1. Select the column you want to hide (either the whole column, or any cell within the column).
2. Select **Format→Hide Columns**.

After hiding one or more columns, you may find yourself wanting to show them again, at some later point in time. To show a column that you have hidden, follow the steps below.

STEPS

Showing a Hidden Column

1. Select **Format→Show Columns...**. The dialog box illustrated in Figure 13.42 will be displayed. Columns which are visible, have a check next to them. Columns that are hidden, have no check.
2. Select a column you would like to show.
3. Select **Show**. You can also hide fields using the **Hide** button.

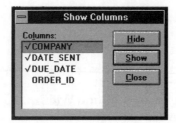

FIGURE 13.42
Show Columns dialog box.

4. Repeat Steps two through three until all of the columns you want to show have checks next to them.
5. Select **Close**.

Output

Printing

MS Query does not offer the capability to print queries. That is because Query was designed to get data into another application. You can, however, print by either copying and pasting data to another application, or using an application like MS Word 6.0 or Excel 5.0 which allow you to use Query to bring data into their environments.

Saving the Query Results

You can also save the query results as a table in one of the formats that Query supports. In other words, if you have the proper drivers and the correct server environment (if required), Query can save the results as virtually any data source supported by ODBC. To save the query result as a table in the format of one of your data sources, follow the steps below.

STEPS   Saving the Query Result as a Table

1. Select **File→Save As...**. The **Select Data Source** dialog box seen earlier in Chapter 12 will be displayed.
2. Select the data source you want to save the table to from the **Save As** list box.

> **X-REF** *If you would like to use a data source that is not listed, Select **Other**.... See Chapter 12, **An Overview of Using External Data**, for more information on selecting or setting up a data source.*

3. Select **Save**. Depending on the data source that you choose to save to, a different dialog box will be displayed. You might also be prompted with an additional dialog box which will prompt you for a user ID and password.
4. Type the name of your table in the **Table Name** edit box. Fill in any other options, as is appropriate for the data source you are saving to.
5. Select **Save** (for table-based data sources) or **OK** (for file-based data sources).

You can now access this table through Query, or any other application which works with the data source.

CHAPTER 14
Structured Query Language Basics

Introduction

This chapter is an introduction to **relational database technology** and **Structured Query Language (SQL)**. SQL has a relatively free-form English-like syntax, and is the industry standard language for interaction with relational databases. Extensions to the ANSI[1] SQL standard, which are specific to Microsoft SQL Server, are discussed in Chapter 15. In this chapter you will learn:

- Relational database fundamentals.
- The relational model.
- Basic data retrieval.
- How to join multiple tables in a query.
- How to summarize information in a relational database.
- Using row or scalar functions in a query.
- Basic data updating using SQL.

Topics such as relational database design, advanced query techniques (such as subqueries), and performance issues are beyond the scope of this book.

---

[1] ANSI is the American National Standards Institute. This group has established a standard level of SQL features.

Relational Database Fundamentals

SQL is an industry standard language that is used to interact with relational databases. All **relational databases** represent logically related sets of information. A relational database is organized into **tables**, with each table containing columns. Tables are in turn related to each other through **primary** and **foreign** keys.

Primary keys uniquely identify a row in a table and can be more than a single column. **Foreign keys** are columns used to link to other tables (**joins**). A join can be made to either a primary key or a foreign key.

The model often used to describe relational databases is called the **relational model**. In this model, **entities** are modeled as tables in the database. **Relationships** represent the links or joins between entities. A relationship can be one of three types:

- One to one
- One to many
- Many to many.

Relationships are modeled as either columns or tables, depending on the type of relationship. **Many to many** relationships are modeled as tables since the number of rows returned depends on the number of matching rows in both related tables. All other relationships are modeled as columns. The last portion of the relational model is the attribute. **Attributes** are qualities or descriptions of entities in the database, and are modeled as columns of tables.

In all of the examples that follow, the **pubs** database is used. This database is shipped with Microsoft SQL Server. If this database is not available, please contact your database administrator, and she or he can install it for you. An **ER** diagram of the pubs database is shown in Figure 14.1.

Rather than focusing purely on the version of SQL that is available in MS Query, this chapter uses ANSI SQL, and the extensions that are part of Transact SQL. This is to give you an idea of some of the functionality that is available with more robust database servers, such as SQL Server and Oracle. Chapter 15, specifically focuses on using SQL Server. All examples in this chapter are based on SQL Server syntax.

Basic Data Retrieval

In SQL, the **SELECT** statement is used to retrieve data from a relational database.

The general syntax of **SELECT** is:

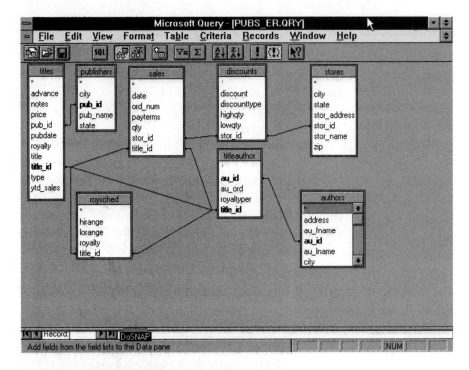

FIGURE 14.1
ER diagram of pubs database.

SELECT $\begin{bmatrix} \text{ALL} \\ \text{or} \\ \text{DISTINCT} \end{bmatrix}$ select_list[INTO table_name]

FROM table_name [,table_name ...]

[WHERE search_conditions]

[GROUP BY group_list][HAVING group_search_list]

$\left[\text{ORDER BY } column\_name \begin{bmatrix} \text{ASC} \\ \text{or} \\ \text{DESC} \end{bmatrix} \left[,column\_name \begin{bmatrix} \text{ASC} \\ \text{or} \\ \text{DESC} \end{bmatrix} ... \right] \right]$

[COMPUTE row_function(column_name)[,row_function(column_name)...]]

In the notation above, any element in square brackets ([]) is optional. The words in upper case are **keywords.** In the **SELECT** statement, as in all SQL statements, all optional keywords must be included in the same order as shown in the syntax diagram.

Choosing Columns to Retrieve

In the syntax diagram above, the first required element is the **select_list,** which is how you specify the columns (or attributes) needed for the query. The simplest form of the **select_list** is *. This is a wildcard and selects all columns in the table or tables specified in the **FROM** clause. The columns are selected in the order the columns are defined in the table. The SQL clause illustrated in Figure 14.2 will retrieve the entire **authors** table.

> **HINT** *Although wildcard selection (using the *) is done here for illustrative purposes, it is less likely to be used in actual applications than a list of columns. Specify the columns required to improve Query performance.*

The **select_list** may also be a list of columns that exist in the table you are querying. The column names must be separated by a comma. The SQL clause illustrated in Figure 14.3 will retrieve the first and last names for the entire **authors** table.

Choosing Rows to Retrieve

The next clause in the **SELECT** statement is the **WHERE** clause. Using this clause and specifying **search_conditions** will restrict the rows chosen for the result set. Only the rows matching the **search_condition** specified in the **WHERE** clause will be returned. The general form of the **search_condition** is:

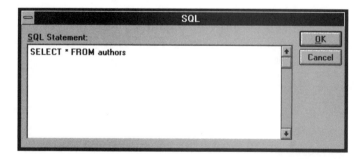

FIGURE 14.2
A basic **SELECT** statement.

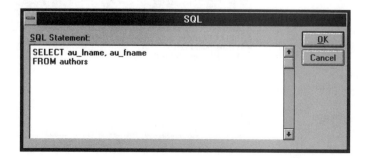

FIGURE 14.3
A **SELECT** statement with a column list.

WHERE *expression1 comparison_operator expression2*

where:

- **expression1** and **expression2** are column names, calculations, or constants (text constants are enclosed in " ").
- **comparison_operator** is one of the operators listed in Table 14.1, which compare two expressions.

The SQL clause illustrated in Figure 14.4 will retrieve all the infor-

TABLE 14.1 Comparison Operators

Operator	Meaning
=	Equal to
>	Greater than
<	Less than
>=	Greater than or equal to
<=	Less than or equal to
<>, !=	Not equal to
!>	Not greater than
!<	Not less than
()	Precedence control
NOT	Logical negative
LIKE	Pattern matching
BETWEEN	Inclusive range
NOT BETWEEN	Exclusive range
IS NULL	Checks for data
IN	List matching
AND	Joins two search conditions, returning true when both are true
OR	Joins two search conditions, returning true when either is true.

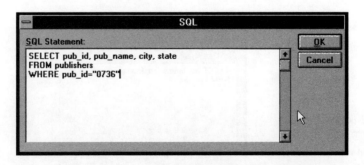

FIGURE 14.4
A **SELECT** statement which included a **WHERE** clause.

mation about publisher "0736". The result of this query is illustrated. Additional examples of search conditions are presented in the next sections.

Advanced Searching Techniques

The following advanced searching techniques can give you more precise results.

AND/OR

Often a single search condition is not sufficient to produce the proper result set. When this is the situation, **multiple search conditions** can be combined with the **AND** and **OR** conjunctions. If all conditions joined by **AND** clauses are **True,** the row is selected. In contrast, the row is selected if any condition joined by an **OR** is **True.** SQL's order of evaluation is:

- Expressions in parenthesis.
- Expressions modified by **NOT.**
- Expressions joined by **AND.**
- Expressions joined by **OR.**
- Reading from left to right.

HINT *Queries using multiple search conditions joined by **AND/OR** operators can be very difficult to interpret. To make sure SQL interprets a query the way you intended, always use parenthesis to control the order of evaluation.*

The next example will use multiple search conditions to further restrict the result set. The SQL clause illustrated in Figure 14.5 will retrieve all business and computer books from the **titles** table.

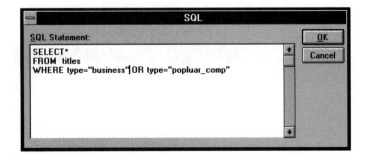

FIGURE 14.5
An Example of an
OR clause.

NOT

The **NOT** clause is used to negate or reverse the normal result of a query. For example, the query used in the section above selects all computer and business title information. The SQL clause illustrated in Figure 14.6 will retrieve all titles except computer and business titles. The parenthesis is used to ensure the query produced the expected results.

> **HINT**
>
> Using **NOT** can dramatically increase the execution cost of a query. **NOT** forces a complete scan of either the index or the table in order to select the rows. Use **NOT** when the result set has already been reduced by other constraints on indexed columns, where possible.

LIKE

The **LIKE** clause provides a very powerful tool for querying tables. **LIKE** allows the use of patterns in the data to select rows. Simple examples include selecting any name starting with **A** or any name ending in **son.** LIKE accomplishes this pattern matching through the use of wildcards. A **wildcard** is a character or group of characters that can stand for another character or group of characters. The **LIKE** wildcards and their use are defined in Table 14.2.

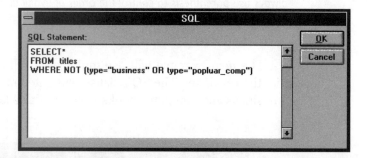

FIGURE 14.6
An example of a NOT clause.

TABLE 14.2
LIKE Wildcards

Wildcard	Use
%	Match any group of one or more characters.
_ (Underscore)	Match any one character.
[]	Match any one character in the range or set.
[^]	Match any one character not in the range or set.

STRUCTURED QUERY LANGUAGE BASICS

The SQL clause illustrated in Figure 14.7 will retrieve all titles having **computer** or **Computer**.

Table 14.3 shows several additional examples of the use of the wildcard facility provided by **LIKE**.

> **HINT** *The wildcards used in SQL queries do not function the same way DOS wildcards do.*

BETWEEN and NOT BETWEEN

Some queries require selecting rows based upon a range of values, either inside or outside of the end points. In SQL, **BETWEEN** and **NOT BETWEEN** provide this facility. **BETWEEN** selects rows based upon a range of values inside the end points. **NOT BETWEEN** selects rows based upon a range of values outside the end points.

Advanced readers will notice that the same result can be achieved by using standard comparison operators (i.e., $<=, >=$ **and** $>=, <=$). While this is true, using these keywords will make code easier to understand and maintain, with no impact on performance. The SQL clause illustrated in Figure 14.8 will retrieve all the books published between June 1, 1985 and June 30, 1985, inclusive.

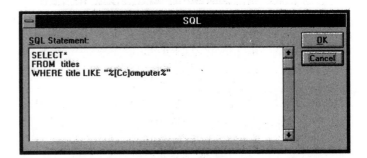

FIGURE 14.7
An example of a **LIKE** clause.

TABLE 14.3
LIKE Wildcard Examples

Wildcard	Results
'Mc%'	Any data beginning with 'Mc'.
'%son'	Any data ending with 'son'.
'M[cC]%'	Any data beginning with either 'Mc' or 'MC'.
'____'	Any item with exactly 4 characters.
'%chocolate%'	Any item containing the string 'chocolate'.

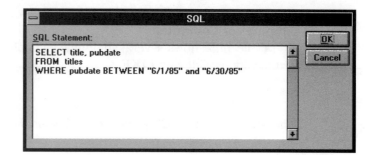

FIGURE 14.8
An example of a **BETWEEN** clause.

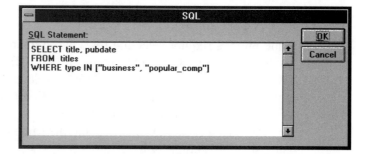

FIGURE 14.9
An example of an **IN** clause.

IN

The **IN** keyword allows the query to specify a list of values that should be chosen from. This can also be accomplished by using the **OR** conjunction to chain together a group of equality tests. As with **BETWEEN,** using **IN** makes the code easier to read and maintain in the future. The SQL clause illustrated in Figure 14.9 is the query from Figure 14.4, realigned to use **IN** rather than **OR.**

Joining Multiple Tables

The definition of a relational database is that data is divided into tables. Therefore, there must be a way of combining these tables back into information rather than disjointed bits of data. In SQL, this is done by joining tables together. A **join** is accomplished by adding the additional table or tables to the **FROM** clause of the **SELECT** statement, and then specifying how the tables are to be matched in the **WHERE** clause. The columns used for this matching process are called **keys.** In this section, four primary types of joins will be covered:

- Equi joins
- Outer joins

- Self joins
- Unrestricted joins.

Equi Joins

An **equi join** is one where the columns being joined are compared for equality. All columns from both tables are returned in the result set if the columns compared are equal. If the **SELECT** statement is modified to exclude the duplicate join column, the query is then called a **natural join.** This form of join effectively combines the information from the two tables.

The SQL clause illustrated in Figure 14.10 will retrieve all titles, prices, and the publishers' names. Since the publishers' names are contained in the **publishers** table, the query will join the **titles** table to the **publishers** table. Note that the **WHERE** clause doesn't just specify the column names to compare. Since the column names are the same, they must be qualified with the table name in order for SQL to distinguish them. This form of qualification can be used anywhere a column is used. The full form of qualifications is actually *database.owner.table.column_name*. This allows the use of columns from other databases as well as other tables in this database.

Outer Joins

In equi joins, or normal joins, any rows that do not match the search conditions are excluded from the result set. Often, however, it is useful to see these rows. For example, in a human resources database, a query listing employees and dependents should list an employee regardless of whether that employee has dependents or not. A normal join would exclude any employees without dependents. This form of join is an outer join.

Few SQL implementations allow this form of join, though Microsoft Query, Access, and SQL Server do, as does ODBC. In SQL Server, this is done by introducing two new join operators. These operators, *= and =*,

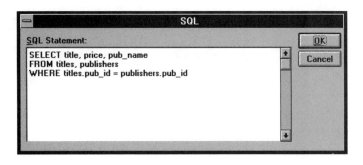

FIGURE 14.10
An example of an **equi join**.

include all rows from the left or right table respectively. **NULL** values are used to fill in the missing columns. Since this is an extension to ANSI SQL, different implementations of SQL may implement this capability differently. Query and Access use the notion of a RIGHT and LEFT OUTER JOIN to accomplish the same effect. A LEFT OUTER JOIN is equivalent to * = and a RIGHT OUTER JOIN is equivalent to = * in Query and Access.

The SQL clause illustrated in Figure 14.11 will retrieve all titles, with sales information, using SQL Server syntax. Figure 14.12 shows how Query performs this outer join. The result set is the same.

Self Joins

Self joins allow the linking of a table to itself. While this may seem odd, it is often quite useful. For example, in a database containing monthly sales figures for various branch offices, a self join is one way to calculate the monthly percentage change in sales for each branch. The SQL clause illustrated in Figure 14.13 will retrieve all rows that have sold in more than one store. In a self join, the table name appears twice in the **FROM** clause.

In order to allow SQL to distinguish the two tables, the query introduces the use of a feature called **table aliasing**. A table alias is specified after the table name in the **FROM** clause and is separated by a space from the table name. These are used for two main reasons:

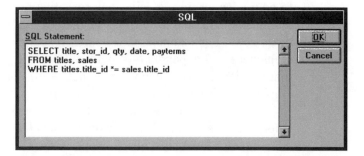

FIGURE 14.11
An SQL Server outer join.

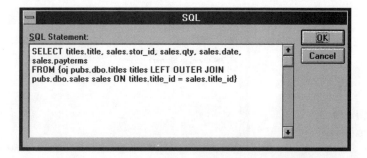

FIGURE 14.12
A Query outer join.

- To distinguish the role of a table in a self join (where it is required).
- To shorten the amount of typing in a query (because the alias can be used anywhere the table name can be).

Unrestricted Joins

The final form of the join function is the **unrestricted join,** or **Cartesian product.** This form is not often used in practice, but is an important part of the theoretical model of relational databases. Conceptually, the first step of creating a join is to create the Cartesian product. This result set contains all possible combinations of rows from both tables, regardless of matching columns. From this intermediate temporary table, the search conditions are applied to produce the desired results. In practice, all relational databases implement this more efficiently.

The SQL clause illustrated in Figure 14.14 will retrieve all stores and publishers. This query results in the implication that all stores carry all publishers, which is clearly not the case. In fact, there is no direct relationship between these two tables in the database! By using the **stores** table you could find out which stores sold which publisher's titles, but not if the book was in stock and never sold.

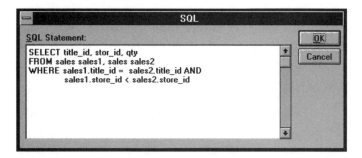

FIGURE 14.13
Example of a **self join.**

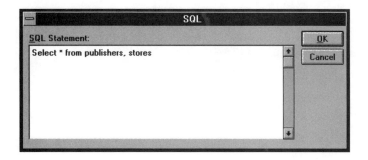

FIGURE 14.14
An example of an **unrestricted join.**

> **HINT** *This type of operation is very expensive in terms of processing overhead. The number of rows returned is the product of the number of rows in both tables. In the example above, **publishers** has four rows and **stores** has six rows. The Cartesian product of these two sets gives twenty four rows in the result set. A **WHERE** clause should always be used to reduce the processing overhead of joins.*

Sorting Information with SQL

SQL normally returns rows in the result set in the order in which they are stored in tables. Often, you will need to reorder the result set into a more effective order. In SQL, you use the **ORDER BY** clause. The syntax of **ORDER BY** is:

ORDER BY *column_name1 [DESC] [, column_name2 [DESC], ...]*

where:

- **ORDER BY** is a required keyword.
- **column_name** is the column being sorted by.
- **DESC** indicates the result should be sorted in descending order. **ASC**, or ascending order is the default.

The SQL clause illustrated in Figure 14.15 will retrieve the list of the titles in alphabetic order.

Summarizing Information with SQL

In SQL, the means for generating summaries is the **GROUP BY** clause, modified by the **HAVING** phrase. In general, any columns you specify in the **GROUP BY** clause should also be included in your **select_list** as well

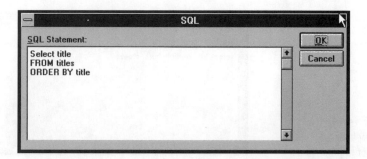

FIGURE 14.15
An example of an **ORDER BY** clause.

Structured Query Language Basics

to generate correct results. Table 14.4 lists several functions that may be used to aggregate information with the **GROUP BY** clause. The **HAVING** phrase allows restriction of the groups processed by the **GROUP BY,** and is only available with the **GROUP BY** clause.

The SQL clause illustrated in Figure 14.16 will retrieve the list of the stores which have sold more than 100 books.

This example joined the **sales** table to the **stores** table on **stor_id.** This result was then grouped by **stor_id,** and **qty** was totaled. Finally, only those stores where the total **qty** was greater than 100 were selected for the final result set.

The SQL clause illustrated in Figure 14.17 will retrieve all store names and the quantity sold.

Microsoft SQL Server provides several extensions that provide

TABLE 14.4
Aggregate Functions

Function	Description
SUM	Calculate a total.
MIN	Calculate the minimum.
MAX	Calculate the maximum.
AVG	Calculate the average.
COUNT	Calculate the number of non-null rows.

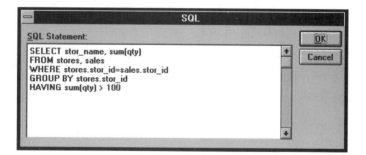

FIGURE 14.16
An example of a **GROUP BY** clause, modified by a **HAVING** clause.

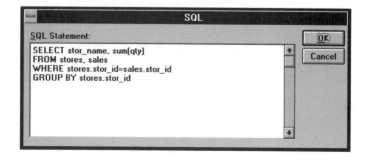

FIGURE 14.17
An example of a **GROUP BY** clause.

greater capability for summarizing information. These are described in Chapter 15.

Scalar Functions

Scalar functions are also called **row functions** because they act on data in rows to create calculated columns. The aggregate functions presented in the previous section are also known as column functions, since they act vertically on an entire column of data. In SQL, the standard arithmetic operators are available and can be used on any numeric column. The SQL clause illustrated in Figure 14.18 will retrieve all titles and prices after a 10% discount.

In addition, several other types of functions are generally provided. The specific functions provided will vary from vendor to vendor. This is the list provided with Microsoft SQL Server. The functions below will be grouped into four broad categories:

- Character
- Date
- Numeric
- System.

The following sections list some of the more commonly used functions. A complete list is provided with the documentation for your relational database.

Character Functions

The functions described in Table 14.5 are provided with SQL Server and are used to manipulate character data. Character data is stored in SQL Server as CHAR, VARCHAR, or TEXT. Other implementations of SQL may provide other capabilities.

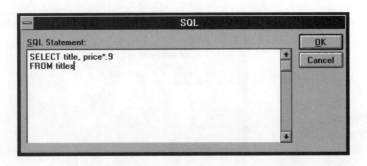

FIGURE 14.18
An example of a simple **scalar** function.

Date/Time Functions

The date and time functions shown in Table 14.6 are based on ANSI/SQL. The expressions below may be either **TIMESTAMP** columns, or strings with valid dates or times. Microsoft SQL Server provides different and more powerful date and time handling capabilities. These are defined in Chapter 15.

Numeric Functions

Table 14.7 lists functions provided by SQL Server for common numeric calculations. This is a partial list of available numeric functions. Other relational database products may provide a different capability.

TABLE 14.5 Character Functions

Function	Arguments	Description
+	text1 + text2	Concatenates text1 and text2. String constants should be enclosed in single or double quotes.
ASCII	(text)	Returns ASCII Code value of first character.
CHAR	(integer)	Converts Integer ASCII Code value to character.
CHARINDEX	(target, text)	Returns the starting position of target in expression.
LEFT	(text, integer)	Returns the leftmost integer characters of text.
LOWER	(text)	Converts the expression to lower case.
LTRIM	(text)	Removes leading blanks.
RIGHT	(text, integer)	Returns the rightmost integer characters of text.
RTRIM	(text)	Removes trailing spaces.
UPPER	(text)	Converts the expression to upper case.

TABLE 14.6 Date/Time Functions

Function	Arguments	Description
DATE	(expression)	Returns a date from the expression.
DAY	(expression)	Returns the day (1–31) from the expression.
DAYS	(expression)	Returns the Julian date representing expression.
HOUR	(expression)	Returns the hour portion of expression.
MINUTE	(expression)	Returns the minute portion of expression.
SECOND	(expression)	Returns the seconds portion of expression.
TIME	(expression)	Returns the time portion of expression.
TIMESTAMP	(expression, [expression])	Returns a timestamp.

System Functions

The functions in Table 14.8 provide a handy way to access information in system tables. These functions will be dependent on the relational database used. These are some of the functions delivered with Microsoft SQL Server.

Data Updating

This section will provide a brief overview of using SQL to maintain and update a database. In SQL, there are four commands used to maintain a database:

- INSERT
- UPDATE
- DELETE
- SELECT INTO.

TABLE 14.7 Numeric Functions

Function	Arguments	Description
SIGN	(numeric)	Returns +1, 0, or -1, depending on whether the argument is positive, zero, or negative.
ABS	(numeric)	Returns the absolute value.
ROUND	(numeric, integer)	Returns the numeric expression, rounded to integer places.
POWER	(numeric, y)	Returns numeric to the **y** power.
RAND	(integer)	Returns a random number between 0 and 1. Integer is an optional argument providing the seed.
SIN/COS/TAN	(numeric)	Returns the appropriate trigonometric result.

TABLE 14.8 System Functions

Function	Arguments	Description
DB_NAME	(database_id)	Returns the database name for the ID, or the current database if omitted.
ISNULL	(expression, value)	Returns value if expression is NULL.
USER_NAME	(user_id)	Returns the user name for the user ID, or the current user if omitted.
SUSER_NAME	(server_user_id)	Returns the server user's name for the ID, or the current server user if omitted.

INSERT

INSERT, which adds new rows to a table, has the following syntax:

INSERT [INTO] *table_name [(column_list)]*
VALUES*(constant,...)*

where:

- **INTO** is an optional keyword.
- **table_name** is the table being added to.
- **column_list** is an optional subset of the columns in **table_name** for which data is being provided.
- **VALUES** is a required keyword.
- **(constant,...)** is the list of constants (text values must be enclosed in double quotes, **""**).

The **INSERT** statement adds one row for each statement executed. Values must be entered in the same order as the **column_list,** or the table definition. Character data must be quoted. Since you must use a single **INSERT** statement for each row, this method is not efficient for large volumes of data. Every relational database provides a method for bulk data input. These tools are beyond the scope of this book. The SQL clause illustrated in Figure 14.19 will add a row to the stores table.

UPDATE

The **UPDATE** statement allows you to change the values of columns in existing rows in a single table. **UPDATE** has the following syntax:

UPDATE *table*
SET *column = expression*
WHERE *search_condition*

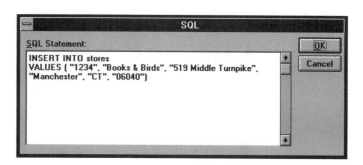

FIGURE 14.19
An **INSERT** statement.

where:

- **SET** is a required keyword.
- **column** is the column being modified.
- **expression** is a formula or constant which is the new value for column.
- **WHERE** specifies the row(s) being modified.

Therefore, with **UPDATE,** you can affect a single row, groups of rows, or all rows. The SQL clause illustrated in Figure 14.20 will increase the selling price of all books by 10%.

DELETE

The **DELETE** statement allows you to delete one or more rows from the specified table. The **DELETE** statement has the following syntax:

DELETE *table_name*
WHERE *search_condition*

where:

- **table_name** is the table affected.
- **WHERE** specifies the row(s) being deleted.

The **DELETE** statement allows you to delete one or more rows from the specified table. If the **WHERE** is omitted, all rows in the table will be deleted. The SQL clause illustrated in Figure 14.21 will delete the row inserted above.

SELECT INTO *tablename*

This section describes the use of the **INTO** *tablename* clause that is part of the general syntax for the **SELECT** statement, which was presented at the start of this chapter. This clause creates a new table (called *tablename*)

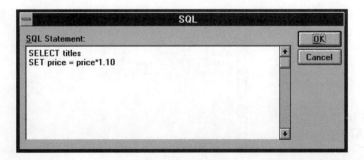

FIGURE 14.20
An **UPDATE** statement.

Structured Query Language Basics

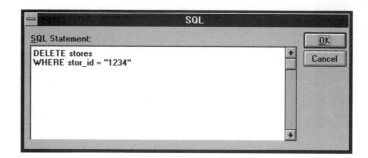

FIGURE 14.21
A **DELETE** statement.

based upon the columns listed in the **select_list.** This is a two-step operation. SQL Server first creates the empty table. The second step fills the table with the rows generated by the **SELECT** statement. If processing fails during this second step, the table will exist but be empty.

In order to create tables in your database with this statement, the **selectinto/bulkcopy** option must be turned on. Since this option effects database backup strategies, your database administrator is the only person who can enable this option. Figure 14.22 illustrates an example in which a database is selected, *selectinto/bulk copy* is enabled, and a new table is created using **SELECT INTO.**

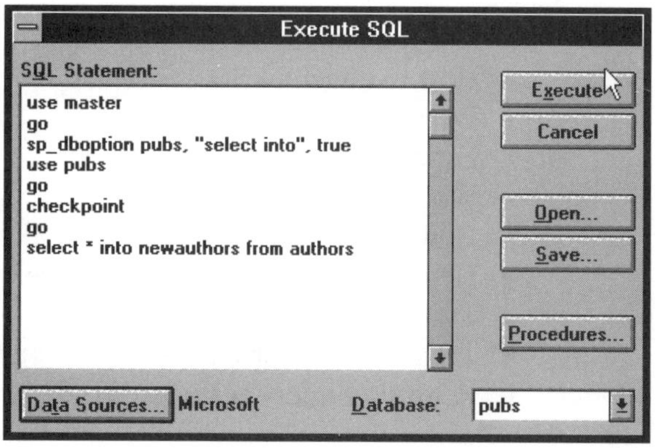

FIGURE 14.22
An example of **SELECT INTO**.

CHAPTER 15
Using SQL Server

Introduction

This chapter provides additional information specific to using SQL Server. The ANSI SQL standard allows extensions to the basic language, which most vendors make use of. This section will provide basic information on several important extensions available in SQL Server. More complete information is contained in the *Transact-SQL Reference* manual, available from Microsoft.

In this chapter you will learn:

- About client/server computing.
- How to attach to SQL Server.
- What a view is.
- How to create a view.
- What a stored procedure is.
- How to use stored procedures.
- How to create a stored procedure.
- Transact/SQL Query extensions.
- Transact/SQL programming language extensions.
- Returning query results to EXCEL.

Introduction to Client/Server Computing

Microsoft SQL Server for Windows NT is a database server which is used in a client/server environment. Using SQL Server differs from most personal computer databases in several ways. SQL Server is based on the client/server principle. This means, in most cases, that SQL Server will not be running on your personal computer but will be part of an enterprise-wide computing solution. Your queries will be packaged and sent on the network to SQL Server, which will process your request, as well as those of others, and return results to the appropriate user. Your interaction with SQL Server will typically be with a front-end program, such as Microsoft Access, Microsoft Query, or a custom application built for your organization, which manages the dialog with SQL Server.

Client/server applications imply that several components are already in place. These applications imply that your workstation (the client) is connected to another workstation (the server), which may or may not be more powerful than your workstation (the client). The connection between these two workstations is the network, a necessary component of client/server technology. This design also enables you to better control where processing is done. In the typical shared database application (file-server based, not client/server), the server provides only basic file services. All processing is done on your workstation, in many cases with the entire database being copied to it across the network. Client/server allows you to split processing between a client application (or front-end) and a server (or back-end) application. Only the results of a query need to be sent over the network to the client.

This architecture requires several pieces of information to correctly identify a query and return the results to the proper user. In addition, security information may be required to ensure the integrity of the underlying information. Depending on your configuration, some or all of these pieces of information may be optional. The first item needed is the name of the SQL Server. Your enterprise may be using several SQL Servers, so you need to know which one contains the information you need.

Secondly, in order to verify security, you will need to identify yourself with a user ID and password. This is necessary to grant you access to all appropriate objects and databases. In many installations, your user ID is the same as you use to log in to your network, and is supplied by default. If you are using Windows/NT, Windows/NTAS, or Windows for Workgroups v3.11 or later, with integrated or mixed security, you don't need to provide either your user ID or password. The security mechanisms of Windows/NT will be used to verify your security based on your login ID.

In order to attach to SQL Server, you will need to work with your enterprise's information technology support area. This group can provide you with the information and software you will need to use SQL Server.

Attaching to SQL Server

To connect a client workstation using Excel through Query to SQL Server, you must have an ODBC data source set up for your server. An overview of ODBC and how to define data sources was covered in Chapter 12, An Overview of Using External Data. To connect to a SQL Server which already has an ODBC data source defined, follow the steps below.

STEPS

Connecting to a SQL Server from MS Query

1. Launch MS Query.
2. Select **File→New Query....** Figure 15.1 illustrates the **Select Data Source** dialog box.
3. If your data source is in the list of **Available Data Sources,** select it. Otherwise, select **Other....** The ODBC **Data Sources** dialog box will be displayed.
4. Select the data source from the list, and select **OK.** If it is not listed, see Chapter 12, An Overview of Using External Data. Figure 15.2 illustrates the **SQL Server Login** dialog box.
5. Select **Login ID:** and enter your SQL Server ID.
6. Select **Password** and enter your password for SQL Server. Your enterprise's information technology support area can provide you with this information.
7. After successfully logging in, you may start to define your query by

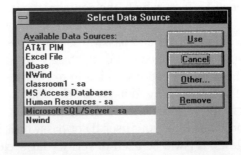

FIGURE 15.1
Query Select Data Source dialog box.

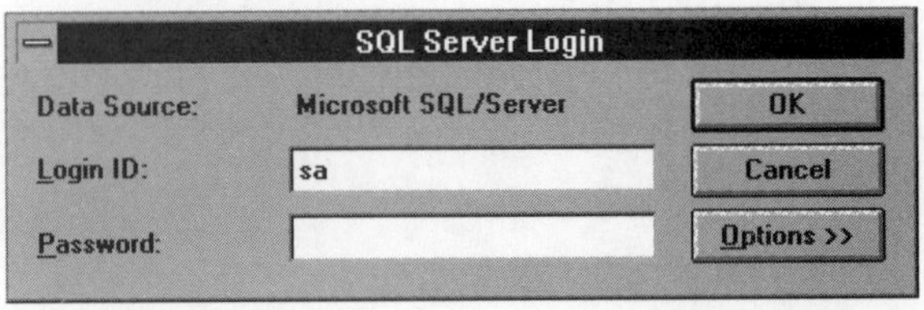

FIGURE 15.2
SQL Server Login dialog box.

selecting tables, opening an existing query, or entering SQL directly into the SQL window.

Views

When you have developed a complex query, you need to have a way to store the query and make it available to others. In Query, this is done by saving the query to an operating system file by selecting **File→Save As...** In order to share your query, however, you must have access to a shared network disk, or otherwise distribute copies of your query.

What a View Is

In SQL Server, the concept of a **view** allows you to store your query as part of the database. Once the view is in the database, anyone with permission can access the query. A person using your view will see it as if it were another table in the database, even if the view is a multi-table join.

As a result, views are often used to store queries joining several tables with complex **WHERE** logic. Views can also be used as a security device by restricting access to sensitive information. In SQL Server, permissions can be set on views in addition to tables. This allows, for example, a personnel system to restrict access to salary information while allowing broad access to phone numbers and mail codes.

How to Use a View

Views are used just like tables. Any place you can use a table name in Transact SQL, you can use a view name. When you use the **Add Tables** dialog box, to add tables to a query, views are also listed in the **Table Name** list box.

How to Create a View

Views are added to the database catalog by the **CREATE VIEW** statement. The syntax of the **CREATE VIEW** statement is:

CREATE VIEW *view_name*
[*(column_name$_1$, column_name$_2$,...)*]

AS
select_statement

where:

- **CREATE VIEW** is required.
- **view_name** is the name of the view (query).
- **column_name** is the optional list of column names. This list is necessary only when calculations are included in the *select_statement,* or when you want to rename a column.
- **AS** is a required keyword.
- **select_statement** is the **SELECT** statement that defines the query results desired.

Views can be created on base tables, other views, or any combination of tables and views. In SQL Server, you can update through a view, which is an extension to the ANSI standard. However, you can only update one table at a time through a view. Also, if the SELECT statement uses a wildcard (i.e., **SELECT ***) and the structure of the table used is changed, new columns will not appear in the view. This occurs because the wildcard is evaluated and expanded when the view is created. To create a view, follow the steps below.

STEPS Creating a View

1. Write and test the **SELECT** statement that will produce the results required. In this example, the query demonstrated in Chapter 13, in the section, **Equi Joins**, will be saved as a view.
2. Type the text illustrated in Figure 15.3 into the **SQL Statement** control in the **Execute SQL** dialog box to create the view.
3. Select **Execute**.

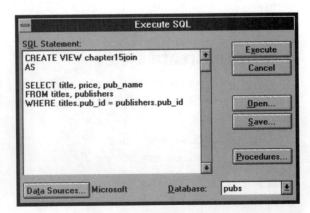

FIGURE 15.3
SQL code to create a **View**.

4. Test the new view by typing the text illustrated in Figure 15.4 into the **SQL Statement** control box in the **Execute SQL** dialog box.
5. Select **Execute**. The query will be executed, and the result set returned to the Data pane.

Stored Procedures

Stored procedures are equivalent to functions or subprograms in traditional programming languages. They allow the developer to build complex logic once and then reuse it as needed. A stored procedure is compiled when it is written and an execution plan is stored in the database. This process makes running a stored procedure more efficient when compared to re-entering the SQL code each time. This is especially true for procedures that are executed frequently and return similar amounts of information each time.

SQL Server provides many stored procedures that are helpful in the administration of a database. Some of these may only be used by the database owner, while others are available to everyone. These system-stored procedures also provide an excellent source of programming examples, as some of the logic is quite complex. Figure 15.5 shows the results from the system-stored procedure **sp_help**, which lists the objects in the current database, *pubs*.

How to Use a Stored Procedure

There are four ways to execute a stored procedure from MS Query:

- The Transact SQL EXEC statement, followed by the procedure name and parameter list.

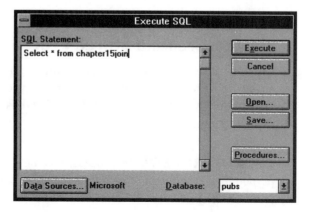

FIGURE 15.4
Testing the **View**.

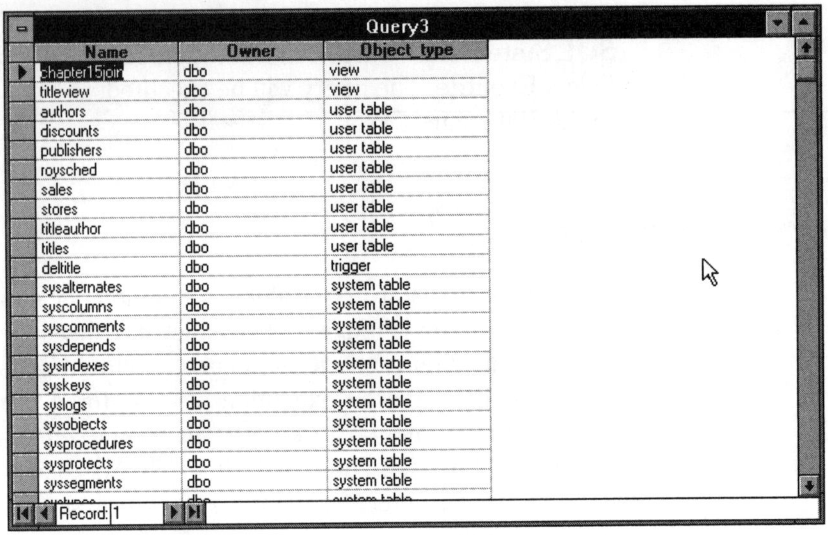

Name	Owner	Object_type
chapter15join	dbo	view
titleview	dbo	view
authors	dbo	user table
discounts	dbo	user table
publishers	dbo	user table
roysched	dbo	user table
sales	dbo	user table
stores	dbo	user table
titleauthor	dbo	user table
titles	dbo	user table
deltitle	dbo	trigger
sysalternates	dbo	system table
syscolumns	dbo	system table
syscomments	dbo	system table
sysdepends	dbo	system table
sysindexes	dbo	system table
syskeys	dbo	system table
syslogs	dbo	system table
sysobjects	dbo	system table
sysprocedures	dbo	system table
sysprotects	dbo	system table
syssegments	dbo	system table

FIGURE 15.5
Partial output from **sp_help,** *pubs* database.

- Typing the procedure name and parameter list in the **SQL Statement** control, and selecting **Execute.**
- Using the unique MS Query syntax of {**CALL procedure (*parameter_list*)**}, and then selecting **Execute**.
- Pasting the procedure in from a list of stored procedure in the current database (which uses the **CALL{}** syntax), and selecting **Execute.**

The **EXEC** statement allows the user to execute an existing stored procedure. Stored procedures can have parameters passed into them, as well as returning values to user local variables. These optional parameters may be passed either by position or by name. Passing parameters by name is always the safest, especially for stored procedures where the number or order of parameters might change.

How to Create a Stored Procedure

Creating stored procedures is an involved topic. This chapter will provide an overview to creating and using stored procedures. Stored procedures are created with the **CREATE PROCEDURE** statement. The syntax of this statement is:

CREATE PROCEDURE *procedure_name*
[@parameter_name, parameter, datatype [= parameter, defaultvalue]
[OUTPUT]

[,@*parameter_name₂ parameter₂ datatype [= parameter₂ defaultvalue]*
[OUTPUT]...]]
[WITH RECOMPILE]

AS
SQLStatements

where:

- **CREATE PROCEDURE** is required
- **procedure_name** is the name of the stored procedure.
- **@parameter_name** is the name of an input to, or output from, the stored procedure. Parameters are optional and must start with @.
- **OUTPUT** is an optional keyword indicating that the preceding parameter is an output parameter.
- **WITH RECOMPILE** is an optional phrase indicating that the stored procedure should always be recompiled before use.
- **AS** is a required keyword.
- **SQLStatements** is the SQL logic that accomplishes the stored procedure's goal.

STEPS Creating a Simple Stored Procedure

1. Determine the task the stored procedure will do, the input parameters needed, and any output parameters desired. This example will take one input parameter—*state*, and return the list of authors in the input state.
2. Write and test the SQL logic needed for step 1.

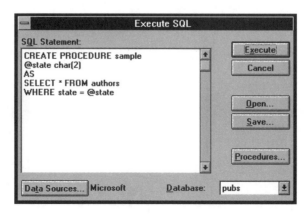

FIGURE 15.6
Create stored procedure.

3. Use the **CREATE PROCEDURE** statement to enter the stored procedure into the database catalog. Figure 15.6 illustrates the creation of the stored procedure.
4. Test your stored procedure (see Figure 15.7).

Transact/SQL Query Extensions

SQL Server provides several additional query capabilities in its implementation of SQL (Transact/SQL or T-SQL). These additional capabilities improve the functionality available in queries and fall into two categories:

- Data format conversion
- Sub-totals and grand totals.

Data Format Conversion

Data format conversions are achieved through two means in SQL Server:

- Implicit conversion
- Explicit conversion.

Implicit Conversions

SQL Server provides many built-in datatypes. Table 15.1 provides a list of the built-in SQL Server datatypes. Conversions between many of these datatypes are done implicitly, that is, without the use of a conversion function.

Explicit Conversions

Explicit conversions are done through the use of the **CONVERT** function. The general format of the **CONVERT** function is:

CONVERT *(resultdatatype[(length)], expression [, style])*

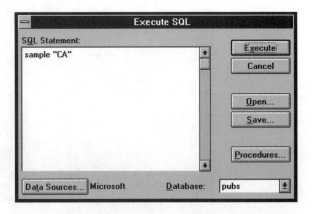

FIGURE 15.7
Testing a stored procedure.

TABLE 15.1
SQL Server Datatypes

Data Type	Valid Values
int	Integer values +/- 2,147,483,647.
smallint	Integer values +/- 32, 767.
tinyint	Integer values 0-255.
float	floating point values; 1.7 E-308 to 1.7 E308.
real	floating point values; 3.4 E-38 to 3.4 E38.
money	money values; +/- 922,337,203,685,477.5807 accurate to 4 decimals.
smallmoney	money values; +/- 214,748.3647 accurate to 4 decimals.
char(n)	character values, up to n characters, n<256.
varchar(n)	character values, variable length up to n characters, n<256.
text	character values, up to 2,147,483,647 characters.
binary(n)	binary values, up to n bytest, n<256.
varbinary (n)	variable binary values, up to n bytest, n<256.
image	binary values, up to 2,147,483, 647 bytes.
datetime	date and time values, 1/1/1753 to 12/31/9999.
smalldatetime	date and time values, 1/1/1900 to 6/6/2079.
bit	integer values, 0 or 1.
timestamp	column automatically updated when row is inserted or updated.

where:

- **CONVERT** is required.
- **resultdatatype** is the datatype that is returned.
- **length** is the optional length of the returned data.
- **expression** is a column, constant or calculation to convert.
- **style** is an optional parameter used to reformat **datetime** data.

This function can be used to convert different data formats, as well as to reformat dates into several formats. The data format conversions which require explicit conversion are in the following categories:

- **char** or **varchar** to any numeric or binary format
- **text** to **char** or **varchar** format
- **image** to **binary** or **varbinary** format.

The **CONVERT** function is also used to reformat **datetime** columns to **char** or **varchar** formats conforming to any one of several standards for date and time. Table 15.2 shows the value of the style parameter and the output produced, assuming the date and time is 1/1/94, 3:12 PM. To use

TABLE 15.2
Data Formats Available with CONVERT

Style	Result
0	Jan 1 1994
1	01/01/94
2	94.01.01
3	01/01/94
4	01.01.94
5	01-01-94
6	01 Jan 94
7	Jan 01, 94
8	15:12:05
9	Jan 1 1994
10	01-01-94
11	94/01/01
12	940101
13	01 Jan 1994
14	15:12:05:880

the **CONVERT** function to produce the results in the first row of the table below, the following syntax is used:

CONVERT*(varchar(12), datecol, 0).*

where **datecol** is of **DATETIME** format containing the value *1/1/94 3:12 PM*. Adding 100 to the style number above results in a four digit year (e.g., 1/1/1994). Styles 0, 9, and 13 always return a four digit year.

SubTotals and Grand Totals

T-SQL provides an important enhancement to the SQL standard by allowing both summary and detail information to be produced in a single query. However, this capability results in nonrelational output that front-end programs, including MS Query, may not handle properly. All standard SQL queries produce output that is a regular matrix, i.e., all rows have the same number of columns. However, using this facility, subtotals are produced on separate lines, only for those columns subtotaled. This is non-relational output and causes many front-end programs difficulty.

T-SQL provides this capability with the **COMPUTE BY** clause as part of a **SELECT** statement. This allows producing subtotals, grand totals, and detail lines in a single pass of the data. If **COMPUTE BY** is used, **ORDER BY** must also be used. The columns specified in the **ORDER BY** clause determine the subtotal levels available to **COMPUTE BY**. For example, if the result set is to be sorted by the columns **alpha, beta,** and **gamma,** the **COMPUTE BY** clause can be any of the following:

- **COMPUTE** expression *BY* alpha
- **COMPUTE** expression *BY* alpha, beta
- **COMPUTE** expression *BY* alpha, beta, gamma.

The columns determining the subtotal groups must be in the **ORDER BY** clause and specified in the same sequence. The SQL clause illustrated in Figure 15.8 will show sales subtotaled by stores, with a grand total. Query, and other front-end tools, will not be able to handle this type of query, since it produces nonrelational output. The example below was produced using ISQL/W, a tool provided with SQL Server. The **ISQL/W** icon is located in the **SQL Server Tools** program group by default. If you don't have this program group, contact your organization's information technology support group.

Transact/SQL Programming Language Extensions

Unlike many versions of SQL, T-SQL provides a broad array of extensions that allow programming within your queries. In this section, the objective is to provide an overview to the most common T-SQL statements:

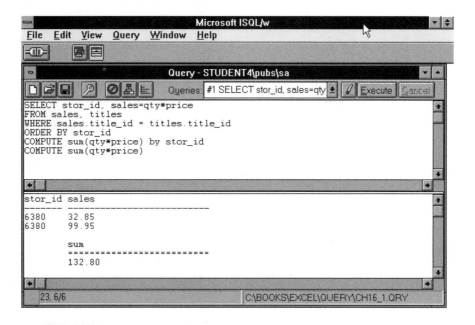

FIGURE 15.8
Subtotals and grand totals.

- **BEGIN/END**
- **BREAK**
- **CONTINUE**
- **DECLARE**
- **GOTO**
- **IF/ELSE**
- **PRINT**
- **RETURN**
- **WAITFOR**
- **WHILE.**

Below is a simple example showing the use of the T-SQL programming language extensions. The statements in the example will be covered in more detail below. This example will simply loop five times, and print the loop counter each time.

```
DECLARE @counter int
DECLARE @msg char(30)
SELECT @counter=0
WHILE @counter < 5
BEGIN
SELECT @counter = @counter + 1
SELECT @msg = CONVERT(char(30), @counter)
PRINT @msg
END
```

BEGIN/END

BEGIN marks the start of a block of SQL statements while **END** marks the termination of a block. These statements function like {} in the C programming language and are used whenever flow control statements affect entire blocks of SQL.

BREAK

BREAK is used to stop the processing of a loop started with the **WHILE** statement. If several loops are nested, **BREAK** in an inner loop returns to the next higher level loop and continues processing there.

CONTINUE

CONTINUE is also used to control processing of statements in a **WHILE** loop (like **BREAK**). After a **CONTINUE** statement is executed, all statements after the **CONTINUE** are skipped. The **WHILE** loop restarts at its beginning.

DECLARE

DECLARE *@variable datatype* where:

- **DECLARE** is required.
- **variable** is the name of the local variable. It must start with @.
- **dataype** is a SQL Server or user datatype.

T-SQL allows the use of local variables in SQL logic. These may be used to store loop counters for **WHILE** loop, messages for users, status values, or any other information a developer requires.

Before using a local variable, T-SQL must be told of its datatype and name to allocate storage for it. This is done with the **DECLARE** statement.

The name must conform to SQL Server's rules for identifiers and start with an @. The datatype may be any system- or user-defined datatype.

The **DECLARE** statement does not initialize or assign values to a local variable. This must be done using the **SELECT** statement. The SQL clause illustrated in Figure 15.9 defines a variable called *@AvgPrice* and sets it to the average price in the **titles** table and displays it as a single row.

GOTO

GOTO label where:

- **GOTO** is required.
- **label** is the name of location declared in the SQL code. When it is declared, it must end with a **:**.

Like the **GOTO** statement in other languages, this causes an unconditional branch to a label defined by the user. This can be used to define loops or to perform conditional processing. A label must follow the rules for identifiers, be used alone and followed by a colon when declared.

Excessive use of **GOTO** statements can make logic difficult to follow and is often considered poor programming style.

Figure 15.9
DECLARE statement.

IF/ELSE

IF *logicalexpression*
    SQLStatement$_1$
[**ELSE**
    SQLStatement$_2$]
where:

- **IF** is required.
- **logicalexpression** returns **True** or **False.**
- **SQLStatement$_1$** is a group of statements executed if **logicalexpression** is **True**
- **ELSE** is an optional clause, indicating what to do if **logicalexpression** is **False.**
- **SQLStatement$_2$** is a group of statements executed if logical condition is **False.**

IF/ELSE allows the programmer to control which SQL statements are executed based on conditions found earlier. If the condition is **True,** the SQL statement following the **IF** statement is executed, otherwise that following the optional **ELSE** statement is used.

Normally, only a single SQL statement is executed as a result of an

IF/ELSE. However, by using a **BEGIN/END** block, any number of statements may be grouped for execution.

PRINT

PRINT *text*
where:

>**text** can be quoted literal constants, or a **char** or **varchar** local or global variable.
>
>PRINT is used to display messages to the user during execution of SQL statements and can only display character data. To display numeric or date/time data, the **CONVERT** function must be used.

RETURN

RETURN *integer_return value*
where:

- **RETURN** is required.
- **integer_return_value** is an optional value that is returned.

The **RETURN** statement causes an unconditional end to a group of SQL statements. Any statements following the **RETURN** are ignored.

Optionally, the **RETURN** statement may return a status code. 0 is reserved to indicate successful completion, while negative values are used to indicate error conditions. Several values are reserved for use by SQL Server and can be found in the T-SQL *Reference Manual*.

WAITFOR

WAITFOR   {**DELAY** *time* |
               TIME *time* |
               ERROREXIT |
               PROCESSEXIT |
               MIRROREXIT }

This statement allows the user to pick a time or event to execute a SQL statement. **DELAY** allows the choice of a relative time, while **TIME** specifies an absolute execution time. Only one of the five events listed above can be used with one **WAITFOR** statement.

WHILE

WHILE
  logicalexpression
  SQLStatement

where:

- **WHILE** is required.
- **logicalexpression** returns **True** or **False**.
- **SQLStatement** is executed if **logicalexpression** is **True**.

The **WHILE** statement will continue to execute the SQL statement it controls until the **logical_expression** is **False.** Using a **BEGIN/END** block can allow **WHILE** to control any number of SQL statements in a loop.

Index

Advanced Filter, 54–56
    comparison values criteria, 63–68
    and criteria range, 57–62
    and list range, 56–57
Aggregate functions, pivot table, 203–11
Aliases in pivot tables, 214–16
Ascending sorts, 14–15, 17–18, 23–24
AutoFilter
    applying, 47, 49, 52–53
    comparison criteria for, 47–49
    copying, 53–54
    custom, 52
    defined, 46–47
    removing, 53
AutoFormat, 7–8, 212–13

Borland Quattro Pro for DOS, 126
Buttons, Query, 259, 260

Calculation functions, pivot tables, 203–11
Case sensitivity and sorting, 32–33
Cell protection, 78
ChartWizard, 179–84
Client/client computing, 318–19
Column fields, 151
Columns
    applying AutoFilter to, 52–53
    labels, 4–7
    in Query, 267–68, 292–96
    sorting, 23–25
Command buttons, 147–48
Comparison criteria, filtering
    for Advanced Filter, 55–56, 57–68
    for AutoFilter, 47–49
    in MS Query, 273–77
Criteria, filter

    See Comparison criteria
Cue cards, Query, 249–50
Customizing
    AutoFilter, 49–52
    data forms, 138–50
    using Excel style dialogs, 149–50
    sort orders, 33–41
    using VBA, 138–49

Data
    combining, 134–35
    different from information, 1–2
    different from lists, 2–3
    exporting, 127–33
    external, 11–12
    formats of, 117–37
    forms of, 69–82, 138–50
    importing, 117–27
    internal, 11–12
    and pivot tables, 156–85
    reading, 117–37
    symbolic link files, 133–34
    trouble-shooting, 135–37
    writing, 117–37
    See also Data forms; Databases; Functions, database
Databases
    custom, 138–50
    defined, 1–12
    filtering, 43–68
    forms of, 69–82, 138–50
    functions of, 83–116
    macros for, 233–37
    and Microsoft Query, 238–48, 249–97
    parts of, 8–9
    pivot tables, 151–85, 186–232

Databases (*continued*)
    ranges, 9–11
    reading, 117–37
    security, 77–82
    sorting, 13–42
    and SQL Server, 318–34
    and Structured Query Language, 298–317
    and VBA programs, 233–37
    writing, 117–37
    See also Data; Data forms; Functions, database; Lists
Data fields, 151, 155–79, 207–11
Data forms
    adding to, 76
    browsing, 73–75
    customizing, 138–50
    defined, 69–70
    deleting, 77
    initializing, 142
    parts of, 70–72
    protection of, 78–82
    restricting entry and editing, 77–78, 78–82
    using, 72–73
Data Interchange Format (DIF) files
    exporting, 134
    importing, 127
Data tables
    adding formulas to, 98–99
    approximate matches, 107–8
    compare values, 108–15
    defined, 93–94
    filling, 96–98, 101–3
    lookup tables, 103–7
    one-input, 94–95, 96
    performance considerations, 103
    setting up, 95–96, 100–101
    two-input, 100–103
    See also Pivot tables
Dates
    in pivot tables, 220–24
    in SQL, 314
dBase files, 39–40
Descending sorts, 15–18, 23–24
Dialog sheets, 139–40
Display_data_form procedure, 143

Excel
    See Microsoft Excel
Exporting data, 127–28
    combining data in, 134–35
    DIF files, 134
    Excel worksheet, 128–29, 129–31
    Lotus 1–2–3 file, 131

    Quattro Pro for DOS, 132
    Symbolic link files, 133
    text, 128–29
    Xbase files, 132–33
Extensions, Transact/SQL
    programming language, 329–34
    Query, 326–29
External data, 11–12, 38–39
Extract ranges, 55, 64–68

File formats, 136
    See also Data, formats of
Filtering
    Advanced Filter, 54–68
    AutoFilter, 46–54
    copying filtered data, 53–54
    criteria for, 47–49, 57–68
    custom, 49–52
    list ranges, 56–57
    mode, 43–46
    QBE grids, 59
    removing filters, 53
    selected columns, 52–53
    selecting list for, 8
    wildcards, 51–52
    See also Comparison criteria, filtering
First_row procedure, 145–46
Fonts, display, 290–91
Functions, database
    DAVERAGE, 88, 89
    DCOUNT, 88, 89
    DCOUNTA, 88, 89
    defined, 83–84
    DGET, 88, 89
    DMAX, 88, 89
    DMIN, 88, 89
    DPRODUCT, 90
    DSTDEV, 90
    DSTDEVP, 90
    DSUM, 90
    DVAR, 90
    DVARP, 90
    Function Wizard, 85–87
    list of, 87–90
    syntax of, 84–85
Function Wizard, 85–87

Grand totals
    in pivot tables, 199–200
    as Transact/SQL Query Extensions, 328–29
Graphics
    cataloging, 25–27
    sorting, 25

Grouping items in pivot tables, 216–28

Hide/show items in pivot tables, 228–32

Importing
    Borland Quattro Pro for DOS files, 126
    data, 117–27
    delimited text data, 123–24
    DIF files, 127
    fixed width text data, 124–25
    lists, 35–39
    Lotus 1–2–3 Spreadsheet files, 125–26
    Microsoft Works files, 126
    Symbolic link files, 127
    text files, 118–25
    TextWizard, 119
    Xbase data files, 125–26
Indexing in data tables, 112–16
Information and data, 1–2
Internal data, 11–12

Joins
    automatic, 283–84
    equi, 281–83, 284–85, 307
    multiple tables, 280–81, 306–10
    outer, 286–88, 307–8
    removing, 289–90
    self, 288–89, 308–9
    unrestricted, 289, 309–10
Keys
    sort, 13, 17, 19–22, 31

Label Identification Rule, 6
Labeling data, 4–6
Last_row procedure, 146–47
Lists
    creating, 4
    customizing, 34–40
    different from data, 1–3
    formatting, 7–8
    identifying, 4
    labeling, 4–6
    ranges, 56–57
    selecting, 8
    See also Databases
Lookup tables, 103–15
Lotus 1–2–3 Spreadsheet files
    exporting from, 131
    importing, 125–26

Macros
    assigning, 148–49
    for text, 233–34

    and VBA, 235–37
Matches in data tables, 107–8, 110–15
Menus, Query, 251–55
Metafiles, 25–27
Microsoft Excel
    advantages of, 3
    AutoFormat, 7–8
    and column labels, 4–7
    data access from, 246–48
    databases in, 1–3
    exporting, 128–30
    and Microsoft Query, 238–40, 246–48
    and pivot tables, 166–81
    previous versions of, 130–31
    style dialogs, 149–50
Microsoft Query
    adding criteria to, 273–76
    adding fields to, 262–68
    building a query, 261–97
    closing a query, 271
    column width, 292–95
    columns in, 268
    control menu, 260–61
    creating a query, 261–62
    criteria pane, 257–58, 276–77
    cue cards, 249–50
    data pane, 258
    defined, 238–40
    display fonts, 290–91
    equi joins, 281–90
    and Excel, 238–40, 246–48
    external data, 238
    formatting query windows, 290–96
    hiding columns, 295–96
    joining multiple tables, 280–90
    menus, 251–55
    modifying records, 269–70
    navigation buttons, 259
    Open Database Connectivity (ODBC), 241–46
    opening a query, 272–73
    outer joins, 286–88
    output, 296–97
    printing, 296
    query window, 255–57
    record selectors, 258
    records menu, 266–67
    removing a join, 289–90
    row height, 291–92
    saving, 296
    saving a query, 270–71
    scroll bars, 259–60
    selecting fields in, 264–66
    self joins, 288–89

Microsoft Query (*continued*)
    sizing buttons, 260
    sorting, 277–80
    starting, 249–50
    table pane, 257
    toolbar, 255
    Windows Open Services Architecture (WOSA), 240–46
    workspace of, 250–61
    See also Structured Query Language
Microsoft Works files, 126
Modules, assigning, 148–49
Move_to_next procedure, 143–44

Nesting sorts, 21
Numbers in pivot tables, 213–14, 225–27

OLE objects
    cataloging, 28–30
    sorting, 28
One-input data tables, 94–99
Open Database Connectivity (ODBC), 241–46
    adding/defining data sources, 242–44
    drivers, 244–46
    and Excel, 241
    setting up data sources, 241–42
Orientation, sort, 31–32
Outlines, sorting data in, 41–42
Output, 296–97

Page field, 151, 166–73, 182–85, 194–98, 227–28
Pivot tables
    adding fields, 186–88
    adjusting fields, 177–79
    aggregate functions, in, 203–11
    aliases in, 214–16
    AutoFormat, 212–13
    calculation function in, 210–11
    cell formatting, 179, 232
    charts from, 179–84
    ChartWizard, 179–84
    column headings, 177–78
    columns, 178, 229–31
    create from another pivot table, 173–75
    create from consolidated data, 163–73
    create from external data, 160–63
    create from internal data, 155–60
    data sources, 155–79
    dates and times, 220–24
    defined, 151
    displaying pages, 194–97, 197–98
    and Excel, 166–71
    formatting, 212–16
    grouping items in, 216–28
    hiding and displaying items, 199–200, 228–32
    layout of, 188–94
    links, 175–76
    moving items in, 191
    and multiple pages, 197
    numbers in, 213–14, 225–27
    orientation of, 191–94
    page fields, 166–73, 185, 227–28
    pivot toolbar, 151–53
    PivotTable field, 151–52
    PivotTable Wizard, 151–52, 186–87
    printing multiple pages, 198–99
    query toolbar, 151–52
    refreshing data, 176–79
    removing fields, 186, 188
    removing grouping from, 227–28
    shortcut menu, 153–55
    showing and hiding items, 199–200, 228–32
    storing pages as separate worksheet, 198
    subtotals in, 200–203
    toolbars, 151–53
    totals in, 199–211
    and VBA codes, 235–37
Previous_row procedure, 144–45
Printing, Query, 296
Procedures, stored (SQL), 323–26

Quattro Pro for DOS, 132
Query
    See Microsoft Query
Query by Example (QBE), 50–51, 57–62
Query toolbar, 151–53

Ranges, database
    criteria, 57–62
    defining, 9–11
    extract, 55, 64–68
    list, 56–57
Reading data formats, 117–27
Records, Query, 269–70
Refreshing pivot tables, 176–79
Relational databases functions of SQL, 299
Row field, 151, 291, 312–14

Saving a query, 270–71, 296–97
Scalar functions, 312–14
Searching techniques, SQL, 303–6
Selecting
    a list, 8
Server/client computing, 318–19
Show/hide items in pivot tables, 228–32
Sorting

advanced options, 31–33
ascending sorts, 14–15, 17–18
case sensitivity, 32–33
columns, 23–25
command, 18–19, 23, 24–25
custom order, 33–41
defining lists for, 34–35
descending, 15–17
first-key, 31
with graphic objects, 25–27
horizontal, 32
importing list for, 36–40
keys for, 13
in MS Query, 277–80
multiple-key, 19–21, 21–22
nesting, 21–22
with OLE objects, 28–30
order of, 13–17, 33–41
orientation, 31–32
in an outline, 41–42
quick, 17–18
removing custom list, 40
selecting list for, 8
single-key, 17–19
with SQL, 310
of subsets, 22–23
three-key, 20–21
vertical, 32
Structured Query Language (SQL)
    AND/OR, 303
    attaching to server, 320–21
    BEGIN/END, 330
    BETWEEN and NOT BETWEEN, 305–6
    BREAK, 330
    character functions, 312
    CONTINUE, 331
    data format conversions, 326–28
    data retrieval, 299–306
    data updating, 314–17
    date/time functions, 313
    DECLARE, 331, 332
    DELETE, 316
    equi joins, 307
    extensions, 329–34
    GOTO, 331
    IF/ELSE, 332–33
    IN, 306
    INSERT, 315
    introduction to, 298
    joining multiple tables, 306–10
    LIKE, 304–5
    NOT, 303
    numeric functions, 313
    outer joins, 307–8
    PRINT, 333
    relational databases, 299
    RETURN, 333
    scalar functions, 312–14
    searching techniques, 303–6
    selecting columns, 300–301
    selecting rows, 301–3
    SELECT INTO, 316–17
    self joins, 308–9
    server, 318–34
    sorting with, 310
    stored procedures, 323–26
    subtotals, 328–29
    summarizing information with, 310–12
    system functions, 314
    totals, 328–29
    and Transact-SQL, 326–29, 329–34
    unrestricted joins, 309–10
    UPDATE, 315–16
    views, 321–23
    WAITFOR, 333
    WHILE, 334
Subsets, sorting, 22–23
Subtotals
    in pivot tables, 200–203
    as Transact/SQL Query Extensions, 328–29
Summarizing information with SQL, 310–12
Symbolic link (SYLK) files
    exporting, 133
    importing, 127

Tables, data
    adding formulas to, 98–99
    approximate matches, 107–8
    compare values, 108–15
    defined, 93–94
    filling, 96–98, 101–3
    joining in Query, 280–90, 306–10
    lookup tables, 103–7
    one-input, 94–95, 96
    performance considerations, 103
    setting up, 95–96, 100–101
    two-input, 100–103
    See also Pivot tables
Text files
    delimiters, 120–21, 123–24
    dividing into columns, 120–21
    exporting, 128–29
    fixed width, 118–19, 121–22, 124–25
    formatting columns, 122–23
    importing, 117–25
    interpretation, 136
    and macros, 233–34

TextWizard, 119
Times in pivot tables, 220–24
Toolbar
    Pivot, 151–53
    Query, 255
Totals in pivot tables, 199–211
Transact-SQL, 326–29, 329–34
Two-input data tables, 100–103

Views, SQL server, 321–23
Visual Basis for Applications (VBA)
    adding command buttons, 147–48
    assigning macros, 148–48
    defined, 141
    display_data_form procedure, 143
    first_row procedure, 145–46
    global variables, 141
    initializing data form, 142
    last_row procedure, 146–47
    move_to_next procedure, 143–44
    and pivot tables, 235–37
    previous_row procedure, 144–45
    using, 138–40

Windows Open Services Architecture (WOSA), 240–46
Windows, Query, 290–96
Worksheets
    protecting, 78–81
    unprotecting, 78–81
Writing data formats, 177–37

Xbase data files
    exporting, 132–33
    importing, 125

Free Companion Disk!

That's right, you can get a **FREE*** companion disk for **Excel 5.0 Spreadsheet Databases** by filling out the coupon below (or making a copy of it, if you don't want to cut your book up!), and enclosing $9.95 to cover shipping and handling.

_____	_____	_____
First Name	Last Name	Area Code/Telephone
_____	_____	_____
Company	Title	
_____	_____	_____
Street	P.O. Box	
_____	_____	_____
City	State	ZIP

Please make check payable to Logic Control

Send to: Logic Control
21 Bridge Square
Westport, CT 06880

* This offer is good only in the United States and Canada. John Wiley & Sons, Inc., is not responsible for orders placed with Logic Control.

Who Is Logic Control?

Logic Control is a Microsoft Training Channel Partner and Consulting Channel Partner that specializes in the development of missions critical and client/server applications, developer education, and on-line help systems.

Mission Statement

Logic Control's mission is to provide creative business solutions using leading-edge technologies. Logic Control does this by offering:

- Developer Education
- Custom Software Development
- Technology Mentoring

Authorized Technical Education Center

Developer Education

To help you meet your software education needs, Logic Control offers:

- **A State-of-the-Art Training Facility:** One 66 Mhz 486DX2 workstation with a 17" monitor for each student.
- **Small Classes:** Maximum class size is limited to ten students.
- **Faculty with Real-World Experience:** All Logic Control faculty are actively involved in custom software development projects, and come from a variety of business disciplines.
- **Faculty Certification:** All Logic Control faculty are certified by Microsoft to deliver Microsoft University courseware.
- **Developer Oriented Curriculum:** Offerings include Logic Control and Microsoft University courses on:
  - Microsoft/Sybase SQL Server
  - Microsoft Visual Basic
  - Microsoft Windows NT
  - Microsoft Windows NT Advanced Server
  - Microsoft Access
  - Microsoft Excel
  - Microsoft Word
  - Microsoft Mail
  - Microsoft Visual C++
  - Information Modelling
  - Relational Database Design
  - User Interface Design

- **Convenient Location:** Logic Control's facilities are located in beautiful Westport, CT, on the shores of the Saugatuck River, between the Merritt Parkway and I-95, and are within walking distance of the Westport Metro North train station. This location makes our facility easy to reach from New York City, Westchester, and Connecticut.

Software Development

Logic Control has real-world experience in building custom solutions based on the products found in Microsoft Office. OLE, DDE, MAPI, and ODBC are the foundation technologies which are part of solutions that we have delivered to clients in recent engagements.

Technology Mentoring

By providing software development, and education services, Logic Control is in a unique position to help you take control of your environment, and harness new technology for the benefit of your organization.

21 Bridge Square, Westport, CT 06880
203•454•3663